Systematic
Observation
of
Teaching

SYSTEMATIC

OBSERVATION

OF

TEACHING

an
interaction analysis-instructional strategy
approach

Richard L. Ober
University of South Florida

Ernest L. Bentley
Metro Atlanta Supplementary Educational Center

Edith Miller
University of Georgia

PRENTICE-HALL, INC., ENGLEWOOD CLIFFS, NEW JERSEY

PRENTICE-HALL INTERNATIONAL, INC., *London*
PRENTICE-HALL OF AUSTRALIA, PTY. LTD., *Sydney*
PRENTICE-HALL OF CANADA, LTD., *Toronto*
PRENTICE-HALL OF INDIA PRIVATE LIMITED, *New Delhi*
PRENTICE-HALL OF JAPAN, INC., *Tokyo*

*Dedicated to the many teachers
of the cities of Atlanta, Decatur, and Marietta,
and of the counties of Clayton, Cobb and Gwinnett
who learned to use the RCS and the ETC and
were so helpful to us in developing a book of this type.*

Contents

Foreword, xi

Preface, xiii

1

Awareness
and
Control, 1

The Teaching-Learning Process	*3*
Observing the Teaching-Learning Situation	*5*
Questions—Prospective Teachers	*7*
Strategy	*11*
A New Look	*13*

2

Systematic
Observation
as a Concept, 15

Systematic Observation	*16*
Observation Systems	*19*
Exemplary Systems	*21*
Uses of Observation Systems	*29*
Selecting an Observation System	*34*

3
Reciprocal
Category
System, 37

Data Collection	*40*
Data Preparation	*59*
Data Interpretation	*66*
The Observer and Valid Observation	*79*
Summary Reflection	*85*

4
Equivalent
Talk
Categories, 87

Observing and Recording	*93*
The Equivalent Talk Categories	*97*
Practice Opportunities	*108*
Collection Procedures	*111*
Preparation Procedures	*119*
Data Interpretation	*131*

5
Instructional
Strategy
Building, 139

Functions, Strategies, and Planning	*141*
The Process of Strategy Building	*143*
Simulated Instructional Strategy Development	*155*
Conclusion	*170*

6
Modification
and
In-Practice Uses, 171

Practice Techniques 172
"Control" Variations for
the Fifteen-Minute Micro-simulation 195
Systematic Observation:
A Tool for Strategy and Self-Evaluation 196

Appendix, 201

Keys to Drills 201
Instructions for the Two-Minute Micro-simulation
(Without Video or Audio Recording) 217
Directions for Preparing the Fifteen-Minute
Micro-simulation Critique 220

Bibliography, 225

Books and Monographs 225
Articles 228

Glossary, 231

Index, 233

Foreword

For many decades, progress toward better instruction in the schools has been held back by the widespread and uncritical adoption of a faulty definition of teacher competence. Too long it has been assumed that the competent teacher is one who has mastered a set of skills, methods, ways of behaving that are universally effective or "good." Research in teacher effectiveness has spent its energy in an unsuccessful search for these key behaviors; teacher educators have vainly tried to teach them to students without knowing what they are.

This book is notable in that it abandons this untenable position for one that is fully consistent with the results of recent research in the area. The large number of studies of teacher behavior carried out during the last two decades have made it more and more apparent that the effect achieved by a given way of behaving is specific to the teacher, the pupil, and the situation. If there are any universally effective behaviors, their number is small indeed.

The competent teacher, then, is one who possesses a large repertory of strategies and tactics which he can use at will. As the authors of this book point out, he must first acquire an awareness of and control over his own behavior. Then he can go out into the schools and develop his own individual way of being effective in his own situation. Becoming a fully competent teacher is, then, a life-long process rather than a point to be reached.

In this book the reader will find sound practical methods for developing the awareness and control of behavior that is so necessary a prerequisite to teacher competence. This is the first book that I have seen which addresses itself directly to this problem. It deserves to be widely used—and widely imitated.

Charlottesville, Virginia   DONALD M. MEDLEY
February, 1971

Preface

A sprinkling of interest in the topic of systematic observation, evident about the turn of the century, has been followed during the 50s and 60s by the frontierlike experimenters. Now in the 70s, systematic observation is operationally available as a legitimate, proven technique. This book focuses on systematic approaches to observation, planning, and assessing teaching-learning, primarily for the pre-service teacher. Pre-service teachers, for whom the techniques hold great promise, include those in courses that require observation of actual classroom settings, courses generally described as concerning basic methods in which lesson planning and strategy building take place, and course experiences in the assessment of planned and actual teaching. An additional use for the materials will be found at the graduate level by those engaged in research entailing systematic observation of teaching-learning situations.

Most traditional classroom instruction has consisted of trial and error selection of content, strategy, and implementation. Systematic observation presents means of accountability, both for the actions of the teacher and the continuous interactions within the classroom. Awareness and control are the theme and motif. *Awareness* is the greater cognizance of actual verbal behaviors, and the more sensible, sensitive decisions about instructional strategies—based on the most current evidence concerning human capabilities, personality attributes, environmental variables, relevant content, and methodology. *Control* is utilized in a management sense—that is, by establishing feedback loops through systematic observation techniques, such as the RCS and the ETC, data-based modification is possible. The intuitive leaps that have emphasized the trial and error nature of teaching-learning give way to organized plans, feedback, and alteration.

Materials are organized so that the reader will become familiar with the theoretical bases on which the work is predicated and so he will be fully aware of the practicalities of the observational tools as well as their suggested applications. Because of the relative newness of systematic observation as a field, the rationale and illustrative examples of observation systems will prove particularly useful as a general overview of the field and its approach. Two observational tools—the Reciprocal Category System (RCS) and the Equivalent Talk Categories (ETC)—are thoroughly discussed so that the reader will learn to understand and to apply the systems in practical ways and subsequently improve his instructional repertoire. The authors have considerable personal experience in guiding pre- and in-service experience with the RCS and view it as a means for developing awareness and control related to the socio-emotional climate of the classroom. The ETC system, an outgrowth of the work with the RCS, is based on the need for ways of viewing quality in verbal interaction and increased facility by instructional agents in their use of functions such as, questioning, answering, reacting and structuring.

Considerable emphasis is placed on learning how to observe with the result that planning for teaching (lesson plans) is more a science than an art, and therefore, a major strength for the reader, whether pre- or in-service, is derived from the treatment of strategy building. The particular roles played by each observational system in strategy development provide useful guides when planning effective instruction.

The book is unique in that it presents in an understandable and practical fashion a field that has tended to be esoteric and research-oriented.

Chapter 1 concentrates on *awareness and control* in the classroom situation. The use of observational techniques in developing awareness and control is discussed, as well as questions concerning the practical application of this approach. This chapter introduces the book by presenting strategy development in the context of awareness and control fostered by systematic observation techniques.

The basic rationale of using awareness and control, brought about by the use of systematic observation, is further developed in Chapter 2. The concept of systematic observation is explained, systems in general and in particular are discussed, uses of observational systems are related, and the framework of interactional analysis is established.

Chapters 3 and 4 are devoted to specific observation systems—tools that the reader can understand and apply. The Reciprocal Category System (RCS) focuses primarily on the climate of the classroom setting described in Chapter 3. Chapter 4 presents the Equivalent Talk Categories (ETC), a system that is designed to classify interaction and that places particular emphasis on the quality of verbal action and on reacting behaviors.

Chapter 5 is an examination of potential strategies based on learning theory implications. Practical applications are suggested to illustrate the use of observation categories in strategy building.

Skill development through practice approaches is the major emphasis in

Chapter 6. Laboratory and classroom uses of the systematic observation techniques are delineated so that extensive simulated and actual trial are possible.

Among those who have been of significant assistance as these ideas were formulated and the manuscript developed were the teachers who participated in the many training experiences utilizing the systems presented in the book. Robert K. Bane, Betty A. Bentley, R. Robert Rentz, Jeaninne N. Webb, and Samuel W. Wood were valuable participants and reactors throughout the experience. The scripts in the book were developed with suggestions from Virginia Purcell, Gail Speer, Betty A. Bentley, Edith Miller, and Richard L. Ober. The efforts of the typists Penny Newton, Linda Reagan, and Ann Sammons made the manuscript possible.

Complete references for all sources cited by author and date in this book can be found in the Bibliography. Special recognition and appreciation are given to the following authors and their publishers for permission to use their ideas and/or data in the preparation of this text: Ted Amidon and John Hough (Addison-Wesley), Arno Bellack (Teachers' College Press), Bob Brown (Harper & Row), Jerome Bruner (Harvard University Press and John Wiley & Sons), Robert Gagné (Holt, Rinehart & Winston), Ned Flanders (Paul Amidon and Associates), Ira Gordon (John Wiley & Sons), Marie Hughes, Ted Parsons, Norris Sanders (Harper & Row), B.O. Smith and John Withall (*Journal of Experimental Education*).

R.L.O.
E.L.B.
E.M.

Systematic
Observation
of
Teaching

1

Awareness
and
Control

For both the avid and the casual moviegoers of America, the release of
Bonnie and Clyde in 1968 was a hallmark. The final scene of the movie,
the grotesque overkill of Bonnie and Clyde, immediately comes to the minds
of most people when the movie is mentioned. While the reviews of the
movie ranged from disgust and repulsion to praise and adulation, the movie
attracted a great deal of serious attention and was considered by many to
be a significant advance in moviemaking. One of the movie's most outstanding features was the combination of talent that went into its produc-
tion and the fascinating combination of scripting, music, cinematography,
acting, and directing.

What does *Bonnie and Clyde* have to do with a classroom? Nothing and
everything. The real impact that this movie has for education lies in the
story of its direction. Arthur Penn, the director of *Bonnie and Clyde,* in
an ETV interview [1] recently told of a revolution in his approach to moviemaking. In the early days—the Playhouse 90, Omnibus, Philco Theatre
days—of television, Penn was a very busy, productive, and sought-after
television writer-director. His strategy as a director in a medium that was
new and unstructured was to have everything nailed down. Every lighting
detail, every nuance of the actor's voice, every move of the action, every
camera angle was predetermined and set from Penn's point of view. He
was very successful and admired.

As television became less creative and more commercial, Penn left the
medium and moved into the legitimate theatre and moviemaking. His
strategy, for a while, remained the same. Nail everything down. Leave no

[1] Channel 8, Georgia Educational Television, Athens, Georgia, May 26, 1970.

1

room for misunderstanding, overinterpreting. However, in moviemaking, he soon found that he was missing something by being so inflexible. Not only was it difficult for him to communicate his ideas to the people involved in the process of making the movie, but also he felt that the creativity of the situation was stifled. At this point, he began to structure less and observe more. Over a period of time, he developed a new strategy— one that allowed him to set the frame of reference, to establish the philosophical point of departure, and to bring the talent and creativity of all the involved people to relate to and become involved in the situation. He began to explore and discuss every possible aspect of the picture. Hence, he evolved a strategy that builds on the best in every situation, with the director both aware and in control of the outcome.

Just as the director brings the skill of giving life and form to a movie, the teacher brings to the teaching-learning situation the *skill* with which he is able to control and use his teaching expertise and therefore, influence the other variables of the situation. This skill does not automatically come to a teacher with certification or a teaching contract. Rather, it is a skill developed through awareness of the interacting elements in a teaching-learning situation, planning strategies for teaching based on this awareness, and sound objectives, assessing the results, and modifying these objectives in terms of the assessment.

To the casual, uninitiated observer, a teaching-learning situation might appear to be a rather smooth, operational process in which the teacher and students calmly and confidently move from one activity to another with ease and facility. To someone else, the same situation might appear to be one of confusion and disorganization, in which the teacher and students move haphazardly from one uncontrollable crisis to another. The disparity between the two observations is due precisely to what each observer was looking for and how he saw it. Both interpretations may be accurate descriptions of what was really happening; both may be completely inaccurate. One thing is certain—the interpretation of any given situational observation is in the eye and mind of the observer.

Teacher role has been studied, defined, restudied, and redefined so thoroughly that there is probably documentation available to support any description of the teacher that one wishes to suggest. All of these role descriptions may be accurate in part or they may be irrelevant and inaccurate. Regardless of whether observers are able to describe what the teacher does in definite terms, teachers keep right on "doing their thing"— seemingly without the slightest concern that what they are doing apparently defies definition and is extremely complex.

The teaching-learning situation can be viewed as an interaction among teacher, student, and content. If well planned and executed, this interaction consists of three steps:

1. Developing objectives
2. Planning and executing instruction
3. Measuring and evaluating results

The development and value of sound objectives—in measurable, behavioral terms—is at the apex of interest in educational thought.

The new methods of measurement that are a result of working toward understandable and reachable goals have been impressive, and the trends toward improving the teaching-learning situation itself are heartening. The use of techniques such as simulation and systematic observation are moving the teaching process away from the realm of unexplainable, "hit-or-miss" interaction toward a process that can be objectively planned, observed, assessed, modified, and executed.

The Teaching-Learning Process

Any statement concerning the teaching-learning process is influenced substantially by predilection for which the following serve as basic assumptions:

1. The complex teaching-learning situation can be divided into a series of related, yet separate variables that can be identified, classified, measured, and studied.
2. The role of the teacher as he operates within the framework of this situation can be described in terms of three sets of functional variables:
   a. establishing learning objectives
   b. facilitating learning/instruction
   c. measuring and evaluating learning
3. The instructional-learning situation, as it relates to the instructional phase of teaching, consists of three basic elements:
   a. the learner
   b. the learning stimuli (content, climate, involvement)
   c. an instructional agent—in this case, the teacher
4. In terms of the instructional-learning situation, two important sets of variables in the learning stimuli are content or instructional approach and the socio-emotional climate.
5. Within the framework of the instructional-learning situation, the instructional agent (teacher) has two very important functions:
   a. To create a positive socio-emotional climate in which the learner will feel comfortable and learning will be facilitated.
   b. To manipulate and control the content in ways that will facilitate learning to the ends determined by the learning objectives.

6. The creation of a positive socio-emotional atmosphere and the manipulation and control of the learning stimuli are contingent upon skills that can be identified and described in functional and strategical terms and, in turn, that can be learned and measured.

7. Observers can be trained to acquire and sharpen certain skills that will enable them to study the classroom in a systematic and objective fashion.

8. Teachers can be trained to acquire and sharpen certain skills that will enable them to be aware of and control their own behavior in the instructional-learning situation.

9. Teachers can—with awareness and control—develop strategies of teaching that can be true both to their philosophies and to learning theory.

This book attempts to accomplish two major goals: First, it will describe skills and/or techniques that have been found to be useful for studying the behavior of a teacher as he operates in the classroom. These skills and techniques employ the use of precision-like instruments—observational systems—that allow the observer to identify and classify specific variables that are a part of the teaching-learning situation. Second, as a result of studying the classroom as an observer, one will be able to formalize his own conceptualization of the teaching-learning situation in separate, descriptive terms that can be identified, studied, and understood. Then, when actively engaged in a classroom situation as a teacher, he will be consciously aware of these interacting variables, and, in turn, will be better able to control them in ways that will facilitate and result in maximum learning.

Frequent use is made of the phrase "to be aware of, able to control." "To be aware of" is used in the sense that the teacher has acquired a satisfactory understanding or awareness of both the composition of the classroom and of the interaction that takes place in it. "Able to control" refers to the manipulation and control of the learning *stimuli* [2] and the teacher's own behavior—not dominant control of the student or the student's attitudes. In other words, in this book, "control" refers to the teacher as he plans and manipulates his own behavior in the classroom.

This approach, in fact, arbitrarily refrains from dealing with *what* the student is to learn within the instructional-learning situation and addresses itself to *how* the teacher can best facilitate learning once the learning objectives are determined and set forth. Obviously, the establishment of learning objectives is a vital role of the teacher and is not to be neglected.

---

[2] The whole array of possible stimulus increments into which the content can be broken down and made available to the student or learner (i.e., written page, model, demonstration, film, etc.).

The teaching-learning situation is the focus—how it can be observed and how a teacher operates within it. There is exclusive concern with how to *achieve* learning objectives, not how to *determine* them. This posture in no way detracts from the importance of establishing learning objectives. Rather, it serves to emphasize the significance of learning objectives and their establishment, for it points out that the establishment of learning objectives and the achievement of them are separate and different activities—both of which are vital to learning.

Instructional-learning situations have three fundamental sets of variables in common—the learner, the learning stimuli (something to be learned), and the instructional agent (teacher). Obviously, the learner as a variable is considered, but he is not considered in terms of his individuality and peculiarities. Instead, the concern is related to how to: 1) manipulate and control learning stimuli and, 2) create a positive socio-emotional climate in which the learner feels comfortable and is motivated to learn. Consequently, the main focus becomes the instructional agent—the teacher—and how he behaves, rather than on the learner and how he behaves.

While a teacher is usually the instructional agent in a teaching-learning situation, it should be pointed out that this is not always the case. Within the stated definition of an instructional agent—"a facilitator of learning"—can be found a variety of agents and/or devices. For example, a programmed text, computer-assisted instruction, teaching machines, free discovery (in the absence of the teacher), and another fellow-learner are examples of instructional agents that fit our definition. Even the possibility that learning in a particular situation can be facilitated if the teacher removes himself from the situation represents an instructional strategy that meets the qualifications of the stated definition.

Specific *skills and techniques* that will help the beginning observer to study and analyze the teaching-learning situation in a systematic and objective fashion are presented. In turn, the analysis will help him to become aware of and better able to control his own behavior in order to facilitate classroom activities and strategies leading to maximized learning. Those parts of the instructional situation which can be classified and observed are the factors over which control can be exerted, and these very same factors are the ones which can be used to facilitate learning.

Observing the Teaching-Learning Situation

Merely to go into a classroom to observe without any definite purpose or preconceived plan of operation can be both tiresome and rewardless. Perhaps, for a short while, such an experience might be rather interesting, even entertaining to the novice, but over any length of time, the whole experience becomes an ordeal, an endless series of "teacher-student skirmishes and encounters," with little rhyme or reason.

Unfortunately, classroom observation experiences are too often meaningless and essentially wasted ventures because the observer has neither a rationale from which to operate, nor a specific plan of operation for carrying out his task—a "look and see" exercise with a "catch what you can" outcome. If the observer is prepared to enter the observational experience with an understanding of what he is about to witness and equipped with techniques for accomplishing his task, he can secure valuable first-hand information that can be quite beneficial. But to acquire such an understanding of what he is about to witness and to learn the necessary techniques require that at least two basic conditions be met:

First, the observer needs to know precisely for what he is looking. He must have clearly in mind his own personal conceptualization of what constitutes the instructional-learning situation. He must be able to recognize and identify the "principal characters" in the situation and, in turn, be able to recognize the role of each. Moreover, the observer needs to be aware of what is supposed to happen as a result of this activity—what are the objectives to be achieved? (Again, the concern is not *how* the objectives were determined or whether or not they are worthwhile and/or meaningful; rather, the concern relates to *what* the objectives are.) *Second,* in order to develop a plan of action for observing the classroom setting, the observer needs to be able to see variables both as separate, discrete phenomenon and as they interact with each other within the dynamics of the classroom operation.

Both the conceptualization of what the classroom setting really is and the development of a plan of action can be greatly assisted by *systematic observation.* The concept of systematic observation is described and developed in some detail in Chapter Two. However, for the present it will suffice to say that systematic observation represents a useful means of identifying, studying, classifying, and measuring specific variables as they interact within the instructional-learning situation. Operationally, systematic observation adds meaning and precision to observational experiences. By using the observational techniques that are provided by systematic observation, the observer is able to conceptualize the interaction of the variables that make up the instructional-learning situation. Finally, he is able to study these interacting variables in a live, on-going situation.

One of the prerequisites of an observational system is that it include and describe specific item variables that are a part of the classroom setting. It is the descriptions of identified variables that provide the observer with a theoretical framework for the instructional-learning situation from which he operates. These same item variables permit the observer to record and measure what he sees happening when he observes. Systematic observation brings the classroom interaction into focus so that it can be studied and described. As a result, classroom observation experiences take on new meaning. Observational exercises are planned and, in turn, yield data that can be interpreted and that are valuable to the observer. He can understand what he sees because he observes with both a purpose and a means for observing.

Observational systems are built and developed so that a person can be trained to use them for studying classroom behavior and for planning and analyzing his own teaching. To be most useful to the individual, an observational system must be simple enough to understand and manageable enough to be used by the typical classroom teacher. The system must yield data that are meaningful and relevant and it must make these data immediately available, with little or no statistical treatment. The key here is "immediate feedback." If the teacher has to wait to receive data describing a particular teaching performance, the activity loses much of its impact.

Both of the observational systems—the RCS and ETC—featured in this book qualify favorably in terms of the above criteria. Both are simple enough to be easily understood, both can be managed by the typical classroom teacher, and both immediately yield data that, with minor statistical treatment, provide real, concrete feedback to the teacher concerning his teaching performance.

The RCS—the Reciprocal Category System—is an adaptation or modification of Flanders' interaction analysis. The system contains nine categories that can be reciprocally applied to student or teacher talk and one general category that refers to silence or confusion. The RCS makes possible the observation of classroom verbal interaction, with particular emphasis on the socio-emotional climate of the classroom. The system provides a means of looking at the warming and cooling behaviors of the students and teachers as well as the positive and negative reinforcement factors.

The ETC—Equivalent Talk Categories—focuses on the level of cognitive interchange. Developed as an outgrowth of extensive work with the RCS, the ETC makes possible the systematic observation of the functions that directly affect the level of cognitive interaction in a classroom. The basic functions of informing, questioning, and responding are observable as well as the reacting and structuring behaviors that, to a great degree, determine cognitive level.

Questions—Prospective Teachers

Several questions are commonly asked by prospective trainees as to why they should learn to use an observational system. How can it benefit a teacher? What will it do for me? Can I use it in my teaching? Will it make a difference in my teaching? Experience and research have provided some rather definite answers to such questions.

Studies concerning the effectiveness of observation systems in shaping teacher behavior have been conducted, and a large proportion report favorable and positive results. One such study was conducted in 1965–66 at Ohio State University by Hough and Ober (1966). The study was designed to investigate the effectiveness of two different training designs for shaping the verbal behavior of undergraduate, preservice teachers who were enrolled in a general methods course. A total of 420 subjects, divided into two groups according to training in verbal behavior control, was studied. Regardless of training in verbal behavior control, all subjects received training in several skills: stating learning objectives in behavioral terms, selecting learning strategies, constructing testing instruments, and human relations. Only the training methods used to analyze and control verbal behavior were different for the two groups. One group was formally trained in the skill of interaction analysis (a modified version of the Flanders' system). The other group learned to consider verbal behavior in a more traditional fashion without the assistance of any formal observational system. In order to demonstrate their teaching skill, each of the subjects planned, taught, and analyzed a 20-minute lesson under simulated conditions while interaction analysis data were collected by a reliable observer.

Findings from the study indicated that there were distinct differences between the two groups:

> Subjects taught interaction analysis were found to use, in their teaching simulation, significantly more verbal behaviors that have been found to be associated with high student achievement and more positive student attitudes toward their teachers and school. These same subjects were found to use significantly fewer behaviors that have been found to be associated with lower achievement and less positive attitude.

The Hough-Ober study was followed by two additional studies conducted while the subjects were involved in student teaching experiences. Both follow ups studied the same sixty subjects—thirty each from both of the trained and untrained groups in the Hough-Ober study.

In the first follow up, Lohman (1966) found that there were several differences between trained and untrained student teachers with respect to their observed verbal teaching behavior:

> . . . the student teachers who had been trained in interaction analysis: 1) accepted and clarified student feelings more; 2)

praised and encouraged student action and behavior more; 3) accepted and clarified student ideas more; 4) lectured less; 5) gave fewer directions and spent less time giving directions; 6) used more verbal behaviors associated with motivation of students.

In addition, there was significantly more spontaneous student talk in classes taught by student teachers who were trained in interaction analysis:

> . . . the ratio of indirect verbal behavior to direct verbal behavior and the ratio of student talk to teacher talk were significantly different. This indicates a greater use of indirect verbal behavior and more student talk.

Findings of the Ober study produced a total of twenty-one significant multiple correlations—eleven related to indirect (warm, acceptant) teacher verbal behavior and ten related to direct (cool, aloof) verbal behavior. In addition, nine of the eleven correlations related to indirect verbal behaviors were found within the group of student teachers who had been trained previously in interaction analysis. In contrast, seven of the ten significant multiple correlations related to direct verbal behavior were found within the untrained group. Interpreted, these findings support the hypothesis that interaction analysis training is an effective means for helping teachers to control their verbal behavior to be in closer agreement with their own declared preferences for either an indirect or a direct style of teaching.

The three studies reported above (Hough-Ober, Lohman, and Ober) make it possible to say that: formal training in an observational system (in this case, interaction analysis) helps teachers to become aware of and better able to control their verbal behavior to be in closer agreement with (1) their own preferences for a particular style of teaching behavior, and (2) the prevailing philosophy that is brought to light while they are involved in a general methods course.

In another study, conducted at Temple University, Hough and Amidon (1965) designed a training program involving forty student teachers: twenty who were trained in interaction analysis concurrently with their student teaching and twenty who were involved in a conventional general methods course concurrently with student teaching. All subjects reacted to the Dogmatism Scale [3] (1966) and the Teaching Situation Reaction Test [4]

---

[3] The Dogmatism Scale is an instrument designed to measure the "openness-closedness" of the mind (belief-disbelief system).

[4] The Teaching Situation Reaction Test is an instrument reported to be valid for measuring a number of variables normally related to a person's preference to use either an "indirect" or a "direct" style of teaching.

(1965) prior to the beginning of the study. Findings indicated that the interaction analysis group showed a significant positive pre- to post-training change in terms of the Teaching Situation Reaction Test (i.e., they tended to prefer a more "indirect" style at the end). Furthermore, the greatest change was made by interaction analysis subjects who were more open minded. The researchers concluded that positive pre- to post-training change is related to both the dogmatism factor and training in interaction analysis.

Shortly after the Hough-Amidon study, Furst (1965) studied three groups of ten student teachers. One group received interaction analysis training *prior* to student teaching, a second group received interaction analysis training *concurrently* with student teaching, and a third group had *no* training in interaction analysis. Findings of the study indicate that student teachers who were taught interaction analysis used more acceptance of students' ideas and less rejection of student behavior. In addition, they tended to use more extended (prolonged) acceptance of students and more extended questioning. There was more total student talk and more student initiated talk in classes taught by student teachers who were taught interaction analysis concurrently with student teaching. Furst concluded that the timing or sequencing of interaction analysis training apparently had no effect on verbal behavior differences—rather, it was whether or not the student teachers received training in interaction analysis that made the difference.

Kirk (1964) used interaction analysis to compare the behavior of fifteen student teachers who were trained in interaction analysis with fifteen counterparts who were not trained. Each subject was observed for two 20-minute periods of teaching while interaction analysis data were collected by a reliable observer. Results of the study indicate that an operational understanding of interaction analysis (training) helps students to control their behavior—trained subjects talked less, gave fewer directions, and asked more questions following student voluntary contributions than did the untrained subjects.

The six studies summarized above have several characteristics in common. First, each involved pre-service teachers (undergraduates) as subjects. Second, each involved an observational instrument as a training tool. Third, each produced results that show differences between trained and untrained subjects with respect to their verbal teaching behavior. And fourth, the differences in each study tend to point in a favorable direction; that is, the teachers who were trained to use interaction analysis were able to control their verbal behavior in ways that are more congruent with either their own personally stated beliefs concerning teaching philosophy and/or the fundamental, underlying philosophy upon which their previous training was predicated. In conclusion, findings of these six studies support the general hypothesis that training in an observational system helps a teacher to become more aware of and better able to control his teaching behavior.

Strategy

At the risk of oversimplification, then, for learning to be facilitated two basic conditions must be met:

1. A positive socio-emotional climate in which the student feels comfortable and is motivated to learn must exist.
2. The instructional agent (teacher) must manipulate and control the learning stimuli in ways that will result in maximum student learning.

The phrase "manipulate and control" implies that the teacher will conduct the classroom learning activities according to a predetermined plan, rather than haphazardly. He needs to assess a given instructional-learning situation well ahead of time. From this assessment, the teacher must make certain professional judgments concerning what he will do instructionally in order to facilitate learning in that particular situation. The teacher selects instructional strategies that he judges to be most appropriate to that situation.

The notion of *instructional strategy* is certainly not a new one in educational circles. The approach of developing strategies through the use of systematic observation is more recent, however, and this union stimulates some very interesting possibilities. Chapter 5 develops and discusses both of the concepts of planning and executing instructional strategies in more detail.

As used here, a strategy refers to the use of one or more related functions that, together, provide a means for facilitating and/or accomplishing a particular learning objective. That is, strategy is a whole, made up of several related functions. In turn, a function is a teacher (or learner) behavior as described by an item or category of an observational system.

The following three tables (1.1, 1.2, 1.3) are samples of strategies that

Table 1.1

DRILL STRATEGY USING THE RCS *

Code

Teacher Question	4	"What is 3 + 5?"
Student Response	15	"Eight."
Teacher Reinforcement	2	"Correct!"

* The purpose of this strategy is the learning of sums.

Table 1.2

CLARIFICATION STRATEGY USING THE RCS

Code

Student Initiation	16	"My father says he is an individualist."
Teacher Request for Clarification	3	"What does he mean by that, Joan?"
Student Initiation to Amplify	16	"Well, he says that he always votes for the man, not the party."
Student Request for Amplification	13	"How does that make your father an individualist?"
Student Initiation to Amplify	16	"Well, he thinks as an individual himself, not like the rest of the public."

Table 1.3

MAINTAIN-EXPAND STRATEGY USING THE ETC *

Code

Teacher Introducing the Learning Situation   9
  "Now we have isolated the major elements of a piece of fiction—plot, theme, character, tempo. I would like us to take the story John suggested we all read and explore the story for these elements and the way that the author uses them."

Teacher Questioning—Restricted   2
  "What did we decide was the most outstanding characteristic of the plot, Susan?"

Student Responding—Restricted   14
  "The fact that the plot centers around one character."

Teacher Reacting—Maintain   6
  "Yes, we did discuss the fact that the main character of Dolly reveals the plot. What other general decision did we reach about the plot?"

Student Responding—Restricted   14
  "Well, Jim seemed to think that the plot was a puzzle, like Dolly's mind was a puzzle."

Teacher Reacting—Expand   7
  "Yes, we did talk about the possibility of the plot being developed like a puzzle. Is there any other way the author reveals this puzzle idea to us?

Student Responding—Expanded   15
  "Well, I think he uses some symbolism. For example, in the first paragraph, he talks about the jigsaw edges of Dolly's mouth. Then he has Dolly complaining about the maze of problems that beset her. Both of those words—jigsaw and maze—have puzzle associations."

* This strategy is designed to raise the level of thinking related to the topic in question.

could be developed using the functions isolated by the observational systems presented in this book. Following the description of the function or behavior is the appropriate category symbol.

In the examples given above, the strategies consist of several behaviors as described by an observation system, in this case the RCS and the ETC. It should be made clear that wherever a strategy is presented in this book, there is no intent on the part of the authors to purport it as an appropriate technique. Rather, the relationship of the awareness and control fostered by the systematic observation and strategy development is illustrated. Strategies are not "tongue-in-cheek" lesson plans, but should reflect not only the objectives of the situation, but also the learning theory upon which the objectives are based.

Later in the text, several positions on learning are presented and discussed along with examples to illustrate how strategies and behaviors described in terms of observational systems can be used to demonstrate their rationale and implementation. Again, it is not intended that a particular learning theory be identified as better than another or as a foolproof technique. This book does not defend the soundness of a particular learning theory, but rather it presents and defends the use of systematic observation as a means for putting a learning theory into practice. In all cases, it remains the task of the individual reader to determine whether or not he chooses to adopt and use a particular learning theory and/or strategy in his own teaching.

A New Look

The idealistic purpose and practical goal of this book is to present systematic observation as a method of strategy building and instructional improvement. It is directed at the teacher, whether a beginning pre-service teacher or an experienced in-service teacher. More specifically, the book is designed to accomplish at least two objectives:

1. To prepare the observer (teacher) to study classroom behavior in an objective and systematic way, through the use of two observational systems—the RCS and the ETC.
2. To present to the teacher a variety of teaching techniques—functions, strategies—that he will have under his control for use as he performs his own teaching activities.

In order to accomplish the goals and objectives above, the book is organized to acquaint the reader with the field of systematic observation, to teach the reader to use the RCS and the ETC, and to develop for the reader the relationship between systematic observation and strategy building.

In Chapter 2, the notion of systematic observation is presented and discussed in detail. Different kinds of systems are outlined with examples.

Chapter 3 deals with the Reciprocal Category System. The basic rationale and mechanics are outlined, along with instruction for learning and using the system. Chapter 4 presents the Equivalent Talk Categories (ETC), similar to the RCS, with the rationale and mechanics for learning and using the system.

Chapter 5 deals with functions and strategies of teaching as they relate to learning and learning theory. Documentary evidence is included to clarify and support the various strategies discussed.

Chapter 6 explains how the RCS and ETC can be used in planned observational experiences and in laboratory microteaching experiences. In this chapter, the theory and rationale that have been featured and discussed in the previous chapters of the book are operationalized with clearly outlined learning experiences. Directions and explanations are given for establishing controlled teaching situations, both in the lab and in the classroom, so that a teacher may select and plan instructional strategies and execute them for subsequent analysis through systematic observation.

2

Systematic
Observation
as a Concept

The scientific mode of inquiry has centered on the systematic observation of selected phenomena for years, or at least since Sir Francis Bacon died of pneumonia in the eighteenth century following the renowned chicken preservation experiment. In the world of the classroom, likewise, the alert, well-prepared teacher has observed characteristics of children and of interactions involving aptitude, methodology, and content. Unlike the carefully systematized and controlled laboratory approaches in science, the classroom teacher has largely depended on emotional reactions to independent, isolated incidents rather than substantial, systematically collected samples of participation and performance.

The work of Withall (1949), Flanders and Amidon (1960), Medley and Mitzel (1948), and Galloway (1968) has pioneered the utilization of systematized approaches in the study of children in classrooms in the United States and around the world, and since 1960, these efforts have received wide attention.

Observational systems, developed for the purpose of identifying, classifying, quantifying, and analyzing specific classroom behaviors and interactions, are in use throughout the profession, by the teacher, researcher, and teacher trainer. Systems do not, however, produce evaluative judgments, but rather, serve as tools for obtaining data that can be used to compare action with intent—what actually happens in the classroom with objectives.

Through the use of various observational systems, classroom interaction can be analyzed from points of view such as verbal interaction, non-verbal behavior, levels of cognition, and types of questions and answers. It is important to note that no single system purports to measure the total classroom situation and that more than one system must be used to obtain a comprehensive view of the teaching-learning situation.

Systematic Observation

Systematic observation is an accepted method of organizing observed teaching acts in a manner which allows any trained person who follows stated procedures to observe, record, and analyze interactions with the assurance that others viewing the same situation would agree, to a great extent, with his recorded sequence of behaviors. Furthermore, the observer would know that he or others would record the same behaviors in the same way though viewing in a wide variety of classrooms or interaction settings. As an accepted frame of reference, systematic observation serves in much the same way that rules in bidding and defending apply in playing bridge, or, perhaps more analogously, the rules in a sport where a foul is a foul, a score is a score. The basic purpose of systematic observation is to help operationalize teaching objectives in teaching strategies.

Certain assumptions form the base of this approach to improving teaching strategies. In order to improve, teachers need awareness and control of their teaching strategies. Teachers can achieve such awareness by evaluating their own teaching-learning behaviors. An important concept and perhaps the key to using systematic observation procedure is that through the assaying process—identifying and classifying—inconsistencies in behavior and perceptions can be alleviated, unsuccessful approaches abandoned, and new approaches identified.

An observational system usually includes some type of carefully defined items or categories so that observers can become skilled in identifying and recording brief codes to represent behaviors occurring in classrooms. Discussions of systematic observation in general and the in-depth explication of two systems have been designed to direct practitioners toward developing skills that are useful in planning and improving behavior. The two systems—RCS and ETC—utilize audio or video tapes made in the classroom and a coding system representing categories of instructional-situation behaviors or functions, mechanics for the application of collection, preparation, and interpretation, and practice exercises to encourage skill reinforcement. Each category focuses the teacher's attention on identified types of classroom behavior and makes it possible to record observed behaviors in quantitative terms. For example, after gaining understanding and skill to a criterion standard, teachers are then ready to prepare audio or video tapes of themselves and their classes and to begin self-evaluation activities.

Two illustrative items or categories are helpful to understanding a coding system. Wrightstone's efforts to record pupil responses in group situations in the 1930s included the following categories of student talk:

	Code
Initiative in prepared voluntary report or exhibit	3a
Initiative in extemporaneous contribution from real experience *	3b

   * Wrightstone, 1935, pp. 33–34.

The student categories in Flanders' (1965) Interaction Analysis further illustrate the category concept:

	Code
Student Talk—Response: talk by students in reponse to teacher. Teacher initiates the contact or solicits student statement.	8
Student Talk—Initiation: talk by students that they initiate. If "calling on" student is only to indicate who may talk next, observer must decide whether student wanted to talk. If he did, use this category.	9

As an observer of live interaction or in coding taped sequences as the illustrated behaviors occurred, a code would be recorded according to *a priori* instructions.

Observers learn to apply established procedures including the mechanics of data collection through observation, analysis of recorded behavior sequences or behaviors, and the interpretation of the collected evidence. Individual teachers can learn the skills, collect feedback information, and render their own judgments.

A simple example of systematic observation was recently developed by a group of Georgia teachers interested in the problem of interpersonal relations for trainable and educable mentally retarded children of elementary and middle years in mental maturity. Depicted below is the Interpersonal Relations System (IRS) as devised by these teachers. This system is not a carefully tried and tested approach; however, it represents the concept of isolating elements into observable segments.

INTERPERSONAL RELATIONS SYSTEM (IRS)

1. Name calling
2. Taking turns
3. Following directions
4. Compromising
5. Respecting personal property
6. Other acceptable manners

Observation systems are organized, objective ways of looking at classroom behavior, i.e., recording in a fashion that teachers and theoreticians can readily recognize the acts and/or actions in a sequence. Mutually understandable sets of terms are available. They are tools, techniques for objectivizing self-evaluation. Self-confrontation becomes a source of feedback data on which judgments can be sensibly based.

No one observation system is presently capable of classifying or presenting the total picture of the classroom—more than one system is necessary to gain a comprehensive picture. Ober reports that in a Nassau County, Florida research study, the design required the use of three systems: the Reciprocal Category System, the Teacher Practices Observation Record, and the Florida Taxonomy of Cognitive Behavior.[1] Results indicated that, with respect to a particular home economics class, one system revealed limited verbal patterns, one failed to reveal substantial experimentalism in the Dewian tradition, but the third system indicated that "the learning activities tended to cluster at the higher levels of cognitive behavior." Even though an outside-observer, research approach was utilized, the carry-over value implied that in self-evaluation, it is important to use more than one system to measure thoroughly the aptitude-treatment interactions.

Direct observation can and should be used in the search for effective patterns of teaching-learning behavior. Basic elements in the classroom generally include the teacher, the students, the content, the plan, and the interactions. In recent years, considerable interest and attention have been devoted to modification or refinement of "the plan" now commonly known as "the treatment." Student aptitudes and teacher behaviors are now characteristically studied as they interact with content within specified treatments or teaching strategies. Observation allows individual teachers to study and analyze their own teaching strategies in the privacy of classroom and home. Systematic observation provides the opportunity for continuous monitoring of teaching behavior—the examination of class-relevant variables, in light of activities necessary to teach as planned.

Birch (1969) has indicated that as teaching behaviors are reviewed, there are usually varying degrees of discrepancy between what was planned for and what actually occurred, resulting in cognitive dissonance (inconsistency or imbalance in perceived and actual). Birch and Parsons [2] indicate that change involves the disintegration-reintegration process and that dissatisfaction with results leads to replacement of the cause for dissatisfaction. Thus, dissonance in cognitive structures should be expected, identified, and faced. (The level of frustration that can be expected is an important

---

[1] Brown, Ober, and Soar, "Florida Taxonomy of Cognitive Behavior" (Gainsville, Fla.: University of Florida, 1968); an observation system for assessing cognitive content level in the classroom. B. Brown, *The Experimental Mind in Education* (New York: Harper & Row, 1968)(TPOR).

[2] Statements in Grand Rapids, Michigan to Guided Self-Analysis study group, November, 1969.

consideration in that there must be some feeling by the teacher that remediation and improvement are practical possibilities.)

This book focuses primarily on verbal interactions. An early Flanders' study (1960) revealed that two-thirds of the time in a classroom, somebody is talking, two-thirds of *that* time is the teacher talking, and two-thirds of *that* time is direct teacher talk. The influence of the verbal dimension on learning processes is an important index and, therefore, teaching strategies planned to encourage and trigger increasingly sophisticated thinking depend largely on verbal presentation and interchange.

Two systems are emphasized within the present discussion—one to assess the classroom atmosphere and the other to sequentially identify teaching strategies as they occur in the classroom. Although the systems suggested are not evaluative, they do foster identification, classification, quantification, and analysis of classroom actions. Awareness of the actual leads to control in strategy selection and implementation—a benefit of accurate feedback. Behaviors in the classroom are empirically nothing until they are identified, hopefully, so that, regardless of who is observing, agreement and communication are possible. Such agreement and communication are facilitated by observation systems.

Observation Systems

There are two basic kinds of observation systems: *sign* and *category*. A sign system is composed of a list of behaviors. During a given period of time, the observer simply checks or marks in some manner each behavior that occurs. Regardless of the frequency of occurrence, the behavior is checked only once during the observation period. The category system provides classifications of behaviors that the observer learns. At regular intervals within the observation period, the observer determines in what category the observed behavior falls and records that category number.

A sign system lists a number of specific incidents of behavior that may or may not occur during the observation period. The Florida Taxonomy of Cognitive Behavior, a sign system, is composed of fifty-five behavioral items. These items are grouped, basically, in seven levels of cognition as defined by Bloom (1956) and Sanders (1966).

1.10 Knowledge of specifics
1.20 Knowledge of ways and means of dealing with specifics
1.30 Knowledge of universals and abstractions
2.00 Translation
3.00 Interpretation

4.00   Application
5.00   Analysis
6.00   Synthesis
7.00   Evaluation

Under each level appear specific behaviors such as those presented in Figure 2.1.

Figure 2.1

FLORIDA TAXONOMY OF COGNITIVE BEHAVIOR
(SAMPLE LEVELS)

2.00 TRANSLATION

						18. Restates in own words or briefer terms
						19. Gives concrete example of an abstract idea
						20. Verbalizes from a graphic representation
						21. Translates verbalization into graphic form
						22. Translates fig statements to lit statements, or vice versa
						23. Translates from lang to Eng, or vice versa

3.00 INTERPRETATION

						24. Gives reason (tells why)
						25. Shows similarities, differences
						26. Summarizes or concludes from obs of evidence
						27. Shows cause and effect relationship
						28. Gives analogy: simile, metaphor
						29. Performs a directed task or process

During each observation period, the observer checks each behavior as it occurs. Behaviors are checked only once per six-minute observation period.

Observing classroom interaction through a category system is quite different: observations are limited to one facet of classroom behavior. A convenient unit of behavior is determined and a discrete set of categories is constructed into which behavior units can be classified. Thus, an observation record would contain the units of behavior, classified by category, occurring during an observation period. A category system should be exhaustive—inclusive of behaviors of the types to be recorded.

Withall's system (Table 2.1), one of the earliest examples of systematic observation and a category system, focuses on teacher behaviors in the social-emotional climate. It consists of seven teacher categories on a continuum ranging from teacher centeredness to learner centeredness. This category system, the forerunner of several popular systems, ignores pupil behavior and concentrates on teacher actions which are then placed in one of these seven categories.

Table 2.1

WITHALL'S CATEGORIES

1. Learner-supportive statements that have the intent of reassuring or commending the pupil.
2. Acceptant and clarifying statements having an intent to convey to the pupil the feeling that he was understood and help him elucidate his ideas and feelings.
3. Problem-structuring statements or questions which proffer information or raise questions about the problem.
4. Neutral statements which comprise polite formalities, administrative comments . . . no intent inferrable.
5. Directive or hortative statements with intent to have pupil follow a recommended course of action.
6. Reproving or deprecating remarks intended to deter pupil from continued indulgence in present unacceptable behavior.
7. Teacher self-supporting remarks intended to sustain or justify the teacher's position or course of action.

In using an observation system to analyze the classroom situation, the teacher serves as an abstractor. He identifies and selects from the continuous flow of classroom events units of behavior that are relevant to the idea or behavior under investigation. If his focus is verbal behavior, the teacher selects a system that measures this dimension, and, through this system, views classroom interaction, makes qualitative judgments, and records behaviors.

Exemplary Systems

Although general use of observation systems in research and teacher self-evaluation is a relatively recent development, systematic observation appeared in educational literature as early as 1935 with Wrightstone's study of schools in New York using "Newer Practices." The many educators who have investigated and developed observational approaches include: Anderson, Withall, Hughes, Flanders, Amidon, Ober, Brown, Galloway, Medley and Mitzel, Ryans, Gallagher and Aschner, Combs. A brief summary of some illustrative observational approaches is presented in Table 2.2.

The theoretical base or instructional theory on which the various systems are constructed determines, to a great degree, the applicability of the instruments to certain objectives. The Teachers' Practices Observational Record (TPOR) (Brown, 1968), for example, is a system based on the teachings of Dewey and is pragmatic in content. (See Figure 2.2.) The use of this instrument allows one to see the kinds of practices the teacher brings to

Table 2.2

ILLUSTRATIVE OBSERVATIONAL APPROACHES

System		Objective of Study	Illustrative Contributions
Wrightstone (1935)	Category	Study of schools in New York using "Newer Practices"	Form of items
H. H. Anderson (1945, 1946)	Category	Observation of interaction Integrative and dominative teacher contacts	I/D Index (dimentialization) System of Coding Behaviors
Withall (1949)	Category	Teacher behavior in social-emotional climate	7 teacher categories Continuum (teacher centeredness to learner centeredness)
Bales (1950)	Category	Individual behavior in selected social and psychological education	"Interaction" recorder or timing
Medley and Mitzel (1958–61)	Sign and Category	Observational study of teacher graduates	Scales derived from factor analysis; Empirically tested items; Verbal and Non-Verbal Observed
Hughes (1959)	Category	Teacher functions	Verbal and Non-Verbal Observed
Flanders (1963)	Category	Verbal interaction	Combined I.D., teacher categories, timing, and dependence factor, added student talk, analysis techniques including 100 all matrix
Ryans (1960)	Sign	Teacher characteristics	Identified differentiating patterns of teacher characteristics
B. O. Smith and Associates (1962)	Category	Behavior of teachers in teacher presentations of analysis of classroom discourse	Describing, designating and explaining most frequent occurrences

System (cont.)		Objective of Study	Illustrative Contributions
Bellack (1963)	Category	Language in classroom	Research application
Kounin (1965)	Category	Student and teacher behavior patterns	Practical application
Hough (1966)	Category	Effect of training	Modification of i.a. (added categories)
Amidon (1966)	Category	Emphasis on teacher behavior	Modification of Flanders i.a. (added categories and stressed patterns)
Ober (1967)	Category	Teacher verbal behavior, student verbal behavior, teacher-student behavior	Modification of i.a. (reciprocal factor)
Brown, et al. (1967)	Sign	Levels of cognition	Empirical look at levels of thinking
Galloway (1969)	Category	Non-verbal communication	Emphasis on importance of non-verbal actions

the classroom—individualization of instruction, for example. The Florida Taxonomy of Cognitive Behavior (Brown, et al, 1967), on the other hand, provides for a measure of the levels of cognitive behavior of both teacher and student. Flanders' interaction analysis is based on assumptions concerning direct and indirect influence of teacher behavior on classroom climate. Consequently, the system chosen for a specific purpose [3] must be determined by the nature of that purpose.

If the teacher is the focus of the observation, several systems are specifically directed at teacher behavior. The early Withall system listed seven categories of teacher actions. Hughes' (1959) categories (Table 2.3), similar to Withall's, focus on teacher functions.

---

[3] Three resource books usually quite accessible in bookstores, school system professional libraries, and college library collections provide additional discussion. Ira J. Gordon's *Studying the Child in School* contains a section on the Ecology of the Classroom in which observation techniques are identified and described. *The Handbook of Research on Teaching* edited by N. L. Gage has two sections, 6 and 13, that concern observation techniques. Section Six treats Measuring Classroom Behavior by Systematic Observation, while Section Thirteen deals with Social Interaction in the Classroom. Amidon and Hough are editors of a book of readings, *Interaction Analysis: Theory, Research, and Application,* that contains several reports on systematic observation, particularly interaction analysis.

Figure 2.2

TEACHER PRACTICES OBSERVATION RECORD

TOT	I	II	III	TEACHER PRACTICES A. NATURE OF THE SITUATION
				1. T makes self center of attention.
				2. T makes p center of attention.
				3. T makes some *thing itself* center of p's attention.
				4. T makes *doing something* center of p's attention.
				5. T has p spend time waiting, watching, listening.
				6. T has p participate actively.
				7. T remains aloof or detached from p's activities.
				8. T joins or participates in p's activities.
				9. T discourages or prevents p from expressing self freely.
				10. T encourages p to express self freely.
				B. NATURE OF THE PROBLEM
				11. T organizes learning around Q posed by T.
				12. T organizes learning around p's own problem or Q.
				13. T prevents situation which causes p doubt or perplexity.
				14. T involves p in uncertain or incomplete situation.
				15. T steers p away from "hard" Q or problem.
				16. T leads p to Q or problem which "stumps" him.
				17. T emphasizes gentle or pretty aspects of topic.
				18. T emphasizes distressing or ugly aspects of topic.
				19. T asks Q that p can answer only if he studied the lesson.
				20. T asks Q that is not readily answerable by study of lesson.
				C. DEVELOPMENT OF IDEAS
				21. T accepts only one answer as being correct.
				22. T asks p to suggest additional or alternative answers.
				23. T expects p to come up with answer T has in mind.
				24. T asks p to judge comparative value of answers or suggestions.
				25. T expects p to "know" rather than to guess answer to Q.
				26. T encourages p to guess or hypothesize about the unknown or untested.
				27. T accepts only answers or suggestions closely related to topic.
				28. T entertains even "wild" or far-fetched suggestion of p.
				29. T lets p "get by" with opinionated or sterotyped answer.
				30. T asks p to support answer or opinion with evidence.

Hughes suggests optimal percentages of time to be spent in the various functions. However, the identified functions do not discriminate between the judged "good" and "representative" teachers in the major study (Medley and Mitzel, 1963).

Table 2.3

HUGHES' FUNCTIONS

1. Controlling functions, such as standard setting, intervening, routine regulating.
2. Imposition of teacher, such as moralizing, informing.
3. Facilitating functions, such as clarifying, checking, demonstrating.
4. Functions that develop content, such as generalizing, summarizing, stimulating, evaluating.
5. Functions that serve as response, such as meeting requests, interpreting, acknowledging teacher mistakes.
6. Functions of positive affectivity, such as supporting, encouraging, soliciting.
7. Functions of negative affectivity, such as admonishing, reprimanding, ignoring, threatening.

Smith's (1962) categories look at teacher behavior in presentations; and though not directly concerned with subject matter, they come closer to dealing with content than most. (See Table 2.4 for a brief listing of categories.)

Table 2.4

CATEGORIES USED BY SMITH

1. Defining
2. Describing
3. Designating
4. Stating
5. Reporting
6. Substituting
7. Evaluating
8. Opining
9. Classifying
10. Comparing and contrasting
11. Conditional inferring
12. Explaining
13. Directing and managing a classroom

If verbal interaction is the focus of the observation, there are systems which are directed at this dimension of classroom behavior. Gallagher-Aschner (1963), Bellack, *et al.* (1963), Parsons (1969), and Flanders (Amidon and Flanders, 1963) will be presented in simplified terms.

The Gallagher-Aschner System approaches the verbal dimension of class-room behavior by examining questions in five categories:

—Cognitive memory
—Convergent thinking
—Divergent thinking
—Evaluative thinking
—Routine

Cognitive-memory operations generally represent recall of facts using processes such as rote memory and selective recall; verbal behavior such as divergent thinking should be characterized by the taking of a new direction or perspective (what one personally thinks) in a given topic.

In an extensive study of classroom language, Bellack *et al.* (1966) analyzed the pedagogical moves and classified them in terms of pedagogical functions. Four functions were isolated:

1. Structuring—the context.
2. Soliciting—questions, commands, requests.
3. Responding—answers to questions, moves related to soliciting.
4. Reacting—reactions that modify by clarifying, synthesizing, or expanding; reactions that rate prior behaviors either positively or negatively.

While this study developed the functional categories from the process of analyzing extensive recordings of classroom interaction, it can be considered a post-facto observational system. The study also revealed four types of moving in student teacher discourse:

1. Substantive—deals with the subject matter of the class.
2. Substantive—logical—deals with the cognitive processes involved in dealing with subject matter.
3. Instructional—deals with matters such as assignments, materials, and routine classroom procedures.
4. Instructional—logical—deals with didactic verbal processes such as negative or positive rating, explaining procedures, and giving directions.

Ted Parsons (1969) has developed a system that also looks at the teaching process. His system, entitled Guided Self-Analysis, concentrates on teaching for inquiry and includes six schedules or six sub-systems. These sub-systems are related to:

1. Questioning strategies
2. Response patterns

3. Teacher talk patterns
4. Teacher-pupil talk patterns
5. Experience referents
6. Levels of thinking

Each schedule is a guide for analyzing and interpreting a sequence of teaching-learning behaviors. The first schedule, for example, assists the teacher in analyzing the questioning strategies used in the classroom and contains five categories of questions:

1. Rhetorical
2. Information
3. Leading
4. Probing
5. Other

The teacher is encouraged to videotape a teaching-learning sequence and then to review it in terms of each of the schedules. The second schedule, for example, extends the teacher's analysis by concentrating on teacher responses to pupil statements. The schedule is composed of four types of responses:

1. Closure
2. Verbal reward
3. Sustaining
4. Extending

Parsons' rationale of dividing the instructional concerns into small, manageable schedules, so that the teacher can concentrate on one function at a time, supports the point that no *one* system can completely reveal what happens in a classroom.

The well-known observation system of interaction analysis, developed by Ned Flanders to measure the verbal behaviors in the classroom, is a category system, consisting of ten categories. (See Table 2.5.) Interaction analysis—as developed by Ned Flanders and modified by Amidon, Ober and several others—is specifically directed at the verbal aspects of classroom behavior.

Categories 1–7 pertain to teacher talk; categories 8 and 9 refer to student talk; and category 10 indicates silence or confusion. The first four categories of teacher talk are concerned with indirect influence exerted by the teacher and reflect behavior that tends to stimulate student freedom and participation by accepting feelings, praising and encouraging, accepting

Table 2.5

CATEGORIES FOR INTERACTION ANALYSIS [1]

Teacher Talk

Indirect Influence

1. *Accepts feeling:* accepts and clarifies the feeling tone of the students in a nonthreatening manner. Feelings may be positive or negative. Predicting or recalling feelings are included.
2. *Praises or encourages:* praises or encourages student action or behavior. Jokes that release tension, not at the expense of another individual, nodding head.
3. *Accepts or uses ideas of student:* clarifying, building, or developing ideas or suggestions by a student. As teacher brings more of his own ideas into play, shift to category five.
4. *Asks questions:* asking a question about content or procedure with the intent that a student answer.

Direct Influence

5. *Lecturing:* giving facts or opinions about content or procedure; expressing his own ideas, asking rhetorical questions.
6. *Giving directions:* directions, commands, or orders to which a student is expected to comply.
7. *Criticizing or justifying authority:* statements intended to change student stating why the teacher is doing what he is doing; extreme self-reference.

Student Talk

8. *Student talk—responses:* talk by students in response to teacher. Teacher behavior from nonacceptable to acceptable pattern; bawling someone out, initiates the contact or solicits student statement.
9. *Sudent talk—initiation:* talk by students which they initiate. If "calling on" student is only to indicate who may talk next, observer must decide whether student wanted to talk. If he did, use this category.
10. *Silence or confusion:* pauses, short periods of silence and periods of confusion in which communication cannot be understood by the observer.

* There is *no* scale implied by these numbers. Each number is classificatory; it designates a particular kind of communication event. To write these numbers down during observation is to enumerate, not to judge a position on a scale.
[1] Developed by Ned A. Flanders, University of Minnesota, 1959.

and clarifying ideas, and soliciting participation. Direct influence, which tends to limit or restrict student participation by lecturing, giving directions, rejecting student behavior, and justifying authority, is reflected in categories 5, 6, and 7. Student verbal behavior is divided into two categories: teacher initiated (8) and student initiated (9). Category 10 is used to indicate silence or confusion.

Interaction analysis, as developed by Flanders, devotes a great deal of attention to teacher talk—seven of the ten categories. The system also provides for looking at the indirect and direct nature of the teacher's verbal behavior. While these are two strong points of the Flanders' system, they are also its greatest drawbacks. The system devotes little attention to student talk and focuses a great deal of attention on the direct/indirect nature of the teacher's performance.

Interaction analysis incorporates knowledge gained about integrative and dominative contacts, dependence proneness, timed intervals on behavior units, and categories of teacher behavior. Additional contributions are identifiable in student talk categories, a silence or confusion category, and extensive analysis procedures. For a full treatment, the reader should consult references listed in the bibliography to this publication. (See Appendix.)

In an effort to strengthen this aproach, Richard L. Ober developed a modification of interaction analysis—the Reciprocal Category System (RCS). Ober's adaptation provides nine common categories that can be used reciprocally for student and teacher talk. The system is handled in much the same manner as Flanders' system. Data are recorded at three-second intervals and when the behavior changes and are then transferred to a matrix or chart-like form for interpretation.

Each researcher, in his own efforts, provided helpful approaches and findings that made, in retrospect at least, for orderly progression in technique refinement (Figure 2.3). Masterful combination of known with new has led many to refer to Flanders as the "father of interaction analysis." Much of the literature reports studies or theoretical exposition by proponents of interaction analysis, though often in modified form—the Reciprocal Category System, for example, is a modification.

Most observational systems reported in this book have adaptability potential for the classroom teacher. They present systematic aproaches to analyzing dimensions of the teacher-learning situation. Gordon (1966) says it well in *Studying the Child in the Classroom* (John Wiley & Sons):

> What we have today are essentially process-oriented procedures for the observation of classroom behavior, while such behavior is occurring. Although the procedures attempt to be non-judgmental, placing behavior in categories requires some modicum of judgment of the event, even if it does not necessitate an evaluation of the teacher as 'good' or 'bad.' These schedules are simply means of describing a portion of what is taking place in the classroom. The teacher, then, can use the information to assess his own behavior and make his own judgments.

Uses of Observation Systems

The usefulness of observation systems runs the gamut from self-evaluation efforts of the classroom teacher to highly controlled, experimental research.

Figure 2.3

ILLUSTRATIVE CONTRIBUTIONS TO INTERACTION ANALYSIS

H. H. Anderson _____
Integrative and Dominative Contacts
I/D ratio

      Lippitt and White _____
      Dependence-Independence

           Withall _____
           7 Teacher Categories

               Bales _____
               Timing

                    Flanders _____
                    Categories of student talk;
                    Combined Categories, time and I/D;
                    Procedures for Analysis, Matrix

                         Ober _____
                         Equal Emphasis on
                         Student Behavior and 361
                         Cell Matrix

Amidon (1969) lists several basic purposes for interaction analysis when applied in student teaching:

— Developing skill in observation of teaching.
— Providing a tool for the analysis of teaching.
— Providing a tool for feedback about one's teaching.
— Setting a framework for practicing and learning specific teaching skills.
— Providing a framework for conceptualizing and developing various teaching styles.

Ober (1967) enumerates six specified teacher operations in which systematic observation procedures are positive influences.

— Identifying and separating the contributing elements that constitute a given teaching-learning situation.
— Conceptualizing the relationships between these interacting elements.
— Selecting and planning instructional strategies that will facilitate maximum student learning in a variety of teaching-learning situations.

—Developing and sharpening suitable skills in order to transform the selected instructional strategies into practice in the classroom.

—Acquiring reliable and meaningful data that can subsequently be analyzed to provide feedback concerning the quality of the teaching performance.

—Improving the future teaching performance by means of suitable modification and revision.

As a research tool, systematic observation is used in analyzing teacher behavior, investigating pupil-teacher interaction patterns, quantifying verbal behaviors, and studying the relationship between identified teaching styles and pupil achievement.

Three basic areas of schooling are the focus for the majority of reports on applied systematic observation—pre-service internships or student teaching in teacher education programs, in-service instruction or training for teachers and supervisors, and classroom effectiveness related to pupil attitude and academic performance.

Initial Reports

Results from early efforts in the use of systematic observation can be summarized as follows:

—The teacher is the most influential determinant of classroom climate or atmosphere.

—Classroom climate can be assessed through systematic observation techniques.

—Teaching patterns can be identified.

—Pupil performance is influenced by teaching style.

These early reports generally stated that teacher behaviors such as domination tend to produce conformity or resistance and substantial dependence on the instructor. Teacher behaviors identified as integrative encouraged common solution of differences and more individual initiative. (See Table 2.6.)

Table 2.6

TEACHER BEHAVIOR CONCEPTS

H. H. Anderson	Dominative	Integrative
Lippitt and White	Authoritarian	Democratic
Withall	Teacher-centered	Learner-centered
Cogan	Preclusive	Inclusive
Flanders	Direct	Indirect

In-Service Models

During the sixties, investigations have been reported in substantially greater numbers. If interaction analysis is following the S-shaped adoption curve, usually associated with the diffusion of new practices, it would appear from the literature to be out of the slow adoption period and into the middle of the S-curve and its much faster adoption rate.[4] Reports pertaining to interaction analysis and in-service programs focus on training teachers to use systematic observation as a feedback mechanism. Two models are presented for illustrative purposes.

Richmond Unified School District, California. In the December 1968, "Theory Into Practice," Minnis and Shrable discussed a staff development program planned "to improve the quality of both teacher supervision and classroom teaching." Principals learned to use interaction analysis to become more skilled in instructional leadership. These principals learned Flanders' system of interaction analysis, taught classes of public school students for direct experience with its usefulness in classroom teaching, and, as a practicum, worked with volunteer teachers on their own faculties to achieve implementation of the new procedures.

> Teachers were encouraged to acquire skills in (1) identifying patterns of teacher influence on students, (2) analyzing teacher patterns of behavior in light of goals set for a lesson, (3) planning alternative patterns of behavior to replace those not achieving goals, (4) differentiating narrow and broad questions, and (5) identifying levels of thinking required in answering different questions.

The self-help feature was stressed. Teachers used the technique in privacy with the right to erase taped materials until they were ready for the principal or others to offer help in instructional supervision.

Metropolitan Atlanta School Systems,[5] Georgia. During school year 1968–69 approximately 500 Atlanta teachers, principals, and central office personnel participated in laboratories (Bentley and Miller, 1969), based on the Reciprocal Category System of interaction analysis. Emphasis was placed on the *awareness* and *control* factors as influenced by the extent to which the intended teaching-learning model was actually accomplished. Modifications in objectives and procedures were stressed as was practice in

---

[4] See E. Katz, M. L. Levin, and H. Hamilton, "Traditions of Research on the Diffusion of Innovations," *Amer. Sociol. Rev.,* XXVIII, 2 (1963), 237–252, for a discussion of characteristics of innovations and their rates of adoption.

[5] Six school systems have participated—Marietta City, Gwinnett County, Decatur City, Cobb County, Clayton County, and Atlanta Public Schools.

the skills requisite to achievement of intended patterns. Attempts to systematize the laboratory training exercises led to the preparation of a training manual, organization of the two-day training period into approximately ten hours of skill sessions to prepare "good observers" (see p. 79), and development of practice drills related to mastery of identified skills and understanding.

A businesslike controlled approach provided feedback on concepts, category validity, and rater agreement measures. A study of the effect of personal and professional variables on skill development revealed that there is little or no relationship, with the possible exception of age and experience. There is some indication that, as age and number of years in a position increase, the difficulty in becoming a skilled observer increases. In one laboratory involving seventy-six participants, approximately two-thirds learned the RCS well enough for purposes of self-evaluation.

Teachers involved in these sessions informally report the usefulness of systematic observation training to include:

1. Increased awareness of the variety of verbal behaviors occurring in the classrooms.
2. Capability of shifting patterns to achieve goals when verbal interaction indicates that objectives are not achieved.
3. Greater flexibility of verbal behavior, especially in types of questions and ways of accepting student contributions.

Research Efforts

Investigation of effects on teachers have generally been at the pre-service stage. Amidon and Giammateo (1965) in *The Verbal Behavior of Superior Teachers* concluded that, "The results of the present study, as well as the results of Flanders' study, would seem to indicate the verbal behavior patterns of superior teachers can be identified and that these patterns do differ markedly from the verbal-behavior patterns of other teachers." The kind of talk and not the amount of total talk was the differentiating factor.

Furst (1965) looked for differences in student-teacher behavior for trained and untrained samples. She concluded that training resulted in both attitude and behavior differences. Particularly she noted that student teachers trained in interaction analysis used more acceptance of student ideas and less rejection of student behavior. The trained teachers were practicing a positive teacher approach.

A study by Hough and Ober (1966) found that ". . . students who had been taught to use interaction analysis were found to use significantly more verbal behaviors associated with higher student achievement and to have more positive attitudes toward their teachers and school." A follow-up

of this study conducted by Lohman indicated that student teachers who had
been trained in interaction analysis:

1. Accepted and clarified student feelings more.
2. Praised and encouraged student action and behavior more.
3. Accepted and clarified student ideas more.
4. Lectured less.
5. Gave fewer directions and spent less time giving directions.
6. Used more verbal behaviors associated with motivation of students.

Studies of teachers who have been trained in an observation system
indicated intensified awareness of the teaching-learning situation. The ultimate value of observation systems, however, is the use a teacher makes of
the skills and awareness he develops.

Interesting research has been attempted regarding the relationships
among teacher behavior and pupil growth and the use of observation systems. Flanders (1960) found that ". . . if a teacher teaches in an indirect
fashion rather than teaching directly, the kids learn more and feel better
about going to school." This is not to say that all teaching should be indirect. Soar found in a study of Ohio elementary schools that ". . . there
is not a straight line relationship, but children do perform better in some
areas when the teacher is indirect." The Soar study further indicated that
the more abstract the learning, the greater effect of the indirectness of the
teacher. (For example, creativity and vocabulary were reported to be more
positively related to indirectness than reading.)[6]

The June 1969 *Kappan* includes Campbell's and Barnes's discussion of
interaction analysis and the experimental work of New York University's
Interaction Analysis Research Group. Campbell and Barnes review what
they consider to be "some of the more productive research studies" and
conclude, "It is thus apparent that the micro-elements involved in the indirect/direct ratios (indirectness) do affect achievement and attitude development in almost every subject area at almost every grade level from
K-9."

Selecting an Observation System

Two anxieties often arise when attempting to select a system or combination
of systems—that associated with deciding which system(s) provides for
classifying what is selected for study and that related to indecision about
whether any system applies in any area besides social studies. Since an

---

[6] *Interaction Analysis: Theory, Research, and Applications*, Amidon and Hough,
editors, 1967, Addison-Wesley, Reading, Mass.

affirmative is often important to the latter anxiety, in order to make viable the former anxiety, it will be treated immediately.

Although areas such as language arts and social studies are prime targets for application of many systems, Moskowitz has adapted Flanders' interaction analysis for use in foreign language classrooms, Parsons is designing an adaptation of Guided Self-Analysis for mathematics instructors, and the RCS and ETC were designed to be applicable in most areas. With some originality and ingenuity, the basic principles of interaction analysis can become workable in all situations involving human interactions. Elementary school teachers, in particular, have applied the techniques in self-evaluation across subject lines. Industrial arts and physical education instructors at the secondary level, among the more unexpected groups, have acclaimed the applicability.

To determine which system(s) to select for individual teacher use, the teacher must first decide what needs to be investigated, must select some aspect of the classroom situation that is critical to successful teaching strategies.

During the past few years, observational approaches have been refined for assessment of classroom variables such as verbal interaction, non-verbal behavior, levels of thinking in terms of content, and teacher functions. The problem of deciding which behaviors and aspects of the behaviors are to be recorded is usually determined by the purpose for which you undertake the study or analysis.

It should be evident from the sections on Exemplary Systems and Applications that systems are already available for many purposes. Further, the reader should recognize the components of an operational observation system and become aware of adaptations or applications possible in developing his own system for his own classroom needs.

Recent literature stresses the use of the Aptitude-Treatment Interaction Model, for example, of Cronbach (1968) and Fey (1969). In this model, the instructional elements are identified as the teacher ability, attitudes, behavior, student aptitudes and attitudes, the treatment or strategy, and their interactions resulting in student outcomes. With little imagination one can conceive of the identification of critical aspects of each of these areas through systematic observation. Additional information will certainly be available through other means, such as concept scales and achievement batteries.

Ober (1968) suggests four basic considerations for the user of systematic observation: ". . . regardless of a system's intended use or specificity, each displays certain distinct qualities which render it useful to the teacher as well as to the researcher or theoretician. Collectively, these distinct and analytic qualities empower the observer to obtain a clear and accurate picture of specific classroom activities. In order to qualify as a useful observational system it should reflect at least four basic qualities. It should be:

1. descriptive
2. objective
3. in the form of a skill which can be learned and mastered with minimum effort and training time
4. manageable and useful to the classroom teacher as well as to the researcher or theoretician [7]

A category system is preferable when there is only one aspect of behavior to be studied. When several aspects of behavior are of equal importance and also when it is not known which aspects are important, the sign approach is preferable (Medley and Mitzel, 1963).

Probably, the most critical selection factor and most consistently ignored or overlooked is the identification of an observational system that lends itself to systematic implementation. One that has been tried successfully, to the extent that planned training sessions and materials based on substantive studies are available, is superior for widespread implementation in a school system.

One of the most important aspects of learning to use an observational system is learning to use the results. Observation systems do not evaluate— they provide data that can be helpful in evaluation, but in and of themselves are not evaluative instruments. By using the data collected with an observation system, *the teacher can compare his personal perception of what occurs in his classroom with a more objective analysis of what actually occurs. Observation systems are simply means of obtaining meaningful feedback about certain dimensions of the classroom.* The teacher may compare his intent or objectives with the action or data collected, and thereby obtain a basis from which to modify further plans or to change directions entirely to achieve the objectives.

Studies of teachers who have been trained in an observation system indicated intensified awareness of the teaching-learning situation. The ultimate value of observation systems is, however, the use a teacher makes of the skills and awarenesses he develops.

[7] Richard L. Ober, "Theory into Practice through Systematic Observation," *Florida Educational Research Development Council Bulletin,* IV, 1 (Spring, 1968).

3

Reciprocal
Category
System

The Reciprocal Category System (RCS) of interaction analysis was developed by Ober [1] in an attempt to direct more attention to the variety of student talk that occurs in the classroom. The system consists of nine verbal categories that can apply to teacher talk or to student talk. (See Table 3.1.) The nine *reciprocal* categories devote equal attention to

Table 3.1

OBER'S CATEGORIES

Teacher Categories		Student Categories
1	"Warms" (informalizes) the climate	11
2	Accepts	12
3	Amplifies the contributions of another	13
4	Elicits	14
5	Responds	15
6	Initiates	16
7	Directs	17
8	Corrects	18
9	"Cools" (formalizes) the climate	19
10	Silence or confusion	10

student talk and to teacher talk. When teacher talk can be categorized, the single digit number is recorded; for student talk the two-digit number is used. The final category, that is used to indicate silence or confusion,

[1] Richard Ober is presently at the University of South Florida. He developed the Reciprocal Category System while at the University of Florida, 1967.

makes a total of nineteen categories—two times the common nine plus Category 10.

The RCS derives its name from the "reciprocity principal" as it relates to the whole field of systematic observation. According to the reciprocity principal, *for every teacher verbal behavior that can either be observed in the classroom or theoretically conceived, there exists a corresponding student verbal behavior.*

The concern that, in the majority of observational systems, attention is focused essentially on teacher behavior, while student behavior appears to be treated only as an incidental, functionary variable led to the notion of reciprocity in verbal behavior. However, if one believes that students are individuals with unique and distinct concerns, then an observational system designed for studying classroom behavior should provide for the comprehensive study of student behavior within the context of that classroom. Many observational systems fail to provide properly for the assessment of student behavior. For example, the Flanders system of interaction analysis consists of ten categories—seven of which are devoted to teacher verbal behavior and only two are assigned to observed student talk. Consequently, the system is limited with respect to its power to assess the whole spectrum of student verbal behavior. Moreover, because the system includes only two student categories, the theoretician and teacher are both limited in terms of the total number of verbal strategies (patterns) that can be theoretically conceived and/or generated in the classroom. This is critical. It limits drastically the total number and variety of verbal patterns that the teacher can plan and produce in the instructional-learning situation. For example, suppose a particular category—"student asking a question"—is not included in the system. Then a teacher might overlook the possibility of creating situations in which the student will initiate questions. There is good evidence to suggest, therefore, that training in an observational system is a powerful means for shaping teaching behavior, and the direction in which that behavior is shaped is a crucial concern. The observational system, therefore, should be both theoretically sound and appropriate in the classroom setting. The introduction of the reciprocity principal represents an attempt to inject theoretical soundness and a dimension of practicality that can greatly improve the total effectiveness of a system. By learning to use the Reciprocal Category System (Table 3.2), the teacher not only becomes more aware of his own verbal teaching behavior, but he also becomes more aware of the verbal behavior of his student.

A discussion of theoretical assumptions based on materials supplied by Ober explaining the subdimensions and their dualistic qualities appears in the Appendix.

There are three basic sets of operations involved in mastery of the Reciprocal Category System: data collection, data preparation, and data

Table 3.2

THE RECIPROCAL CATEGORY SYSTEM [1]

Category Number Assigned to Teacher Talk	Description of Verbal Behavior	Category Number Assigned to Student Talk
1	*"Warms" (informalizes) the climate:* Tends to open up and or eliminate the tension of the situation; praises or encourages the action, behavior, comments, ideas, and/or contributions of another; jokes that release tension not at the expense of others; accepts and clarifies the feeling tone of another in a friendly manner. (Feelings may be positive or negative; predicting or recalling the feelings of another are included.)	11
2	*Accepts:* Accepts the action, behavior, comments, ideas, and/or contributions of another; *positive reinforcement* of these.	12
3	*Amplifies the contributions of another:* Asks for clarification of, builds on, and/or develops the action, behavior, comments, ideas and/or contributions of another.	13
4	*Elicits:* Asks a question or requests information about the content, subject, or procedure being considered with the intent that another should answer (respond).	14
5	*Responds:* Gives direct answer or response to questions or requests for information that are initiated by another; includes answers to one's own questions.	15
6	*Initiates:* Presents facts, information, and/or opinion concerning the content, subject, or procedures being considered that are self-initiated; expresses one's own ideas; lectures (includes rhetorical questions—not intended to be answered).	16
7	*Direct:* Gives directions, instructions, orders, and/ or assignments to which another is expected to comply.	17
8	*Corrects:* Tells another that his answer or behavior is inappropriate or incorrect.	18
9	*"Cools" (formalizes) the climate:* Makes statements intended to modify the behavior of another from an inappropriate to an appropriate pattern; may tend to create a certain	19

[1] Developed by Dr. Richard Ober, University of Florida, 1967.

Table 3.2 (*cont.*)

THE RECIPROCAL CATEGORY SYSTEM

Category Number Assigned to Teacher Talk	*Description of Verbal Behavior*	*Category Number Assigned to Student Talk*
	amount of tension (i.e., bawling out someone, exercising authority in order to gain or maintain control of the situation, rejecting or criticizing the opinion or judgment of another).	
10	*Silence or confusion:* Pauses, short periods of silence, and periods of confusion in which communication cannot be understood by the observer.	10

interpretation. Collecting data is a relatively simple process based on a knowledge and understanding of the categories and recording observations. Data preparation includes several procedures such as isolating behavior patterns and transferring the "raw" data to a specially designed tabulation form. Data interpretation involves examination and analysis of the quantified interaction.

Data Collection

Collection Procedures

The system of nineteen categories (Table 3.2) can be used to collect interaction analysis data "live" in a classroom, or from audio or video tapes. As the term systematic observation implies, the observer *systematically observes* the verbal interaction in the classroom. A simple *assess-record* pattern is used in collecting the data. Every three seconds, the observer records the kind of verbal behavior that occurs. At the end of each three-second period, the observer records the number of the particular category that most accurately describes the verbal behavior of that period. While recording for one three-second interval, the observer assesses the behavior of the current three-second interval. Consequently, a steady tempo of *assess-record-assess-record* is maintained. The tempo is broken only when more than one type of verbal behavior occurs within a time span. When such rapid changes in verbal behavior occur, the observer records the appropriate category numbers in sequence without regard for the three-second time limit. The speed of the talk—both student and teacher—would make a difference in the number of tallies. It is important to note, however,

Figure 3.1

DATA COLLECTION FORM

	1	2	3	4	5	6	7	8	9	10
1.										
2.										
3.										
4.										
5.										
6.										
7.										
8.										
9.										
10.										
11.										
12.										
13.										
14.										
15.										
16.										
17.										
18.										
19.										
20.										

that the number of tallies is not as important as choosing the correct categories and observing the changes and interactions.

Data collection forms, such as the one above are generally used, although data can also be collected on a regular sheet of paper. The mechanics are quite simple; the appropriate category numbers for the verbal behavior are recorded sequentially in columns (from top to bottom) at three-second intervals or whenever behavior changes.

GROUND RULES

1. Insert a 10 before beginning to collect data and a 10 following completion of data collection. The beginning and ending ten's serve to indicate a beginning and an ending and provide an entrance to the matrix.

2. When a student changes to a different verbal category, a 10 inserted between the two category numbers serves to indicate this change in student verbal behavior.

The following script of a teacher's introduction to a new activity can be used as an example of data collection. The category number of each observation is noted in the script in small handwritten numbers. These numbers correspond with the twenty spaces in a column on the data collection sheet. At the end of the first twenty observations, the observer begins recording on a new column; consequently, the column that appears next to the script is numbered, and a compilation of the observations follows the example. (See Figure 3.2, page 52.)

Classroom Interaction		*Data*
Teacher:	Bob, do you have a report from the group plan- ning sessions today?[4]	1. [10]
		2. [4]
Bob:	Yes,[5] each group has chosen a topic and will	3. [15]
	present a report to the class.[6] The topics are:	4. [10]
	1. Drug Use and Abuse,	5. [16]
	2. The Technology[6] of the Computer Age, and	6. [16]
	3. The World of Genetics.[6]	7. [16]
	Group One will present its report to the class	8. [16]
	with a panel discussion.[6] Groups Two and Three	9. [16]
	haven't yet chosen a method of reporting.[6]	10. [2]
		11. [6]
Teacher:	That sounds good.[2]	12. [6]
	Now, let's see,[6] we agreed on two weeks for pre-	13. [6]
	paring the reports and[6] two days of class time	14. [4]
	for the oral reports.[6]	15. [15]
	Is that correct?[4]	16. [6]
General		17. [6]
Response:	Yes.[15]	18. [6]
Teacher	As I recall, we agreed that the reports would	19. [6]
	have[6] three major purposes:	20. [6]
	1. To present the most current[6] information	2
	about the topic,	
	2. To present the information[6] in a way that	[6]
	has meaning for young adults,[6] and	[19]
	3. To include not only the scientific infor-	[10]
	mation,[6] but also the social implication.[6]	[18]
Robert:	That's what part of the class—and I do mean	[10]
	part[7] of the class—agreed on. I disagree.[8] I	[16]
	think that social implications have no place in	[19]
	a science project.[6]	[19]
Will:	You would think that. You make me think[19] that	[19]
	the myth about scientists having no heart is not	[10]
	a myth.[19]	[16]
Betty:	I think you both are silly. You have missed the	[16]
	whole point.[19]	[16]
	It seems to me that science—in any of its forms[6]	[16]
	—has a profound effect on all mankind.[6] There-	[10]

	Classroom Interaction (cont.)	*Data*
	fore, it is fitting that when discussing problems	10
	or concerns[6]of a scientific nature, we discuss	10
	the social side too.[6]	10
Robert:	I don't understand.[6]. . . (10 second pause) . . .	13
	Betty, what do you mean?[13]	
Betty:	What is science in a vacuum that takes out	3
	mankind?[6]It is my feeling that science is a	
	body of knowledge—to no purpose.[16]	16
Teacher:	Robert, would you like to explain more clearly	16
	what you mean by your statement?[3]Are society	3
	and science mutually exclusive?[3]	3
Robert:	No.[15]	15
	I'm not stupid. I realize that science exists	10
	within[16]. . uh . . . uh . . . society.[16] But,	16
	is a science classroom the place to discuss	16
	society?[14]	10
Teacher:	Does anyone want to try to answer that ques-	14
	tion?[4]	4
(10 seconds of silence)		10
Teacher:	I have a personal opinion, but the suggestion	10
	for these reports[6]came from the class—not me.	10
	So, I think[6]you should resolve this prob-	6
	lem.[6]	6
George:	I think this whole thing is a friendly railroad	6
	job.[1] I wager that the whole point of giving us	11
	the opportunity to work on science[6]reports of	10
	current and *personal* significance was to get us	16
	to realize[6]the inter-relationships of all knowl-	4
	edge and the development of society.[16]	16
	Am I right, Mrs. Breckenridge?[14]	16
		10
		14

Categories

The summary of the categories is very helpful to the observer as he learns to use the system because the key to successful data collection is a thorough knowledge of the categories. Ultimately, the categories should be learned well enough that the observer does not need to refer to the summary. The following discussion further explains the categories of verbal behavior, details rules that are helpful in making distinctions, and presents, in the same manner as the data collection illustration, examples of interactions of each type.

Categories 1 and 11—"Warms" (Informalizes) the Climate.   This type of talk eliminates the tension of the situation; praises or encourages the action, behavior, comments, ideas, and contributions of others; releases tension with casual jokes; and accepts, clarifies, predicts, and recalls the positive or negative feeling tone of others in a friendly manner.

Teacher or student verbal behavior that attempts to alleviate threat and eliminate and release tension falls into categories 1 and 11. The qualities of sincerity and genuineness and the degree of appropriateness are important considerations in dealing with this category. For example, the sentence, "Class, you really are thinking today," might be said sarcastically to cool the classroom climate (Category 9), rather than to warm it. The behaviors in category 1 and 11 are directed at the emotions and feelings of people.

Classroom Interaction	*Data*
Teacher: You know, this is the most fun class I have had in a long time. I can always depend on	*1*
you to be one jump ahead of me.	*1*
I really enjoy working with people who are thinking.	*1*
	2
Yes, George, your guess is right.	*6*
I had hoped you would arrive at that point of understanding.	*1*
I should have known that this good group would beat me to the draw.	*6*
	4
I hope, however, that, having uncovered my ulterior motive, you will enjoy your reports even more.	*4*
	12
Robert, does this idea of discovering the relationship help your understanding or acceptance of the project?	*10*
	16
Robert: Yes, I agree now. I was off on the wrong track. My point is that I don't want to see us *moralize* our time away.	*16*

Categories 2 and 12—Accepts.   This type of talk reinforces positively and accepts the actions, behavior, comments, ideas, and contributions of another. The purpose of the accepting behavior represented by categories 2 and 12 is to reinforce the behavior of another person. The spirit of these categories is *agreement*—positive reinforcement. When a response is automatic and not directly related to the preceding behavior, it is considered a verbal tic and is not recorded. Automatic and frequent "O.K.'s" and "uh-huh's" are examples of verbal tics. Category 2 and 12 behaviors are directed toward the behavior of others.

Classroom Interaction		*Data*
Teacher:	That's a very good caution, Robert.² You have isolated a real concern for us to be watchful³ of—editorializing and moralizing³ Yes, that's a good point.²	_2_ _3_ _3_
Sarah:	I would like to see us leave the moralizing to each individual.⁶I don't ever expect to be a drug user, but⁴I don't want to be told that it is not my right to choose whatever course⁶I want to take.⁶	5 _2_ _16_ _16_ _16_
Teacher:	Sarah, I agree with your desire to retain your personal²rights of choice. That, too, is a good point to consider.²	_16_ _2_ _2_

Categories 3 and 13—Amplifies the Contributions of Another. This type of talk asks for clarification, builds on, and develops the actions, behavior, comments, ideas, and contributions of another. Requests for clarification that emphasize the contributions of others and that specifically refer to verbal behavior indicating that the speaker perceives the contribution as being important are recorded as categories 3 and 13.

GROUND RULE A

Only the *request* for clarification is recorded as a 3 or a 13. The clarification *per se* is not recorded as Category 3 or 13. Instead, it is recorded as another category—responding (Categories 5 and 15) or initiating (Categories 6 and 16), in most instances.

Example: The teacher's question, "What do you mean by that?" would be recorded as Category 3 since he is requesting the student to clarify his last statement. The statement of the response given by the student would not be recorded as Category 13, but rather as Category 15 or 16 depending on the nature of his original contribution.

Classroom Interaction		*Data*
Ron:	I want to know where we are supposed to find the meat for these reports?/⁴	_14_ _3_
Teacher:	What do you mean?³	
Ron:	Where do you get the material for the report?/⁴	_14_ _13_
Louise:	Yes, where are we supposed to get our information?¹³What sources should we use?/³	_13_ _5_
Teacher:	I have no preconceived notion.⁵ You make some suggestions. 7	_7_

Classroom Interaction (cont.)   *Data*

Louise: Books and magazines.[6]   16

Teacher: Yes, those are possible sources.[2] Books, maga-   2
           zines, newspaper, scientific journals and   3
           reports—all kinds of written documents.[3]

Categories 4 and 14—Elicits.   This type of talk asks a question or requests information about the content, subject, or procedure being considered, with the intent that another should answer (respond). The behaviors
that fall into categories 4 and 14 generally assume the grammatical form
of a direct question, although a direction such as, "Tell us the product of
12 and 2," also is a 4. The purpose of the behaviors in categories 4 and 14
is to elicit or secure information or response.

Classroom Interaction   *Data*

Stacey: Are you limiting us to written sources?[14]   14

Teacher: No.[5]   5

Stacey: May we use personal interviews, movies, tele-   14
           vision programs?[14]   6

Teacher: Yes.[5] It sounds like a good idea to me.[2] Does   5
           anyone else have a suggestion?[4]   2

(10 seconds of silence)   4

           Robert?[4]   10
                                                                 10
                                                                 10
                                                                 4

Categories 5 and 15—Responds.   Direct answers or responses to questions or requests for information, initiated by another, and answer to one's
own questions comprise this type of talk. Only *direct* answers to questions
fall into categories 5 and 15. The following ground rule explains the distinction between direct and indirect answers.

GROUND RULE B

To determine whether talk following a question (Category 4 or
14) is Category 5, 15, 6, or 16, the following conditions should be
considered.

Category 5 or 15 follows Category 4 or 14 when the question:
A. Requires either a "yes" or "no" response. The rationale here is
    that yes-or-no propositions limit the student's latitude to an-

swer since he has only these two alternatives from which to choose.

B. Is of the simple recall or memory type. "Who discovered America?" "Tell us how far it is from the earth to the sun." "What is the formula for sulfuric acid?" Each of these requires a memorized answer and is therefore properly recorded as a 15.

C. Is of the convergent type; that is, having only one correct answer. To answer a convergent question normally requires the mental manipulation of two or more items of information rather than memorization of facts. For example: "What is the area of a circle with a diameter of eight inches?" and "How much do seven gallons of water weigh at 60 degrees F?" Both represent convergent questions.

Category 6 or 16 follows Category 4 or 14 when the question:

A. Solicits opinion about or insights into a completely new problem, topic, or discussion.

B. Is of the divergent type; that is, having more than one acceptable answer. Examples of the divergent question are: "How many uses can you think of for a hair pin?" "What are some ways in which we can preserve lumber?" "How might peace be achieved in Viet Nam?"

C. Requires an evaluation. "Should the United States remain in or get out of Viet Nam?" "Which is more suitable, a monetary system based on silver or gold as the standard?" and "Should we abolish the death penalty?" are evaluative type questions.

Classroom Interaction	*Data*
Robert: No, I don't have any ideas. *15*	*15*
John: May we use ordinary magazines such as news weeklies *14* as well as scientific publications? *14*	*14*
	14
Teacher: Of course. Any source is acceptable. *5*	*5*
I would like to caution you here, however. *6* Be	*6*
careful to consider whether *6* the publication is	*6*
presenting facts or opinion. *6*	*6*

Categories 6 and 16—Initiates. This type of talk presents self-initiated facts, information, and opinions concerning the content, subject, or procedures being considered; expresses one's own ideas; lectures; and also includes rhetorical questions not intended to be answered. The verbal behavior represented by categories 6 and 16 is initiated by the individual, and often takes the form of lecture and explanation by the teacher after information has been volunteered by the student. (See Ground Rule B.)

Familiarity with and skill in application of the Gallagher-Aschner System are helpful in distinguishing Category 15 from Category 16. Table 3.3 summarizes the Gallagher-Aschner categories with appropriate examples.

Table 3.3

THE GALLAGHER-ASCHNER SYSTEM

1. *Cognitive-Memory:* anything that can be retrieved from the memory bank.

   What's 3 × 6?
   When did Columbus sail for America?

2. *Convergent:* a question whose single right answer may be obtained by the application of a rule or procedure.

   What's 436 + 21?
   What's 3 to base 2?

3. *Divergent:* more than one acceptable answer is possible. The student is permitted to choose among alternatives or to create ideas of his own.

   What is 10 to three other bases?
   What might have been some effects on the course of history if Columbus had not lived?

4. *Evaluative:* development of relevant criteria, such as usefulness, desirability, social consequences is implied, and then the application of the criteria to the issue.

   Is 10 the best base for a number system?
   How do you evaluate the effects of Columbus' voyage?

DIFFERENTIATION DRILL

RCS Category 15 from Category 16. Cognitive memory and convergent items correspond to RCS Category 5 or 15 while divergent and evaluative items correspond to RCS Category 6 or 16. Thus, in the RCS, analysis of questions pertains to convergence and divergence. To complete Differentiation Drill 2, place a 5/15 or 6/16 and C (convergent) or D (divergent) in the appropriate blank.

15 or 16	*C or D*	*Verbal Responses*
_____	_____	1. T: Why would you smoke marijuana? S: For the kicks of it, to feel "high," to find out if it's as great as everybody says.
_____	_____	2. S: How many vowels are in the word "omniscient"? T: Four
_____	_____	3. T: Who was the god of the underworld? S: Hades
_____	_____	4. S: Do we cross the street when the traffic light is green? T: Yes
		5. T: What would you ask Rod McKuen if you had an hour with him?

15 or 16	*C or D*	*Verbal Responses (cont.)*
_____	_____	S: What makes you "feel" so deeply? What is your favorite poem? Do you like rock music?
		6. S: What would happen if a student revolt occurred in this school?
_____	_____	T: Everyone would be suspended.

Categories 7 and 17—Directs. This type of talk gives directions, instructions, orders, and assignments with which another is expected to comply. Two features of categories 7 and 17 distinguish them from the direction-worded Categories 4 and 14: a direction is given, and compliance is indicated. ("Close the door." "Get out your notebooks.") When such a direction is used sarcastically or as ridicule to cool the climate of the classroom, it is recorded as Category 9 or 19.

Ground Rule

In the event that the direction is either harshly delivered or given for the purpose of regimentation or discipline, it would not be recorded as Category 7, but rather Category 9—"cooling the classroom climate."

Example: The teacher commands, "Sit down immediately!" and, "Wipe that smile off your face!" both would be recorded as Category 9 rather than Category 7, since both tend to have a sharp effect on the feelings and emotions of the student(s).

Classroom Interaction	*Data*
Teacher: Susan, please go to the board and list	7
these suggestions. Write down the following: 7	7
1. Avoid moralizing	7
2. Be aware of type of publication 7	14
3. Prepare definition of terms	5
Susan: Can you read this? 4	7
Teacher: Yes. 5 Now, put the dates we discussed on the	7
board. 7 And . . . go to work on your reports. 7	7

Categories 8 and 18.—Corrects. This type of talk tells another that his answer or behavior is inappropriate or incorrect. Disagreement or corrective feedback that is directed at the behavior of another person is categorized as 8 or 18. ("No, that is not correct." "I disagree." "The correct answer is . . .")

GROUND RULE

Usually, when recording acceptance-correct behavior, only a single category number is recorded.

Example: "No, that's not right. The correct answer is . . ." The first comment, "No, that's not right," is recorded as Category 8. The second part, "The correct answer is . . ." represents additional information and, as such, should be recorded as Category 6. The same holds true for the use of acceptance. The part of the verbal behavior that represents positive reinforcement should be recorded as Category 2 or 12; the remainder, which explains why it is acceptable, constitutes additional information and should be recorded as Category 6 or 16. The concept of following statements of acceptance or correction with a qualifying explanation is sometimes referred to as "public criteria" since it disclosed publicly *why* a given behavior is acceptable or unacceptable.

Classroom Interaction	*Data*
Thomas: I have one more question. May we work individually on these reports?[14]	*14*
	5
Teacher: No.[5] You have the wrong idea.[8] The purpose of dividing into groups is to work together on the project rather than individually.[6]	*8*
	6
	6
A group can cover this topic more thoroughly with little duplication of effort.[6]	*18*
	10
	16
Thomas: Well, I don't agree,[8] but I will do whatever is required.[6] I always wind up doing all the work.[19]	*10*
	19

Categories 9 and 19—"Cools" (Formalizes) the Climate. This type of talk makes statements intended to modify the behavior of another from an inappropriate to an appropriate pattern, and tends to create a certain amount of tension by bawling out someone, by exercising authority in order to gain or maintain control of the situation, or by rejecting or criticizing the opinion or judgment of another. Teacher or student behavior that produces threat or creates tension and serves to cool the climate of the classroom is appropriately placed in Categories 9 and 19. Generally, this cooling behavior entails a statement directed toward the feelings or emotions of someone and tends to alienate that person from the group.

Classroom Interaction	*Data*
Teacher: Let's clear this up right now. I won't have this class waste two weeks. Group work is not designed to take advantage of the industrious student and cover up for the lazy one.	*9*
	9
	9
	9
Your attitude is bad, Thomas. If you expect to be used and put upon, you will be.	*9*

Category 10[2]—Silence or Confusion. This category includes pauses, short periods of silence, and periods of confusion in which communication cannot be understood by the observer.

Classroom Interaction	*Data*
	_10_
(9 seconds of silence)	_10_
	_10_

RECOGNITION DRILL

The first step to becoming a good observer is developing a thorough knowledge of the categories. The recognition drill that follows serves as a sample exercise in identification and classification of verbal behaviors into categories. Read the verbal behaviors, place the appropriate category number in the space provided, and supply the key word in the category definition.

Verbal Behaviors	*Category Number*	*Key Word in Category Definition*
1. Teacher: You are one of my favorite classes of all time.	_____	_____
2. Teacher: The answer to your question is that the gestation period for humans is 10 lunar months.	_____	_____
3. Student: How many problems are you assigning for homework?	_____	_____
4. (Silence)	_____	_____
5. Teacher: That's an acceptable answer!	_____	_____
6. Student: You are a dumb head.	_____	_____
7. Student: Sally, spiders *don't* have six legs.	_____	_____
8. Student: π is approximately equal to 3.1416.	_____	_____
9. Student: I think the best way to do that is through a community survey.	_____	_____
10. Teacher: No, that's not a circle.	_____	_____
11. Student: Willie, lend me your book.	_____	_____
12. Teacher: The causes of World War I are fully discussed in Sidney Bradshaw Faye's *Origins of World War I.* He discusses . . .	_____	_____

[2] Category 10 is also used when making two other distinctions in recording interaction analysis data by the RCS: (1) to begin and close the data collection, and (2) to indicate when the same student changes categories of verbal behavior.

	Category Number	Key Word in Category Definition
Verbal Behaviors (cont.)		

13. Student: Yes, I'll "buy" that. _____ _____

14. Teacher: I don't understand exactly what you mean. _____ _____

15. Student: That report was not only good; it was interesting. _____ _____

16. Teacher: Who put this chalk in my eraser? _____ _____

17. Teacher: Take three straight pins and arrange them along the line. _____ _____

18. Teacher: The only way you will ever pass this course is to stop that eternal goofing off. _____ _____

Figure 3.2

DATA COLLECTION FORM

	1	2	3	4	5	6	7	8	9	10
1.	10	6	16	16	2	5	7	16		
2.	4	19	16	16	16	2	14	16		
3.	15	10	3	10	16	4	5	16		
4.	10	18	3	14	16	10	8	4		
5.	16	10	15	1	16	10	6	16		
6.	16	16	10	1	2	10	6	16		
7.	16	19	16	1	2	4	18	16		
8.	16	19	16	2	14	15	10	10		
9.	16	19	10	6	3	14	16.			
10.	2	10	14	1	14	14	10			
11.	6	16	4	6	13	5	19			
12.	6	16	10	4	13	6	9			
13.	6	16	10	4	5	6	9			
14.	4	16	10	12	7	6	9			
15.	15	16	6	10	16	7	9			
16.	6	10	6	16	2	7	9			
17.	6	10	6	16	3	7	10			
18.	6	10	11	2	14	14	10			
19.	6	10	10	3	5	5	10			
20.	6	13	16	3	14	7	16			

CATEGORY IDENTIFICATION DRILL

Place the correct category number beside the following excerpts from classroom interaction.

1. _____ Entire Class: (*No discernible conversation or interaction.*)

2. _____ Teacher: John, hand in your report today.

3. _____ Teacher: No, John, that substitute for lead won't work.

4. _____ Student: What kind of ceremony or holiday is Guy Fawkes Day?

5. _____ Teacher: I'm not sure I understand what you mean by saying that *Jane Eyre* is a semi-classic. How about clearing up that label.

6. _____ Student: The California capitol is located in Sacramento.

7. _____ Teacher: Yes, that is correct.

8. _____ Student: According to the classic definition, Benet's *John Brown's Body* is the closest thing we have to an epic in American literature.

9. _____ Student: Robert, you always wise off when somebody has an idea that disagrees with your own. Too bad you have to play the "big idea man."

10. _____ Student: Do you mean by *equality* in a democracy that one is given the right to vote? Talk some more about that idea.

11. _____ Student: Mr. Thomas, you did not tell us those papers were due on Monday.

12. _____ Teacher: What does *objective correlative* mean?

13. _____ Student: This is a great day for the memory of Ernest Hemingway. The greatest tenth grade class east of the Mississippi discovered *Old Man and the Sea*.

14. _____ Teacher: George Washington made his farewell address to his troops at Fraunces Tavern, on the island of Manhattan.

15. _____ Teacher: Billy, you have a genius for getting us on the right track again.

16. _____ Student: Tell us what you expect in such a report.

17. _____ Teacher: The classic epic form, in my opinion, has severe limitations. I hope you won't restrict yourself to such a narrow genre.

18. _____ Student: I don't agree. The epic form is ageless.

DIFFERENTIATION DRILL

DIFFERENTIATION requires classification of questions as memory (M), convergent (C), divergent (D), or evaluative (E).

M and C questions should generally elicit Category 5 or 15 responses while D and E questions should elicit Category 6 or 16
responses.

M, C,
D, or E   *15 or 16*

____	____	1. T: Should we abolish the death penalty for first degree murder?
____	____	2. S: How many feet equal one mile?
____	____	3. T: List the ten rules of etiquette for golfers.
____	____	4. T: How does that welder do in efficiency, speed, quality of work in a one hour period?
____	____	5. S: How do you interpret "an eye for an eye and a tooth for a tooth"?
____	____	6. T: Calculate the cost for carpet in this room at $9 a yard.
____	____	7. T: Compute the square root of 436.

	Classroom Interaction	*Data*
Thomas:	I think we should pay particular attention to the reporting/of the space program. I think the political/leaning of news magazines, for example,/could make a real difference in what is said./	16 8 16
Teacher:	Any other suggestions?/	16
Susan:	I would like to ask that we prepare a list of words/and definitions used in the report./In my reading on drug use, I find I'm so unfamiliar with the terms./	16 4 16 16 16 10

Data Collection Drill

In the following script, a slash mark appears to indicate the moment the observer records. As the observer reads the script, he
should note the appropriate category number and transfer these
numbers sequentially to the blank data collection sheet found on
page 58 (Figure 3.3). (See page 59 for end of script.)

	Classroom Interaction	*Data*
Teacher:	All right, first of all, get out your sheets that your discussion/was on, any notes that you took, and your notebooks, too./I'm going to be asking you to refer to them from time to time./ Margaret Strickland, would you please read our problem for us—our small group problem?/Read it for us./	1. ____ 2. ____ 3. ____ 4. ____ 5. ____ 6. ____ 7. ____ 8. ____

Classroom Interaction (cont.)   *Data*

Margaret:	O.K. There are American ambassadors in coun-	9. ____
	tries that are small, underdeveloped nations	10. ____
	ruled by a military dictator/who is friendly to the	11. ____
	United States. A popular revolution has brought	12. ____
	them out./The United States is committed by	13. ____
	treaty to come to the aid of country X/in the	14. ____
	event of outside aggression. Charging out-	15. ____
	side agression by Communism, the dictator of	16. ____
	country X/appeals for American aid in squashing	17. ____
	the revolt. What action should Washington take,	18. ____
	and why?/	19. ____
		20. ____

Teacher: O.K. Let me see. I need some bright, alert
pupil to answer this./Carol Worthen./The first
thing we are going to do is to
list the facts on the board./"What do we know
to be true about this incident? What do we know
for a fact?"/Then we are going to work from
there. Carol, can you give us just one fact?/

Carol: It's a small, underdeveloped nation./

Teacher: All right, that's one./There's hardly any dis-   **2**
agreement there. It's either a small,/under-
developed nation or it isn't. So this will be   ____
our first fact./You might put these down in   ____
your notebooks, too. All right, another fact.   ____
Who had a hand up before?/Ed.   ____

Ed: Friendly to the U. S./   ____

Teacher: Is the country friendly to the U. S.?/   ____

Ed: The dictator is./   ____

Teacher: Steve./   ____

Steve: We had already signed a treaty with them. Or   ____
a pact./   ____

Teacher: All right. Now a treaty was signed./Are we say-   ____
ing what kind of treaty was signed?/   ____

Steve: It described part of it, saying we would go to   ____
the aid of foreign troops. I guess it was . . ./   ____

Teacher: Outside aggression./   ____

Steve: Outside aggression. That's all it told./   ____

Teacher: And so we can say, American aid would be given   ____
in case of outside aggression./Was outside
aggression defined in this problem?/   **3**

Class: No./

Teacher: Is it ever defined for the foreign policy makers?/

Class: No./

Teacher: No./They have to decide from time to time./Is
this or is this not outside aggression?/It's

Classroom Interaction (cont.)   *Data*

not a simple fact that they can look at and say,/
"Well, this is an underdeveloped nation." It
isn't;/you've got to define it each time. O.K.
Any other facts that we can put down? Bert Camp?/

Bert: Ruled by a military dictator./

Teacher: The ruler is a military dictator./O.K., what
            else? Facts that we know to be true. Denise?/

Denise: That the dictator claims that there is outside
            aggression./

Teacher: All right. We know for a fact that the dictator
            claims outside aggression./Anybody argue with
            that? Dean./

Dean: It didn't say that the dictator told us./It
            just states in here that outside aggression by
            the Communists is known. It didn't say by
            whom./

Margaret: It says, "Charging outside aggression by the
            Communists, the dictator of country X appeals
            for American aid."/If he's charging outside
            aggression . . ./

Dean: It doesn't say who said it was./   **4**

Margaret: . . . charging outside aggression, the dictator
            appeals./

Teacher: How many people think you do have to accept it?/

Dean: The trouble is, do you consider that outside
            aggression?/

Teacher: Well, that's a different question./

Denise: Well, you have to start somewhere, and if these/
            are supposed to be the facts that you have, then
            these are supposed to be the facts/that exist,
            and you're supposed to accept them./

Teacher: O.K. So I think we can put this as a fact,
            actually./That Communist elements are known
            to be involved./You see. We're not saying
            whether it's an aggression. We're/not saying
            you know how deeply they're involved. We're
            just saying that we know they are involved./
            O.K. What did your group do, Whit Patterson?/

Whit: We decided to go in and help them in the fight
            to drive out the aggression./

Teacher: O.K. Your solution was to give help./What kind
            of help are you going to give?/

Whit: Military./

Teacher: Military aid./All right, we are not going to
            say now what you assume to be true. We'll get

Classroom Interaction (cont.)   *Data*

	to that later./Chris White, what did your group decide to do?/	___ ___
Chris:	Well, we didn't say./	___
Bob:	I did. Anybody can have a different opinion./	
Teacher:	All right./What was your opinion on it then?/ You would have given them military aid./Who in your group disagreed? You want to point a finger?/	5 ___ ___
Chris:	Glenn and Tommy./	___
Teacher:	Glenn is not here./Tommy, what did you think about it?/	___ ___
Tommy:	I disagree with Chris. I said no military aid. It wasn't outside aggression./	___
Teacher:	Well, how are you going to resolve a situation?/ You get a case like this where someone is saying, "Help us, help us." And here you are the administration. What are you/going to do—just say we're not going to do anything? Is that what you're going to tell the country?/	___ ___ ___
Bob:	It says the dictator is doing it./	
Teacher:	It does state it, doesn't it?/Do you have to accept this as a fact inasmuch as you've got to make a decision?/	___ ___
Tommy:	If they choose./	___
Denise:	Yes, if they choose./	6
Tommy:	In this case they chose not to./	
Denise:	You chose not to./	
Teacher:	Would you choose to do it?/	___
Denise:	Yes,/but not whole scale. Our group decided to give,/to send them weapons and advisors for training their army. And we decided to give them economic/and medical aid, also./	___ ___ ___ ___
Teacher:	Oh, so you're adopting a philosophy that our administration has adopted in the case of Viet Nam./This is what we did today./	___ ___
Denise:	Except that we're not going to send them any troops except those needed to train their own./	___
Teacher:	Oh, so you're just going to send a minimum amount of troops./Right? So that they can train their troops so that they can fight a war. Right?/	___
George:	Going back to Tommy. Didn't he say that we should wait? But isn't this how Communists take over the/country? They don't think that the	

Classroom Interaction (cont.)   *Data*

	government is wrong and that Communism/is the right way. Then they sort of work their own people up into the government?/	———

Jill: That's not aggression!/

Teacher: Yes./

Jill: If we wait, that's what's going to happen./They come so slow, they're going to take over all these little countries./And all these little countries are going to make one great big country; a strong country./

Teacher: Oh, you're operating under a philosophy that un-less we do something about it, the Communists are/ going to take over the world. All right, we're hollering Communists now./Steve?/

Figure 3.3

DATA COLLECTION SHEET

	1	2	3	4	5	6	7	8	9	10
1.	———	———	———	———	———	———	———	———	———	———
2.	———	———	———	———	———	———	———	———	———	———
3.	———	———	———	———	———	———	———	———	———	———
4.	———	———	———	———	———	———	———	———	———	———
5.	———	———	———	———	———	———	———	———	———	———
6.	———	———	———	———	———	———	———	———	———	———
7.	———	———	———	———	———	———	———	———	———	———
8.	———	———	———	———	———	———	———	———	———	———
9.	———	———	———	———	———	———	———	———	———	———
10.	———	———	———	———	———	———	———	———	———	———
11.	———	———	———	———	———	———	———	———	———	———
12.	———	———	———	———	———	———	———	———	———	———
13.	———	———	———	———	———	———	———	———	———	———
14.	———	———	———	———	———	———	———	———	———	———
15.	———	———	———	———	———	———	———	———	———	———
16.	———	———	———	———	———	———	———	———	———	———
17.	———	———	———	———	———	———	———	———	———	———
18.	———	———	———	———	———	———	———	———	———	———
19.	———	———	———	———	———	———	———	———	———	———
20.	———	———	———	———	———	———	———	———	———	———

Classroom Interaction (cont.)   *Data*

Steve: Trouble is, though, from what information we have,   7
the treaty doesn't say that./Just because there's
a few Communists coming in advocating the government's bad./We have that in the United States./
We can't just step in, though they'd like to, if
they could./

_____
_____
_____
_____
_____

Data Preparation

After systematically collecting information on classroom interactions, the observer then prepares the raw data for inspection and interpretation. Skill in preparing data for interpretation includes mastery of four basic activities: bracketing the data into data pairs, entering the data pairs in a 361-cell matrix as tallies, totaling the tallies by rows and columns, and computing category percentages.

Matrix Plotting

The sequential or raw data, collected during RCS observations are bracketed in the following manner:

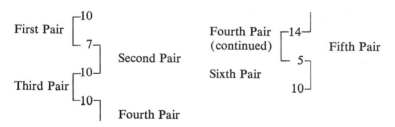

The last numeral in one column of observations and the first numeral in the next column constitute a pair as shown in the above illustration (Fourth Pair).

Bracket data into data pairs (D_1——D_N) so that all recorded category numbers are used twice—first, as the second member of a data pair; and second, as the first member of a data pair. (The beginning and ending 10's are exceptions.)

2nd 10 ⌐
⑦⌐ $1^{st.}$
└10 ⌐
10 ⌐

After the data are bracketed, they are then transferred to a 361-cell RCS matrix by inserting each data pair in its correct cell. The cells are located by row and column numbers. The rows are the horizontal columns in the matrix and are numbered vertically on the left-hand side; the columns are the vertical columns in the matrix and are numbered across the top of the matrix. To enter or tally the 10–7 data pair, one would move down the row numbers to row 10; then one would move across row 10 to column 7. At this point, a tally is entered in the 10–7 cell, as illustrated on the sample matrix (Figure 3.4). Thus, to enter data pairs in a matrix, use the first member of a data pair to locate the row and the last member of the data

Figure 3.4

Matrix Plotting

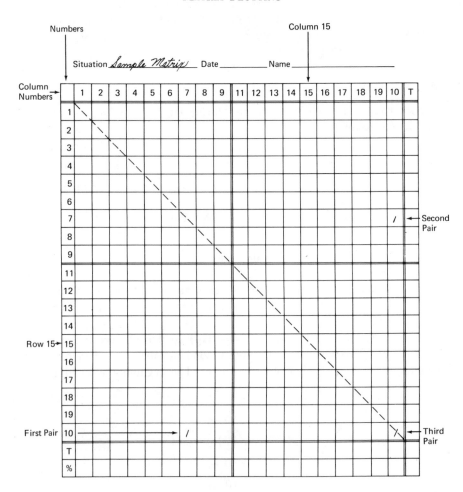

pair to locate the column. Figure 3.4 illustrates the row numbers as they appear vertically on the left side of the matrix and the column numbers printed across the top of the matrix. It is apparent that categories 1 through 9 are followed by categories 11 through 19 and that the 10s are placed last in both rows and columns. Rows, then, extend from left to right; columns from top to bottom.

Three simple formulas are useful for remembering the plotting procedures.

—Formula 1: R. C. Cola
—Formula 2: *R*eciprocal *C*ategory System
—Formula 3: Down and to the right

Formula 1 makes use of a familiar brand name to remind the RCS user that when plotting a data pair one must first locate the row (R) and then place the tally for the data pair (D_1—D_2) in the proper column (C). Formula 2 is another key to remember the *r*ow, *c*olumn order. Formula 3 states the procedure in a "can't miss" method, requiring only that the observer be aware of left as it relates to the matrix and be capable of moving down the left side of the matrix before he moves to the right. This procedure also results in location of the appropriate row in placement of the tally in the correct column.

The same procedure is followed until each data pair is entered as a tally in the matrix. The tallies are then added and converted to Arabic numerals, and the row and column totals are computed. Figure 3.5 presents the data from the sample lesson bracketed before plotting. (Note: The number of data pairs is always one fewer than the number of observations. In this case, there are 147 observations and 146 data pairs.)

Figure 3.6 presents the information from the preceding data sheet plotted in a matrix. The tallies in each cell have been added and converted to Arabic numerals, and the row and column totals have been computed.

To compute the row and column totals, add the tallies across each row and down each column and enter the totals in the provided T row or column. The number of tallies should be the same for the sum of each row and its corresponding column (1 and 1, 2 and 2, 3 and 3, etc.). This provides a useful check on accuracy in the plotting exercise and is a useful guide in locating a lost or misplaced tally. Generally, an errant tally can be located in the row and/or column that fails to replicate its corresponding row and/or column total. Also, it orients the observer to specific overlooked data pairs on the collection form.

The individual cell or square where the T row and T column intersect is the total tallies cell (Figure 3.6). It contains, upon summation of categories 1 through 19, including 10s, the total of all tallies in the matrix.

Figure 3.5

Data Collection Form

	1	2	3	4	5	6	7	8	9	10
1.	10	6	16	16	2	5	7	16		
2.	4	19	16	16	16	2	14	16		
3.	15	10	3	10	16	4	5	16		
4.	10	18	3	14	16	10	8	4		
5.	16	10	15	1	16	10	6	16		
6.	16	16	10	1	2	10	6	16		
7.	16	19	16	1	2	4	18	16		
8.	16	19	16	2	14	15	10	10		
9.	16	19	10	6	3	14	16			
10.	2	10	14	1	14	14	10			
11.	6	16	4	6	13	5	19			
12.	6	16	10	4	13	6	9			
13.	6	16	10	4	5	6	9			
14.	4	16	10	12	7	6	9			
15.	15	16	6	10	16	7	9			
16.	6	10	6	16	2	7	9			
17.	6	10	6	16	3	7	10			
18.	6	10	11	2	14	14	10			
19.	6	10	10	3	5	5	10			
20.	6	13	16	3	14	7	16			

Figure 3.6

Plotted Matrix—Sample Lesson Data

Situation _____ Date _____ Name _____

	1	2	3	4	5	6	7	8	9	11	12	13	14	15	16	17	18	19	10	T
1	2	1				1														4
2		X	2	1		2							1		1					8
3		1	2										2	1						6
4											1			3	1				2	8
5		1				1	2	1					1							6
6	1			2		2				1					-1		1	1		19
7						2							2		1					6
8						1														1
9									4										1	5
11																			1	1
12																			1	1
13				1											1					3
14	1		1	1	5							1								10
15						1							1						2	4
16		4	1	1			1								21			1	4	33
17																				0
18																			2	2
19									1									2	2	5
10				2		1						1	2		7		1	1	10	25
T	4	8	6	8	6	19	6	1	5	1	1	3	10	4	33	0	2	5	25	147
%																				

DATA PREPARATION DRILLS

Preparation. Bracket the following data and plot the matrix (Figure 3.7). Compute the category percentages and totals.

	1	2	3	4	5	6	7	8	9	10
1.	10	4	6	13	16	3	4			
2.	7	15	4	13	3	4	10			
3.	7	4	15	4	3	15				
4.	6	15	6	15	4	2				
5.	4	4	4	10	16	6				
6.	7	15	13	16	16	4				
7.	15	2	6	16	16	15				
8.	15	3	4	16	16	18				
9.	15	16	18	3	4	2				
10.	15	6	10	6	14	4				
11.	15	16	16	16	16	6				
12.	1	3	13	3	16	4				
13.	1	4	13	6	16	15				
14.	6	15	18	16	16	6				
15.	6	4	13	16	2	4				
16.	4	15	13	16	6	15				
17.	15	2	2	18	6	4				
18.	2	6	4	2	6	6				
19.	6	4	15	16	4	6				
20.	6	6	12	16	16	4				

Figure 3.7

Matrix for Data Preparation Drill

Situation_____ Date_____ Name_____

	1	2	3	4	5	6	7	8	9	11	12	13	14	15	16	17	18	19	10	T
1																				
2																				
3																				
4																				
5																				
6																				
7																				
8																				
9																				
11																				
12																				
13																				
14																				
15																				
16																				
17																				
18																				
19																				
10																				
T																				
%																				

Percentages

After the matrix has been plotted and the tallies added, the percentage figure for each category should be inserted in the appropriate column of the percentage (%) row that appears at the bottom of the matrix. Figure 3.8 presents the category totals and percentages for the short story lesson matrix and is followed by an explanation of the calculations. (The cut-away matrix shows only the column numbers and the total (T) and percentages (%) rows. The figures, however, represent the actual totals and percentages for the sample lesson used throughout the manual.)

Figure 3.8

Cut Away Matrix—Sample Lesson

	1	2	3	4	5	6	7	8	9	11	12	13	14	15	16	17	18	19	10	T
T	4	8	6	8	6	19	6	1	5	1	1	3	10	4	33	0	2	5	25	149
%	3	5	4	5	4	13	4	1	3	1	1	2	7	3	22	0	1	3	17	99

Category Percentages = Total no. of tallies on one category
divided by total no. of tallies in matrix

A category percentage represents the portion of the total observed verbal interaction that occurs in that category. An immediate view of the distribution of behaviors or the flexibility is thereby made available to the teacher. The actual computation process is much less important than a teacher's understanding of how to arrange the comparison. Often juxtaposing category totals provides adequate feedback to the classroom teacher.

Data Interpretation

The third step in using the RCS is that of data interpretation—examining and analyzing the data. Since the RCS data are not evaluative, they must be compared with the teacher's objectives before evaluative judgments can be made. By using the RCS data, the teacher can compare his objectives for and his personal perception of what happens in the classroom with a more objective record of what actually occurred—the *intent* or objectives with the *action* or data. This comparison of intent and action can yield a basis for modification of plans or for changing directions entirely, should this be necessary to achieve the objectives.

There are two basic approaches to interpreting interaction analysis data:

1. examining the plotted data from a matrix
2. examining the patterns of interaction within the matrix and the raw data on the collection sheet

---

This training material makes no attempt to make judgments regarding what is *good* or what is *bad* teaching as revealed through RCS data. Rather, the teacher is given the opportunity to learn to use the RCS, observe his own classroom situation, and make his own personal evaluation by comparing objectives and RCS data.

The Matrix

By using the matrix as a means of interpreting RCS data, the teacher has an organized presentation of the verbal behaviors that occurred in a given classroom situation. The matrix reveals the interaction through:

—category percentages
—comparative category ratios
—sub-matrices
—cell loading
—behavior sequences

When preparing the matrix, the observer calculates category percentages for each category (Figure 3.8). An examination of these percentages reveals the *relative* concentration in each of the categories of verbal behavior.[3] These delineations can be very helpful in determining whether or not the planned and expected verbal behaviors actually occurred.

Comparative Category Ratios

Ratios comparing dimensions of verbal behavior are derived when the sum of the tallies in a selected category is divided by the sum of the tallies in another category.

Contrasting categories such as warm–cool (1/11–9/19) provides a good example of the dimensions that can be compared. Ratios such as these simply give a numerical index of the strength of one aspect of verbal behavior as compared with another aspect. Other good comparative categories include:

Accept–Correct (2/8–12/18)
Elicit–Initiate (4/6–14/16)
Direct Response–Divergent Response (5/6–15/16)
Teacher–Student (1–9 Total/11–19 Total)

Because these ratios are computed by dividing the categories (first total by second total), it becomes evident that the lower the ratio, the stronger the second element of the comparison. Figure 3.9 provides category totals from the short story sample lesson for illustrative examples.

---

[3] For classroom use, it is often sufficient to look at the total of tallies in a category compared to the total number of tallies within the matrix to determine what proportion of the behaviors is in that category.

Figure 3.9

CUTAWAY MATRIX—SAMPLE LESSON TOTALS

	1	2	3	4	5	6	7	8	9	11	12	13	14	15	16	17	18	19	10	T
T	4	8	6	8	6	19	6	1	5	1	1	3	10	4	33	0	2	5	25	147
%																				

$$\text{Comparative Category Ratios} = \frac{\text{Total no. of tallies in one category}}{\text{Total no. of tallies in another category}}$$

Examples:

Accept–Correct Ratio for Teacher (2–8)
Category 2 = 8
Category 8 = 1

$$1 \overline{\big)\,8.00}^{\,8.00}$$

Direct–Divergent Response Ratio for
Students (15–16)
Category 15 = 4
Category 16 = 33

$$33 \overline{\big)\,4.00}^{\,.12}$$

Sub-Matrices

It is also possible to look at the data plotted in the RCS matrix in terms of the four basic kinds of talk patterns: (1) teacher talk followed by teacher talk, (2) teacher talk followed by student talk, (3) student talk followed by teacher talk, and (4) student talk followed by student talk. Figure 3.10 illustrates the four sub-matrices, or sections of the matrix, that identify these patterns.[4] By observing the number of tallies appearing in each of these sub-matrices, the frequency of each kind of talk can be determined.

The flexibility within kinds of talk can also be found in the sub-matrices. The number of different combinations that appear in each of the sub-matrices provide an indication of the flexibility of talk that occurs between students and the teacher. For example in Figure 3.11 the Teacher-Teacher sub-matrix contains twenty different data pairs. The Student-Student sub-matrix contains eight different combinations (13–13, 13–16, 14–13, 14–14, 15–14, 16–16, 16–19, and 19–19).

[4] NOTE: The ten columns and rows are not included in the sub-matrices. The total number of talk tallies in the matrix is the sum of those contained in the four sub-matrices. To compute the percentage of total talk that each sub-matrix represents, divide the sum of the behaviors in the sub-matrix by the total talk tallies.

Figure 3.10

MATRIX—SUBMATRICES

	1	2	3	4	5	6	7	8	9		11	12	13	14	15	16	17	18	19
1																			
2																			
3																			
4					Teacher- Teacher Talk										Teacher- Student Talk				
5																			
6																			
7																			
8																			
9																			
11																			
12																			
13																			
14					Student- Teacher Talk										Student- Student Talk				
15																			
16																			
17																			
18																			
19																			

Figure 3.11

FLEXIBILITY IN A PLOTTED MATRIX

Situation _____ Date _____ Name _____

	1	2	3	4	5	6	7	8	9	11	12	13	14	15	16	17	18	19	10	T
1	2	1				1														4
2	X	2	1		2								1		1					8
3	1	2											2	1						6
4				X							1			3	1				2	8
5		1				1	2	1					1							6
6	1			2		2				1					1		1	1		19
7						3							2		1					6
8						1														1
9									X										1	5
11																			1	1
12																			1	1
13				1								X			1					3
14	1		1	1	5							1	X							10
15						1							1						2	4
16		4	1	1		1									X			1	4	33
17																				0
18																			2	2
19							1											X 2	2	5
10			2		1							1	2		7			1	10	25
T	4	8	6	8	6	19	6	1	5	1	1	3	10	4	33	0	2	5	25	147
%	3	5	4	5	4	13	4	1	3	1	1	2	7	3	22	0	1	3	17	99

70

COMPARATIVE CATEGORY RATIO DRILL

Compute the following comparative category ratios from
information on the plotted matrix.

Accept/Correct for Teachers
Warm/Cool for Teachers
Direct/Divergent Response for Students
Teacher/Student

Situation ____ #1 _____ Date _____ Name _____

	1	2	3	4	5	6	7	8	9	11	12	13	14	15	16	17	18	19	10	T
1	X	/		/		2														8
2		X	/	/		3	/													7
3			X												/					2
4				X										2	3		2		/	9
5																				0
6				4		22									/				/	34
7				/																1
8						/			/											2
9																			/	1
11																				0
12																				0
13						/						X								2
14	/												X							2
15		/		/										X						2
16		4				2						/			X				/	15
17																				0
18																		2		2
19																				0
10	2											/		3					X	13
T	8	7	2	9	0	34	1	2	1	0	0	2	2	2	15	0	2	0	13	100
%																				

Behavior Sequence

The matrix simplifies an analysis of behavior sequence. To determine what kinds of, and how often, behaviors precede and follow a specific behavior, turn to the matrix. To locate specific behavior sequences, locate the cell in question by juxtaposing the category numbers in this order:

1. Preceding
2. Following

Therefore, the 6–14 cell, Row 6, Column 14, would reveal how many times teacher initiated talk was followed by a student question (none in Figure 3.11). Likewise, the number of times student requests for clarification (13) preceded student divergent response (16) would appear in the 13–16 cell, Row 13, Column 16 (once in Figure 3.11).

To locate all responses preceding or following a specific behavior, again, turn to the matrix. To determine what kinds of talk followed teacher initiated talk (6), simply go all the way across the sixth row; the tallies in the cells on the sixth row indicate what kinds of, and how often, specific verbal behaviors followed teacher initiated talk. Likewise, to determine what kinds of and how often behaviors preceded teacher initiated talk, one would locate the sixth column and go all the way down the column. The tallies in the cells of the sixth column reveal those behaviors which preceded teacher initiated talk. For example, in Figure 3.12 teacher-warming verbal behavior preceded teacher-initiated talk (1–6 pair) one time and teacher-accepting verbal behavior preceded teacher-initiated talk (2–6 pair) twice, while teacher-initiated talk preceded itself (6–6 pair) twelve times.

Cell Loading

Cell loading provides two kinds of information: (1) it can help the teacher determine whether the planned verbal behaviors occurred to the anticipated degree. (2) It can provide information regarding sequence of verbal behavior and perhaps evidence of teaching style.

The number of tallies that appears in the specific cells is called the loading of the cell. The more tallies a cell contains, the more heavily it is said to load. By isolating specific cells, or blocks of cells, one can determine the loading of these particular verbal behaviors.

Blocks of cells can also provide valuable feedback. If, for example, a teacher were interested in the amount of accepting and clarifying verbal activity, the 2/3–2/3 blocks could be isolated in each sub-matrix in order to study this pattern. (See Figure 3.11 for shaded 2–3 block.)

Figure 3.12

LOADINGS IN MATRIX CELLS AND BLOCKS

Situation _____ Date _____ Name _____

	1	2	3	4	5	6	7	8	9	11	12	13	14	15	16	17	18	19	10	T
1	2	/				/														4
2		X	2	/		2							/		/					8
3	/	2										2	/							6
4											/		3	/				2		8
5	/					/	2	/					/							6
6	/			2		2				/					/		/	/		19
7							3						2		/					6
8						/														1
9									4										/	5
11																			/	1
12																			/	1
13				/											/					3
14	/		/	/	5							/								10
15						/							/						2	4
16		4	/	/		/									21		/		4	33
17																				0
18																		2		2
19							/											2	2	5
10			2			/					/	2		7		/	/		10	25
T	4	8	6	8	6	19	6	1	5	1	1	3	10	4	33	0	2	5	25	147
%	3	5	4	5	4	13	4	1	3	1	1	2	7	3	22	0	1	3	17	99

The cells which lie along the diagonal—steady state cells—contain observations of behaviors of at least six seconds in length or indicate how often the same behavior occurred in sequence. In Figure 3.13 student category 16 was observed twenty-one times in sequence (16–16).

Figure 3.13

Steady State Cells in Plotted Matrix

Situation _____ Date _____ Name _____

	1	2	3	4	5	6	7	8	9	11	12	13	14	15	16	17	18	19	10	T
1	2	1				1														4
2		X	2	1		2							1		1					8
3		1	2										2	1						6
4				X								1		3	1					8
5		1				1	2	1					1							6
6	1		2			12				1					1		1	1		19
7							3						2		1					6
8						1														1
9									X									1		5
11																		1		1
12																		1		1
13					1							X			1					3
14	1		1	1	5							1	X							10
15					1										1				2	4
16		4	1	1		1									21			1	4	33
17																				0
18																			2	2
19								1										2	2	5
10			2		1							1	2		7		1	1	10	25
T	4	8	6	8	6	19	6	1	5	1	1	3	10	4	33	0	2	5	25	141
%																				

Interpretation Drill

Complete these questions from the information on the plotted
matrix (page 75):

_____ 1. What cell loads the heaviest?

_____ 2. How many tallies appear in the heaviest loading
steady-state cell?

_____ 3. Which sub-matrix displays the most flexibility?

_____ 4. How many tallies appear in the 5–6 block?

_____ 5. How many 10–10 behaviors were recorded?

_____ 6. How often does teacher acceptance favor student verbal behavior?

_____ 7. How often is student-verbal preceded by teacher questions?

_____ 8. How many steady state cells load heavily?

_____ 9. How many total talk tallies appear in the sub-matrix?

Situation _____ Date _____ Name _____

	1	2	3	4	5	6	7	8	9	11	12	13	14	15	16	17	18	19	10	T
1	X					/														2
2			/	2		4									/					8
3			X	3		2									/					7
4				X		3	/				/	/	13	2		/			/	24
5																				0
6				12		6									3					21
7						/	X							/						3
8																				0
9																				0
11																				0
12												/								1
13		/		/		/						3				/				7
14														/						1
15	/	4		4		2					/			4		/			/	18
16		/	5	/		/						/			2	/				22
17																				0
18		2										/						/		4
19																				0
10						/									2					3
T	2	8	7	24	0	21	3	0	0	0	1	7	1	18	22	0	4	0	3	
%																				

Patterns

Patterns of verbal behavior can be found in the matrix and in the raw data. Those behavior sequences that appear most often—cells that load most heavily—often reveal specific patterns of behavior. Anytime a cell has four or more tallies, it can be considered to load heavily. Consequently, the interpreter can easily isolate those behavior sequences that occur most frequently.

The patterns that are revealed in the matrix often give some evidence of teaching style or practice. For instance, if a teacher plans to use questions that demand a divergent or evaluative response (16), he must give students time to consider the question. If the student is given time to consider the question, the 4–10 cell and the 10–16 cell will load heavily, indicating silence before and after the question.

Looking at the RCS data from a patterns point-of-view not only gives the interpreter a chance to determine whether or not the patterns planned and attempted were realized, but also an opportunity to discover any other patterns that evolve during the verbal interaction. For example, heavy loading of the 4–10 and 10–4 cells could well indicate that the teacher frequently restates a question before giving the student time to pose an answer. Likewise, heavy and light loading of specific cells can reveal areas where behaviors are occurring—both desirable and undesirable patterns. *However,* only the teacher can determine whether these patterns are desirable or undesirable in working toward the objectives set for the classroom interaction.

While the patterns revealed by the cell loading in the matrix can be very helpful, the raw data can also be extremely valuable to the interpreter. By isolating specific kinds of behaviors of concern, by choosing the behaviors that load most heavily in the matrix, or by simply studying the raw data, the interpreter can discern patterns of behavior that occur in the classroom interaction.

If the teacher's most crucial concern were the questions he asked and the responses that followed these questions, he could go to the matrix—row 4—and find what kinds of behaviors follow a teacher question. If, however, he were interested not only in what kinds of responses followed his questions, but also in the behaviors following the responses (pattern of more than two behaviors), he could most clearly identify those behaviors by looking at the raw data. The matrix does not allow easy study of patterns with more than two behaviors.

To investigate the possible data patterns revolving around teacher questions, the interpreter can take the raw data sheet and isolate these sequences as shown in Figure 3.14.

Figure 3.14

DATA COLLECTION FORM—PATTERNS

	1	2	3	4	5	6	7	8	9	10
1.	10	6	16	16	2	5	16	9		
2.	4	19	16	16	16	2	16	9		
3.	15	10	3	10	16	4	7	9		
4.	10	16	3	14	16	10	7	9		
5.	16	10	15	1	16	10	7	10		
6.	16	16	10	1	2	10	14	10		
7.	16	19	16	1	2	4	5	10		
8.	16	19	16	2	14	15	7	10		
9.	16	19	10	6	3	14	7			
10.	2	10	14	1	14	14	14			
11.	6	16	4	6	13	5	5			
12.	6	16	10	4	13	6	8			
13.	6	16	10	4	5	6	6			
14.	4	16	10	12	7	6	6			
15.	15	16	6	10	16	16	18			
16.	6	10	6	16	2	16	10			
17.	6	10	6	16	3	16	16			
18.	6	10	11	2	14	16	10			
19.	6	10	10	3	5	4	19			
20.	6	13	16	3	4	16	9			

The student response to the first teacher question is at first direct; then the student switches to a divergent or evaluative answer. The third illustration reveals the same pattern of direct and then divergent response. The switching of categories of student verbal response appears in illustrations 1, 2, and 3. This pattern—if continued over a wide sample of observations —could indicate that the student feels a freedom to respond in ways other than directly.

Figure 3.14 illustrates two kinds of behavior patterns: The shaded patterns relate to questioning strategies; the hatched patterns relate to student correction, disagreement, or cooling. In each instance, the questioning strategy differed. In the first sequence, the student gives a limited answer (15) and changes to a more open answer (16) on initiation. The second sequence shows the student giving a limited response (15) followed by teacher lecture (6). The third sequence requires additional information (16) before the student response, while the fourth sequence shows the student response (15) followed by a question (14) from another student. The two disagreement sequences illustrate student use of cooling (19) and correcting (18) behavior.

While it is impossible to draw any conclusions regarding this teacher's questioning patterns from these limited data, it is possible to isolate such patterns to be compared with further observations.

Drill

Isolate from the following data (Data Collection Form), the patterns that illustrate the following styles:

1. Teacher request for direct response
2. Discovery approach
3. Repetition of teacher question
4. Student freedom to disagree

	1	2	3	4	5	6	7	8	9	10
1.	10	6	16	4	16					
2.	6	6	4	15	16					
3.	6	7	15	2	12					
4.	6	10	2	4	16					
5.	6	10	4	15	10					
6.	6	7	4	2						
7.	4	7	10	6						
8.	15	10	4	6						
9.	2	10	4	6						
10.	4	18	10	6						
11.	15	18	6	6						
12.	2	1	6	6						
13.	6	1	6	6						
14.	6	6	6	6						
15.	6	6	6	6						
16.	7	7	6	10						
17.	7	7	6	10						
18.	10	10	4	10						
19.	10	16	4	16						
20.	14	16	4	16						

The Observer and Valid Observation

Both accuracy of judgment in classifying verbal interaction and consistency in judging the behaviors correctly are necessary qualities of "a good observer." Unless recorded behaviors are actual, observed behaviors, a system's usefulness is limited: the greater the disparity between observed and recorded behaviors, the less useful the system. To provide an estimate of an observer's validity or ability to code observed behaviors in the correct category and his reliability or consistency, compute Scott coefficients.[5] Data collected by an observer can be compared to that collected from the same setting by an expert in the RCS (inter-rater agreement), or it can be compared with data previously collected by the observer on the same setting or interaction (intra-rater agreement). Sets of data should be collected under similar conditions, if not identical, for the exact accepted time sample.

Scott's coefficient is classified as a reliability score by many of its users. As a matter of terminology, the authors consider the inter-rater agreement (between observers) as an index of validity, with the term reliability reserved for intra-observer (same observer) repetitions of data collection on the same classroom situation. The individual observer can rate his own accuracy of classification only through comparisons with such criterion measures as expert judgment. Grossly oversimplified, validity as a Scott coefficient is a percentage of rater agreement between the observer and expert, with correction for chance factors and the perfect rating. The expert's data would be considered as the criterion score. Reliability could also be computed as a Scott coefficient and, again oversimplified, can be thought of as the percentage of a rater's agreement with himself with correction for chance factors and the perfect rating. For example, collect data on taped classroom interaction today and again on the same tape for the same length of time and under similar environmental circumstances a month from now. The comparison of these two data collections can be reported as a reliability coefficient and represents how consistently the observer judges the same verbal behaviors to be in the same categories. Audio tapes of actual or simulated classroom behavior and interaction provide readily accessible sources of data when live classroom observations are not possible.

Thus, to be considered a good observer, the student of the RCS should be capable of classifying observed verbal behaviors within categories that an expert would choose as appropriate. In addition, he should be able,

---

[5] W. A. Scott, "Reliability of Content Analysis: The Case of Nominal Coding," 19, *The Public Opinion Quarterly*, 1955, 3, pp. 321–25.

under a variety of circumstances, to demonstrate consistency by classifying the same sequence of verbal behaviors in the same sequence of categories, at different observational periods.

Intra- and Inter-Observer Reliability

Scott's coefficient provides a simple and quick method of estimating intra- and inter-observer reliability. The Scott formula is:

$$\text{Reliability} = \frac{P_o - P_e}{1.00 - P_e}$$

P_o represents the agreement between two observers and P_e represents the agreement between two observers that occurs simply by chance.

In order to use Scott's method, the user must first determine the percentage of each category recorded on two data collections. Two collection sheets are provided as examples (Figure 3.15a&b). These sheets contain

Figure 3.15(a)
DATA COLLECTION FORM

	1	2	3	4	5	6
1.	10	7	4	10	2	6
2.	6	7	4	4	6	7
3.	6	7	6	15	6	10
4.	7	10	4	2	4	10
5.	10	10	15	7	16	10
6.	10	10	16	10	1	10
7.	4	10	2	10	4	9
8.	16	10	7	10	15	15
9.	2	4	7	10	2	10
10.	4	15	10	10	6	10
11.	16	16	10	10	6	4
12.	2	15	10	10	4	15
13.	4	16	10	10	15	18
14.	15	15	10	4	2	15
15.	16	2	10	15	6	16
16.	16	7	4	15	6	8
17.	2	10	15	6	6	2
18.	4	10	7	6	6	4
19.	15	10	7	4	6	15
20.	2	10	10	15	6	10

Figure 3.15(b)

DATA COLLECTION FORM

	1	2	3	4	5	6	7
1.	10	4	7	4	1	6	8
2.	6	15	10	15	6	6	2
3.	6	2	10	7	4	6	4
4.	6	7	10	10	15	6	10
5.	6	7	10	10	2	6	
6.	7	6	4	4	4	6	
7.	10	10	4	15	16	6	
8.	10	10	10	2	8	7	
9.	4	10	15	7	7	7	
10.	15	10	4	7	15	10	
11.	2	10	15	10	6	10	
12.	4	4	6	10	6	10	
13.	15	15	7	10	4	4	
14.	15	15	7	10	15	15	
15.	15	10	10	10	2	10	
16.	2	16	10	10	6	10	
17.	4	15	10	4	6	4	
18.	15	12	10	15	6	15	
19.	15	15	10	15	6	18	
20.	2	15	10	15	6	15	

the data of two observers who have recorded approximately six minutes of verbal interaction in a classroom situation. To compute the percentage of each category for a given period of observation, it is necessary to count the number of tallies recorded for each category and to summarize the results.

A summary work sheet, similar to the one illustrated in Table 3.4, is suggested for this purpose. After the tallies per category have been counted, add these and check against the total number of tallies on the data collection sheet. When the number of tallies per category and the total number of tallies have been determined, the ratio and percentage can be computed. This is accomplished by dividing the total number of observations or tallies into the number of observations recorded in individual categories.

$$\text{Percentage of Category} = \frac{\text{No. of tallies in a category}}{\text{Total no. of tallies recorded}}$$

For example, in Table 3.4, the second observer recorded Category 4 seventeen times and had a total of 124 tallies. The ratio or comparison of

Table 3.4

SUMMARY WORK SHEET

Observer #1

Category Number	Total Tallies	Ratio		Percentage
1	1	1/120 =	.01	1%
2	11	11/120 =	.09	9%
3	17			
4	17	17/120 =	.14	14%
5				
6	16	16/120 =	.13	13%
7	11	11/120 =	.09	9%
8	1	1/120 =	.01	1%
9	1	1/120 =	.01	1%
10	35	35/120 =	.29	29%
11				
12				
13				
14				
15	17	17/120 =	.14	14%
16	9	9/120 =	.08	8%
17				
18	1	1/120 =	.01	1%
19				
TOTALS	120		1.00	100%

Observer #2

Category Number	Total Tallies	Ratio		Percentage
1	1	1/124 =	.01	1%
2	8	8/124 =	.06	6%
3				
4	17	17/124 =	.14	14%
5				
6	21	21/124 =	.17	17%
7	12	12/124 =	.10	10%
8	2	2/124 =	.02	2%
9				
10	35	35/124 =	.28	28%
11				
12				
13				
14				
15	25	25/124 =	.20	20%
16	2	2/124 =	.02	2%
17				
18	1	1/124 =	.01	1%
19				
TOTALS	124		1.01	101%

Category 4 tallies to total tallies is 17:124. This ratio may be converted to a decimal number by dividing 17 by 124 as 17/124 = .137. This decimal has been rounded to the nearest hundredth on the work sheet and this accuracy is sufficient for RCS observers' purposes. The actual computation is illustrated below.

$$124 \overline{\smash{\big)}\ 17.000} = .14 = 14\%$$

with quotient .137 shown above the radical.

Each ratio and percentage has been calculated and is recorded on the work sheet (Table 3.4). The sum of the ratio should be approximately 1.00 and the sum of the percentage should be approximately 100%, though they will vary slightly as a result of rounding.

When these calculations have been completed, a summary sheet similar to the one illustrated in Figure 3.16 should be prepared. Copy the information in the last column (percentage) on the work sheet for each observer in column 2 or 3 of the summary sheet beside the correct category number. The % symbol is recorded as the column heading. Use the fourth column to record the number of percentage points by which the two observers differ in each category. For example, the first observer Category 6 contains 13% of the tallies; 17% of the tallies for the second observer were in Category 6. The difference is: $17 - 13 = 4$. Since the absolute value of the difference is the concern, it will not matter in the fourth column which observer's category total is larger.

The difference column is totaled. This figure represents the total disagreement between the two observers and is used to calculate P_o, the agreement between observers. The total of the difference column would be zero if the two observers agreed (or had the same number of tallies) in each category. The greatest possible agreement would be 100% or 1.00.

or
$$P_o = \text{greatest possible agreement} - \text{disagreement}$$
$$P_o = 1.00 - \text{disagreement}$$

For example, Figure 3.16 shows the total disagreement between the two observers to be 23% or .23. In this case, P_o would be calculated as follows:

$$P_o = 1.00 - .23$$
$$P_o = .77$$

P_e represents the agreement between two observers that occurs purely by chance. For this calculation, use a short method that reduces the work considerably and is accurate enough for general purposes. To calculate P_e, select the two highest percentages for the first observer, square each, and add the two products. The two high percentages for the first observer were

Figure 3.16

SUMMARY TABLE OF VALUES

Category Number	Observation 1 Tallies per category	Observation 2 Tallies per category	Difference
1	1	1	0
2	9	6	3
3	0	0	0
4	14	14	0
5	0	0	0
6	13	17	4
7	9	10	1
8	1	2	1
9	1	0	1
10	29	28	1
11	0	0	0
12	0	0	0
13	0	0	0
14	0	0	0
15	14	20	6
16	8	2	6
17	0	0	0
18	1	1	0
19	0	0	0
Totals	100%	101%	23%

Reliability $(r) = \dfrac{P_o - P_e}{1.00 - P_e}$

$P_o = 1.00 - .23$

$\quad = .77$

$P_e = .29^2 + .14^2$

$\quad = .0841 + .0196$

$\quad = .1037 = .10$

$r = \dfrac{P_o - P_e}{1.00 - P_e} = \dfrac{.77 - .10}{1.00 - .10}$

$r = \dfrac{.67}{.90} = .745$

$r = .75$

29 and 14. The calculation of P_e for the first observer follows; percentages are changed to decimal numerals for calculations, and the result is rounded to the nearest hundredth.

$$P_e = .29^2 + .14^2$$
$$= .0841 + .0196$$
$$= .1037$$
$$= .10$$

Having calculated P_o and P_e, all necessary information is available to apply the formula. The reliability formula is restated here for convenience.

$$\text{Reliability} = \frac{P_o - P_e}{1.00 - P_e}$$

Scott's formula states that reliability is equal to the total agreement between two observers minus the agreement that occurs by chance, divided by the greatest possible agreement minus the agreement that occurs by chance. This reliability is a comparison of the agreement between observers not resulting by chance and the greatest agreement possible that does not result from pure chance.

$$r = \frac{\text{Total agreement between observers} - \text{chance agreement}}{\text{Greatest possible agreement} - \text{chance agreement}}$$

Figure 3.16 illustrates a summary table of values useful in preparing a Scott coefficient for computation. It includes the successive computational procedures involved in deriving this reliability estimate. A reliability of .75 is recorded for this rater agreement example. Generally, an r of .70 or better can be achieved by most serious RCS students. In workshops objectives, an r of .60 is frequently established as an acceptable level to illustrate mastery of the system's collection skills. However, the value of systematic observation is not limited by the observer's inability to compute reliability or validity estimates. The discussion and examples are provided for those intrigued by the accuracy element in quantification of classroom behavior. The desire to be systematic, or even scientific, is increased in many when comparisons such as those illustrated are possible.

Summary Reflection

A systematic observation tool has been explicitly described. Categories of the RCS have been explained, ground rules stated, skills detailed, and practice drills provided. The narrative presentation emphasized the purposes of learning such a tool:

—To make possible organized observation of the socio-emotional aspects of classroom interaction.

—To assist the teacher in planning strategies by providing a set of variables (categories) and suggesting means of organizing patterns of instruction.

—To provide a method of collecting objective feedback on actual instructional segments.

—To lead to sensible evaluative judgments based on quantified, analyzed data related to teacher objectives and strategies.

—To encourage the development of teacher-made observation systems.

Continued stress pointed to the fact that the RCS is not evaluative. In fact, without prior planning by the teacher of a set of learning objectives and the prior selection of strageries, the ability of the teacher to make sensible judgment based on RCS information is doubtful.

A major strength of the entire process is the privacy and lack of threat made possible through audio or video taping of a self-taught lesson and coding at individual convenience thereby, diminishing considerably the threats of outside observers and of a "bad day."

4

Equivalent
Talk
Categories

Regardless of the discipline, technology, or course offering, the development of thinking is central to the educational process. Teachers have, as
their major responsibility, the encouragement, facilitation, and even genesis
of thinking processes of youth assigned to their instructional care. Development of thinking requires a purposeful interaction of teachers, teaching
strategies, content, students, student aptitudes, and environmental forces.

The work of Smith, Hughes, Bellack, Flanders, and others has long since
moved the act of teaching from the realm of the often-misunderstood to
the possibility of objective, realistic analysis. Reviewing the work of those
who have contributed to the development of systematic observation leads
one to reaffirm that it is virtually impossible to devise a system that measures or observes *all* elements of classroom interaction. The literature related
to systematic observation reveals two main concerns in observing the
teaching-learning situation: the climate factor and the teaching (or instructional) processes. The purposeful interaction of the strategy elements of
the teaching-learning situation served as the impetus for the development
of this observational system which focuses on the functions that are present
in teaching strategies.

Teachers who are aware of a planned strategy need accurate feedback
on achievement, partial achievement, or even non-achievement of selected
strategies. Awareness of actual strategies tends to create increased control
for the teacher—management of learning conditions more than mere
regimentation. (Though it does seem evident that teachers who plan strategies that make use of their talents, student aptitudes, and carefully chosen
content promote learning activities, as a general rule, with fewer "discipline
problems.") Sensible modification in an organized fashion is possible when

accurate, objective information on implemented strategies is available. The Equivalent Talk Categories (ETC) system, like the RCS, makes possible such data collection and analysis through systematic observation. (Table 4.1).

Table 4.1

Equivalent Talk Categories [1]

Teacher Code		Student Code
1	*Present Information* Unsolicited information—lecture; explanation related to lesson; demonstration; description; impromptu comments; rhetorical questions.	11
2	*Question—Restricted Thinking* Call for responses that result from restricted thinking —factual knowledge or simple recall; an accepted or pre-determined correct answer; facts previously learned or easy to produce; lower levels of cognition.	12
3	*Question—Expanded Thinking* Call for responses that result from expanded thinking —open-ended responses; generation and application of principles, concepts, and generalizations; solutions generated by application of rules or procedures; answers to how, why, what do you think; higher levels of cognition.	13
4	*Respond—Restricted Thinking* Result from restricted thinking—factual knowledge; an accepted or pre-determined correct answer; facts previously learned or easy to produce; lower levels of cognition.	14
5	*Respond—Expanded Thinking* Result from expanded thinking—open-ended responses; generation and application of principles, concepts, and generalizations; solutions generated by application of rules or procedures; answers to how, why, what do you think; higher levels of cognition.	15
6	*React—Maintain Level of Participation* Verbal behavior that maintains current level of thinking; invitation to continue talking, amplify, clarify, or summarize ideas at the same or a lower level of cognition.	16
7	*React—Extend Level of Participation* Verbal behavior that extends current level of thinking	17

---

[1] Developed by Ernest L. Bentley and Edith Miller, Atlanta, Georgia, 1970.

—request for further information, generation of data or principles, or reconsideration of ideas requiring increased complexity of thinking; obvious utilization of information supplied by another where level of cognitive participation is raised.

8   *React—Terminate Level of Participation*   18
Verbal behavior that brings current topic or thought to a close—termination of responses through comment or intervention; indication that thought sequence is ended; change or introduction of new topic; summation or relationship building activity when new learning is related to old.

9   *Structure—Learning Activities*   19
Comments that organize learning activities—commands; directions; assignments.

0   *Structure—Pause—Silence*   10
Absence of verbalizations utilized to promote the sequence planned.

As previously stated, accurate and objective feedback is available through techniques of systematic observation. Teachers can learn to make audio or video tapes of their own classroom instruction, observe and classify the behaviors in sequence, and analyze and interpret for instructional implications (in the privacy of individual classrooms). Self-evaluation is more likely to lead to changed strategies, modified approaches, and improved teaching of thinking. Rationalizations and excuses often associated with the "outside observer" cannot be used and the teacher must deal with his actual teaching behaviors. Systematic observation tools are means of gathering needed data so that awareness and control are enhanced, strategies can be modified, and thinking more effectively and efficiently pursued.

Basic to the rationale for Equivalent Talk Categories (ETC) as a tool of systematic observation are the beliefs that:

—Teaching of thinking is an important educational activity

—Teaching strategies are important in the development of thinking abilities

—Objective feedback concerning strategies is needed to facilitate awareness and control

—Categories included in the ETC are behaviors important in the development of thinking skills

—Student levels of thinking can be improved in classes where teachers can apply the ETC

—Self-observation is the most appropriate evaluative approach;

teachers will change more readily through self-analysis than through outside supervision

—Equivalent Talk Categories can be learned by most classroom teachers in a relatively short training period

—Ease of teacher use and general applicability across the range of school subjects enhance its usefulness.

Ten Equivalent Categories

Ten categories cannot describe all that transpires in a classroom. However, the ten ETC categories—actually twenty, because of the equivalency factor—make it possible to objectively describe a great many verbal interactions in sequence. (See Table 4.1.) Teaching acts involving teachers and/or students can be scrutinized from the following viewpoints:

—Types of questions

—Types of answers

—Types of facilitative responses

—Sequences of verbal behavior

—Intervention effects of reactions to student contributions

—Levels of thinking generated by selected strategies

—Flexibility of verbal statements (range)

—Quantity of any dimension included as a category.

—Congruency and alignment of intended and actual behaviors

The ten equivalent talk categories are designed for use in classifying, recording, and quantifying classroom verbal behaviors, with each category presenting a distinct behavior. The ten categories may be used in classifying either teacher or student talk; the single digit (teacher code) is used to identify teacher talk; the double digit (student code) is used to identify student talk. (Table 4.3, p. 91.) The system presents no standard and passes no judgment. It simply makes possible the classification and quantification of verbal behaviors so that teaching strategies may be studied in terms of performance as well as theory. The categories focus on five specific types of verbal behavior: (1) presenting information, (2) questioning, (3) responding to questions, (4) reacting, and (5) structuring. (See Table 4.2.)

Presenting behaviors are defined as including all unsolicited initiations of information not covered by other ETC categories. Lectures, anecdotes, rhetorical questions, and unsolicited contributions are examples of verbal comments that should be classified as 1/11 in applying the ETC. Generally, teacher or student verbalizations used in introductions of content or instructional discussions that function as descriptive information, back-

Table 4.2

CATEGORY FOCI

Type of Verbal Behavior	Categories
Presenting	Presentation of information
Questioning	Questions—restricted thinking
	Questions—expanded thinking
Responding	Responses of restricted thinking
	Responses of expanded thinking
Reacting	Continuation of verbal participation
	Extension of verbal participation
	Termination of verbal participation
Structuring	Structure of learning activities
	Structure by pause or silence

Table 4.3

SUMMARY OF EQUIVALENT TALK CATEGORIES

Teacher Symbol		Student Symbol
1	Presentation of information	11
2	Questions—Restricted thinking	12
3	Questions—Expanded thinking	13
4	Responses—Restricted thinking	14
5	Responses—Expanded thinking	15
6	Continuation of verbal participation	16
7	Extension of verbal participation	17
8	Termination of verbal participation	18
9	Structure of learning activities	19
0	Pause or silence	10

ground, or explanation fall in this category. Unsolicited jokes, comments of a personal nature, and reports of individual experience, are generally considered as presentations and are, therefore, classified as 1/11.

Questions are classified as one of two types—those that require the respondent to perform thinking of limited complexity, and those that demand more involved mental effort. The ETC classification for Restricted Thinking questions is 2/12. These elicitations are expected to generate responses described in Sanders' (1966) taxonomy of classroom questions as memory. (Bloom's taxonomical division of knowledge is an equivalent.) The ETC classification for Expanded Thinking questions is 3/13. These elicitations are described in Sanders' *Classroom Questions* (1966) as translation, interpretation, application, analysis, synthesis, and evaluation and are expected to generate responses within these levels of cognitive activity. Bloom (ed.) (1956) lists the divisions as Comprehension, Application, Analysis, Synthesis, and Evaluation.

The division of taxonomical levels by restriction and expansion is arbitrary. It would seem completely reasonable for the user to divide at the point of greatest utility. For example, if the focus is on student or teacher originality (creativity in the Bloom discussion) and judgment, *synthesis* and *evaluation* might be the identifiers for question level discrimination and the other taxonomy levels would be omitted. Teacher decision of cognitive levels to be used may involve any two or three types of thinking as previously identified. (Introductory classes might focus on knowledge and comprehension; more advanced courses on analysis and application.)

A practical way of discriminating for classroom application might be to base decisions about restricted or expanded on the Gallagher-Aschner system of classifying classroom questions as presented in Chapter Three. The categories of Cognitive-memory, Convergent, Divergent, and Evaluative can be used in the same way as Bloom's taxonomy levels. Classify Cognitive-memory as *restricted* (2 or 12) and classify Convergent, Divergent, and Evaluative as *expanded* (3 or 13).

Responding categories are classified on the same basis as the question categories—Restricted thinking and Expanded thinking. Restricted thinking responses (4/14) are those requiring the less complex mental activity as described by the taxonomies or by the Gallagher-Aschner Cognitive-memory category. Expanded thinking responses (5/15) are answers requiring complexities of cognition as defined by the upper five levels of Bloom's (1956) taxonomy, the upper six classes or levels in Sanders' *Classroom Questions,* and the Gallagher-Aschner Convergent, Divergent, and Evaluative categories.

Reacting comments are those verbal behaviors utilized to maintain discussion, extend and raise the level of contribution, or bring about closure. (Closure may be facilitating when it makes it possible for interactions to proceed by beginning another sequence.) Expressions are classified on the basis of interactions and resulting sequences, not on individuals or cases.

Maintaining or sustaining reactions (6/16) include comments intended to result in continuation of a contribution at the same level of thinking. Thus, any verbalizations following a response/answer can be classified as maintaining, if the sequence is continued. To be considered an Extension (7/17), reactions must result in the raising of the level of thinking—from Restricted thinking to Expanded thinking.[1]

Terminating (8/18) verbal behaviors are so identified because they effect closure of a given thought sequence. Even though the statements may

[1] As teachers wish to be more discriminatory in their analysis of levels of cognition, they can modify the ETC categories of questions and answers, the facilitators dealing with levels of thinking through Sanders' taxonomy of questions or Bloom's taxonomy of the cognitive domain, the Florida Taxonomy of Cognitive Behavior, or other appropriate approaches.

be positive in nature and reinforcing in intent, they are classified as 8/18 if continuation (6/16) or extension (7/17) is not effected. Should the teacher fail to recognize or deal with a verbal response, there are functional guidelines stated to explain procedure.

Structuring behaviors are incorporated in the ETC system to identify Structure of learning activities (9/19) and Structure through silence (0/10). Comments requiring compliance and related to instructional acts are classified as 9/19, and are intended to provide operational information and procedures directly related to the progress of the lesson. Pauses and silences are often used to allow a strategy to unfold.

If thinking is what education is about and if talking—presenting questions, giving directions, and handling responses—is important in the teaching act, then the ETC promises the effectuation of meaningful assessment of instructional strategies. Further, it offers systematized guidance in preparing for and modifying subsequent instructional plans.

Observing and Recording

The ten equivalent talk categories are designed for use in classifying and quantifying classroom verbal behavior, representing five basic functions of the teaching-learning process. The system presents no standard and passes no judgment. It simply makes possible the examination of teaching strategy in terms of sequence and levels of thinking. As stated, the categories focus on the following five basic functions:

1. presenting
2. questioning
3. responding
4. reacting
5. structuring

The interplay, juxtaposition, and back and forth of these five functions determine, to a great degree, the success of a teaching-learning situation. The *planned* interaction of these functions is a strategy designed to produce success. The ETC provides a framework, a viewing procedure through which the *strategy* in action can be examined. The first step for the potential observer is to learn the categories. (Table 4.2, p. 91.)

Each of the functions is supported by specific categories, categories that provide for determining the level of thinking required and generated— both by students and the teacher. Presenting is the function of the first category in the system and its symbol is 1. Any time the teacher presents information, volunteers information, or lectures, the behavior is appropriately coded 1. If a student presents unsolicited information, the behavior is recorded as 11. The category is therefore applicable both to student and teacher behavior by adding the prefix to denote a student behavior.

All ten categories may be used in classifying either student or teacher talk. The single digit is used to identify teacher talk, the double digit is used to identify student talk. (See Table 4.4.)

Table 4.4

ETC: FUNCTIONS, CATEGORIES, SYMBOLS

Verbal Functions	Teacher Symbol	Categories	Student Symbol
Presenting	1	Present Information	11
Questioning	2	Question—Restricted thinking	12
	3	Question—Expanded thinking	13
Responding	4	Respond—Restricted thinking	14
	5	Respond—Expanded thinking	15
Reacting	6	React—maintain level of verbal participation	16
	7	React—extend level of verbal participation	17
	8	React—terminate level of verbal participation	18
Structuring	9	Structure—Learning activities	19
	0	Structure—Pause or silence	10

The structuring functions are extremely important as they affect the strategy of the teaching-learning situation. Both presenting and structuring play important roles in the interaction of the functions of questioning, responding, and reacting. The import of the questioning function and the responding function are reflected in two categories for each, one that encourages Restricted thinking and one that encourages Expanded thinking. Furthermore, the role that reacting plays in determining the level of thinking is illustrated in the categories—maintenance, extension, and termination of the level of verbal participation. These functions—presenting, questioning, responding, reacting, and structuring—are good points of departure for understanding the categories.

Sample Classroom Interaction

The following classroom interchange of elementary children and their instructor is presented and coded to illustrate the sequence of functions and their identification by the observer as category codes.

	Interaction	*Code*
Teacher:	Today we shall review our last T.V. lesson on insects that live in groups.	_1_ (1)
	What are these groups of insects known as?	_2_ (2)
Jane:	Social insects.	_14_ (3)
Teacher:	Social insects.	_6_ (4)
	What is one example of insects that live and work together?	_14_ (5)
Bill:	Ants.	
Teacher:	Good.	
	Can you name another?	_6_ (6)
Frank:	Spiders.	_14_ (7)
Sara:	Spiders are not insects!	_11_ (8)
Teacher:	No, Frank, spiders are not classed as insects because they have eight legs instead of six.	_1_ (9)
	Have you thought of another kind, Frank?	_6_ (10)
Frank:	Termites.	_14_ (11)
Teacher:	Termites, yes.	
	Can you recall an interesting fact about the life of a termite? In what way is it very different from an ant?	_6_ (12)
Joe:	The termite cannot digest his own food.	_14_ (13)
Teacher:	Right, can you explain further?	_7_ (14)
Joe:	The termite must depend upon a little one-celled animal that lives in his body to help him digest his food. In return for this catering service the one-celled animal gets free room and board!	_15_ (15)
Tom:	This one-celled animal is a parasite.	_11_ (16)
General Response:	No! You're wrong!	_11_ (17)
Teacher:	Class! Stop shouting and give Tom a chance.	_9_ (18)
	Tom, the little animal is a protozoa, and he is not really a parasite.	_1_ (19)
	Everyone read in your books on page 57. Locate information about the protozoa and see if you believe he should be called a parasite.	_9_ (20)
	(Class reads silently)	_0_ (21)
Tom:	I think I see the difference now. It says here that a parasite lives on or with a host always at the expense of the host.	_11_ (22)
Teacher:	A sort of Freddy the Freeloader, huh?	_1_ (23)
	Can you explain further, Tom?	_3_ (24)
Tom:	Yes, the host would be the plant or animal that has a parasite living on it, but not because it was really wanted. For example, mistletoe is a parasite	

Interaction (cont.)	*Code*

	that lives on trees but gives nothing back to the tree.	_15_ (25)
Jean:	But does the protozoa really help the termite? I should think that he would be an unwanted guest!	_11_ (26)
Tom:	The termite could not live unless the protozoa turned the gnawed wood fiber into material that nourishes the termite. The protozoa in turn is fed.	_16_ (27)
Mary:	If the protozoa is not a parasite . . . then what is he?	_16_ (28)
Teacher:	Does anyone know the term that this alliance between a host and his guest is called?	_0_ (29)
General Response:	No . . .	_14_ (30)
Teacher:	Please read on page 64. Raise your hand when you've located the information.	_9_ (31)
	(Class reads silently)	_0_ (32)
General Response:	I know! I know! I've found it!	_11_ (33)
Teacher:	My directions said to raise your hands not your voices! Sue, read it for us.	_9_ (34)
Sue:	Living things that are associated in this unusual way are called symbionts. The name comes from a Greek word meaning "a living together."	_11_ (35)
Sally:	Does this arrangement go on forever?	_16_ (36)
Teacher:	Often this living together is a lifelong arrangement; occasionally it is temporary. For instance, only in the nesting season does a water bird called the shelduck share the home of a rabbit. The shelduck builds a nest lined with grass and downy feathers at the bottom of a burrow. She may dig one or she may choose the shelter of a rabbit's hole and does not mind if the rabbit is still using it. And apparently the rabbit has no objection to his associate.	_5_ (37)
Anne:	I've just thought of another example of strange companions among the insects!	_11_ (38)
Teacher:	Good. Tell us about it.	_2_ (39)
Anne:	The ants and aphids.	_14_ (40)
Teacher:	Ants and aphids, of course. Tell us about them.	_7_ (41)
Anne:	Aphids puncture the young tips of plants and collect sap. The ants like this sap but cannot puncture a stem with their jaws, so they stroke the aphids and this causes the aphids to give up some of the sweet sap to the ant.	_15_ (42)

Interaction (cont.)   *Code*

Teacher: Very good. You have brought some interesting information to our lesson.   _//_ (43)

Jim: I am going to try to locate some other plants and
animals that live together in this way. I think this
is fascinating.   _//_ (44)

Sam: Could we give some reports on symbi _ _ _ _?
What's it called?   _/2_ (45)

Teacher: The arrangement is called symbiosis.
Yes, the idea of reports is fine.   _4_ (46)
Sam, you and Bill get together (along with anyone
else who would like) and bring us some reports.
I'll be glad to help you locate some materials.   _9_ (47)

Nancy: I agree that reporting is a good idea. I like group
projects. I get a lot from this class period because
the pupils have a chance to plan and participate.   _//_ (48)

Betty: May I make a suggestion?   _/2_ (49)

Teacher: Certainly.   _4_ (50)

Betty: Let's have group work at least once a week. Let
us have a chance to work with these different groups
in the library or any place that is needed.   _/6_ (51)

Teacher: Very good suggestions.   _/_ (52)
Now, Betty, make a chart with the topics of study
and have the pupils sign for the various committees.   _9_ (53)

Betty: I'll do it right away.   _//_ (54)

Teacher: I know I can always expect good results from this
class.   ___ (55)

A major difference between the ETC and RCS is readily apparent—observers code only the functions and do not concern themselves with time.
The ETC is a process-oriented system with emphasis on sequence and
level of cognitive activity. In the ensuing pages, each category is detailed
with appropriate examples, and practice opportunities are provided for
each required set of skills.

The Equivalent Talk Categories

Presenting

The process of presenting information is an integral part of many teaching-learning situations. The most striking concrete example of information
presenting is that of teacher lecture. Many other verbal contributions can,
however, be considered presentation of information—explanations, demon-
strations, and descriptions, for example. The immediate, and often erroneous, assumption is that the process of presenting is reserved for the
teacher. While this is true—too often, perhaps—any information that is

volunteered, rather than solicited, is considered part of the presenting process. A student's volunteered contribution is considered an 11, just as teacher lecture is considered a 1.

Teacher Code		*Student Code*
1	*Present Information*	11
	Unsolicited information—lecture, explanation related to lesson; demonstration; description; impromptu comments; rhetorical questions.	

The presenting behaviors extend from formal lectures or prepared contributions to impromptu comments. Rhetorical questions, or questions to which no answer is expected, are also considered presenting behaviors. Generally, the most helpful distinction in determining which behaviors are presenting behaviors is that they are *offered,* not *solicited* nor *elicited*.

EXAMPLES OF PRESENTING BEHAVIORS

Code

Teacher:	The publishing of books in America is no longer handled only by traditional publishers. Magazine publishers, teaching material manufacturers, and many large corporations frequently publish books.	/
Student: (John)	My father works for a meat packing company. He brings home a magazine called *Meat Packers Monthly*. I'll bet somebody in the meat packing industry does that magazine.	//
Teacher:	Let's clear up one point right here. When we talk about books, we are talking not only about hardbacks but also paperbacks.	//
Student: (Bill)	Even a small number of pages put together can be called a book—like the books we use in Sunday School or Boy Scouts.	//
Student: (Frank)	Well, I don't call the things we read in Sunday School books. I think books have to have at least 100 pages to be considered real books.	
Teacher:	Don't you think this discussion has brought up an interesting point? The personal idea about books. Everybody has a personal idea of what a book is.	/

Questioning and Responding

The functions of questioning and responding are so closely related that they will be combined for the purpose of discussion. Both of these functions are divided into two categories—one of which is characteristic of both expanded and restricted thinking. There are many values that can be applied to restricted thinking and expanded thinking—lower and higher order, cognitively simple and cognitively complex, and so on.

Distinguishing between questions and responses within these two categories can be made easier with a brief review of the Taxonomy of Cognitive Behavior.[2] Sanders (1966), in *Classroom Questions—What Kinds?*, presents a modified version of the Bloom, et. al. Taxonomy.

Table 4.5

TAXONOMY OF COGNITIVE BEHAVIOR[1]

Restricted Thinking	1.	Memory: The student recalls or recognizes information.
Expanded Thinking	2.	Translation: The student changes information into a different symbolic form or language.
	3.	Interpretation: The student discovers relationships among facts, generalizations, definitions, values, and skills.
	4.	Application: The student solves a lifelike problem that requires the identification of the issue and the selection and use of appropriate generalizations and skills.
	5.	Analysis: The student solves a problem in the light of conscious knowledge of the parts and forms of thinking.
	6.	Synthesis: The student solves a problem that requires original, creative thinking.
	7.	Evaluation: The student makes a judgment of good or bad, right or wrong, according to standards he designates.

[1] Data from 7 categories in *Classroom Questions: What Kinds?* by Norris M. Sanders (Harper & Row, 1966).

Thinking skills related to the first level—memory—are considered examples of restricted thinking, and call for little or no expansion or cognitive stretching. The other six levels are considered examples of expanded thinking. Translation, interpretation, application, analysis, synthesis, and evaluation call for expanded thinking and cognitive stretching.

The taxonomy of cognitive behavior is helpful because it distinguishes lower order behaviors from higher order behaviors. Memory, or knowledge requires only recall of information. Application, analysis, synthesis, and evaluation require problem solving, creating, rebuilding, and judging. Therefore, restricted thinking questions and responses are characteristic of the lower level of cognition, and expanded thinking questions are characteristic of higher levels of cognition.

[2] The reader is reminded that these preliminary definitions are by no means adequate for distinguishing the categories. They are submitted only as a necessary background to a discussion of the way that these ideas from the *Taxonomy of Educational Objectives* can be used by classroom teachers.

Teacher Code   *Student Code*

2   *Question—Restricted Thinking*   12
           Call for responses that result from re-
           stricted thinking—factual knowledge or
           simple recall; an accepted or predeter-
           mined correct answer; facts previously
           learned or easy to produce; lowest level
           of cognition.

3   *Question—Expanded Thinking*   13
           Call for responses that result from ex-
           panded thinking—open-ended responses;
           generation and application of principles,
           concepts, and generalizations; solutions
           generated by application of rules or pro-
           cedures; answers to how, why, what do
           you think; higher levels of cognition.

According to many authorities in the field of education, questioning verbal behaviors plays an important role in the teaching-learning situation. From the teaching strategy of Socrates to the modern question strategies, the question has long been an important tool used by the teacher to stimulate thinking, to generate an intellectual exercise. Questions, in and of themselves, may not meet the goal of stimulating thinking. They may, however, be vital to the strategy that does lead to stimulated thinking.

The restricted thinking question calls for a response that can be supplied from the memory bank, looked up in a book, or chosen from a list of alternatives. The expanded thinking question calls for a response that must come from a more complex intellectual exercise—perhaps as complex as conceptualization, or personal solutions to why, how, what do you think. The restricted thinking question calls for a cognitively simple response; the expanded thinking question, a more complex response.

FUNCTIONAL GUIDELINE—QUESTIONING

It is not necessary for a question to take an interrogative form to be considered a question. Often questions sound much like statements or directions, such as, "Please explain your feeling about capital punishment as a moral act." The statement is obviously calling for a response, in this instance an expanded thinking response.

Directions such as "get out your books," "everybody turn to page 7," "let's look at this map for a moment," are not, however, questions. These directions structure the learning activities and, therefore, are not considered questions. They are sometimes referred to as "traffic signals."

EXAMPLES OF RESTRICTED THINKING QUESTIONS

		Code
Teacher:	Who invented the printing press?	*2*
Teacher:	What was the first book to be printed on that press?	*2*
Student:	Why were books bound in leather originally?	*12*
Student:	How do you spell folio?	*12*

EXAMPLES OF EXPANDED THINKING QUESTIONS

		Code
Teacher:	What do you consider to be the most valuable book in this classroom? Why?	*3*
Student:	If the printing of religious literature stimulated the invention of the printing press, how did it spread to other forms of literature?	*13*
Teacher:	What effect can censorship of books have?	*3*
Student:	Why is the printed word considered to be law by many people?	*13*

RESPONDING

Teacher Code		Student Code
4	*Response—Restricted Thinking* Results from restricted thinking—factual knowledge; an accepted or predetermined corrected answer; facts previously learned or easy to produce; lower level of cognition.	14
5	*Response—Expanded Thinking* Results from expanded thinking—open-ended responses; generation and application of principles, concepts, and generalizations; solutions generated by application of rules or procedures; answers to how, why, what do you think, higher levels of cognition.	15

The process of distinguishing between the two types of responses is exactly the same as distinguishing between the two types of questions. Responses that are characteristic of the lower level of cognition are considered restricted thinking responses; responses that are a characteristic of the higher levels are considered expanded thinking responses.

FUNCTIONAL GUIDELINE—RESPONDING

Only those responses that are a result of an elicitation are considered *responses*. Other verbal contributions would likely be presenting or reacting behaviors. Responses are—in every instance —considered to be direct answers to questions, whether or not the question is worded interrogatively.

EXAMPLES OF RESTRICTED THINKING RESPONSES

Restricted thinking answers illustrate the simple cognitive processes that are used in responding—memory, recall, one right answer, or selection from a limited range of alternatives.

		Code
Teacher Question:	Who invented the first printing press?	2
Student Answer:	Johann Gutenberg.	14
Teacher Question:	What was the first book printed on that press?	2
Student Answer:	The Bible.	14
Student Question:	Why were books bound in leather originally?	12
Student Answer:	Because of its durability and availability.	14

EXAMPLES OF EXPANDED THINKING RESPONSES

Responses that reflect expanded thinking are characteristically more cognitively complex.

		Code
Teacher Question:	What do you consider to be the most valuable book in this classroom?	3
Student Answer:	The most valuable book to me, personally, is the dictionary.	15
Teacher Question:	Why?	3
Student Answer:	Because there are lots of ways other than the books in the classroom that you can get information—t.v., oral reports, conversations. The dictionary is valuable in helping one to learn to understand new words, and to look up important people and places.	15
Student Question:	If the printing of religious literature stimulated the invention of the printing press, how did it spread to other forms of literature?	13

Student Answer:	I'm not sure, but I think it might be related to a lessening of interest in the church. As the church became less powerful, the state or government would become more powerful. Therefore, the concentration and interest of the people would be more open to drama, for example.	*15*
Teacher Question:	What effect can censorship of books have?	*3*
Student Answer:	It can either kill a book or make it sell. People seem to react, in extremes, to forbidden things.	*15*
Student Question:	Why is the printed word considered to be law by many people?	*13*
Student Answer:	I think it is so because books are printed and legal documents such as contracts and wills and laws are printed. What is committed to print must be true.	*15*

Reacting

The function of reacting is particularly important in the teaching-learning situation because it serves to build the verbal interchange—the obvious manifestation of thinking. Three categories in the ETC are devoted to reacting behavior—one that maintains the level of verbal participation, one that raises the level of verbal participation, and one that terminates or closes the verbal participation.

Reactions can follow any kind of verbal behavior though, generally, they will be responses and can take any of several grammatical forms. (The one distinguishing feature of all reacting behaviors is that they are directed toward and built on another behavior—generally the one immediately preceding.) The following interchange illustrates such a behavior.

Interaction		*Code*
Teacher:	What is the name given to a large accumulation of books?	*2*
Student:	A library.	*14*
Teacher:	Yes, it could be called a library or a collection.	*1*
	Tell us what kind of books you would include if you were building a personal library.	*7*

The reacting behavior of the teacher (7) was clearly directed toward extending the student response (14). The same student response could generate either of the three kinds of reactions. A teacher reaction designed to maintain the level of the verbal participation would likely take a form similar to one of these:

Code

Tell us more about libraries.   *6*

Have you seen a large library?   _6_

What is the largest library you have ever seen?   _6_

The smallest?   _6_

Please continue your description of your father's law library!   _6_

The distinct feature of these reactions is that they encourage the person(s) to whom the reaction is directed to continue talking. Category 7/17 is devoted to reacting behaviors that call for the speaker to move to a higher cognitive level, a more complex and involved continuation of verbal participation. The following examples are teacher reactions to the sample question designed to extend the level of verbal participation.

                                                                      Code

What makes it possible for people to amass personal libraries?   _5_

What do you think about government restrictions on personal
libraries?   _5_

Why would you like to have a personal library?   _5_

Tell us how your family could use a library in your own home.   _5_

Would the availability of a library in your own home have any specific effect on you?   _5_

These reactions, designed to extend the level of the verbal participation (7), characteristically include suggestions or requests for new ideas, principles, and other more complex verbal behaviors. A reacting behavior that would close or terminate the discussion (8/18) might take one of these forms:

Teacher: Yes, that gets us to the point of talking about research methods.

Teacher: Now another topic of interest . . .

Functional Guideline—Reacting

When reacting behaviors take the interrogative or imperative form, they are still considered reacting behaviors when it is clear that they are directly related to the preceding verbal behavior.

Reacting to Maintain

Teacher Code		*Student Code*
6	*React—Maintain Level of Verbal Participation* Verbal behavior that maintains current level of thinking, invitation to continue, talking, amplify, clarify, or summarize ideas at the same or a lower level of cognition.	16

Maintaining behaviors can be at any cognitive level and are recognized because they cause continued verbal interchange. Should discussion continue as a result of a "react to maintain" behavior (6/16) even though the cognitive taxonomy level is lowered, the verbal interaction is coded as 6/16.

EXAMPLES OF REACTING TO MAINTAIN

Teacher: Correct. And if they didn't have machines then their books had to be copied in other ways. What are some possibilities?

Student: Tell us more about the book binding process.

Teacher: That's good, Jan. Originally, books were held together by stout cords. How can they be held together today?

Student: Books tell us so much about the people of the time in which they were written.

REACTING TO EXTEND

Teacher Code   *Student Code*

7   *React—Extend Verbal Participation*   17
           Verbal behavior that extends current level of
           thinking—request for further information,
           generation of data or principles, or recon-
           sideration of ideas requiring increased com-
           plexity of thinking; obvious utilization of in-
           formation supplied by another where level
           of cognitive participation is raised.

When a reacting behavior is intended to extend the level of thinking, it is considered a 7 or a 17. Reactions to extend behaviors are characteristically probing or prodding verbal behaviors, and may take the form of a challenge or dare, or they may be simple requests for further cognitive processing of the verbal contribution to which the reaction is directed.

EXAMPLES OF REACTING TO EXTEND

Teacher: Yes, books are so plentiful, and the cost is reasonable enough for almost everyone to have them. Do you want everybody to have access to any book they want to read?

Student: Sure, books are important to me. I like to read—fun stuff, anyway. What I don't understand is this censorship business or saying, "that's too old for you." Who can decide what's good for me?

Teacher: Does the old saying that the pen is mightier than the sword make you think a second time?

Student: I think the information we get from books today might as well come from television. What could be the difference?

When closure or termination is effected by failure to react verbally and by moving to another student or idea, that is coded as an 8/18 followed by whatever the new behavior may be.

REACTING TO TERMINATE

Teacher Code   *Student Code*

8   *React—Terminate Verbal Participation*   18
           Verbal behavior that brings current topic or
           thought to a close—termination of responses
           through comment or intervention; indication
           that thought sequence is ended; change or
           introduction of a new topic; summation or
           relationship-building activity when new learn-
           ing is related to old.

The termination of a verbal contribution refers to the closing of an idea, the pulling together of a concept, the drawing of generalizations or conclusions. Reacting behaviors designed to terminate, tend to close out or complete one idea or phase of an idea and move to another.

EXAMPLES OF REACTING TO TERMINATE

Teacher: Yes, I agree that paperback books have really made a difference in the price of books. We have looked at books from the time they were chiseled from clay tablets to the time when they are mass-produced and available to all people at nominal costs.

Student: It is my feeling that we will never decide on one definition of a book. Let's just agree that a book is a collection of printed material.

Teacher: Let's just choose a length that is somewhere between the shortest and the longest ones suggested and work with that definition.

Student: Why bother talking about censorship. We never get to read any of the good books because our parents watch everything we read. I'd like to talk about something else.

Structuring

Structuring behaviors figure in the teaching strategy much like stage directions fit into a drama. While they are not part of the actual content, they are necessary to its progress. The 9/19 behaviors, Structure—Learning Activities, are specifically directed toward building the learning situation. Commands, directions, assignments, or any statement that directs the progress of learning through organizational procedures is a structuring statement, while the 0/10 behaviors are directed toward the use made of a pause or silence.

STRUCTURING-LEARNING ACTIVITIES

Teacher Code   *Student Code*

9   *Structure-Learning Activities*   19
           Comments that organize learning activi-
           ties—commands, directions, assignments.

The behaviors that structure the learning activities most often take the form of directions or commands. They should not, however, be confused with the questioning or reacting behaviors that are related to the thinking skills involved. Structuring of the learning activities is the arranging of the elements of the instructional situation so that the prepared or evolved strategy can be effected.

EXAMPLES OF STRUCTURING OF LEARNING ACTIVITIES

		Code
Teacher:	Let's all move to the library today and look at . . .	9
Teacher:	Please take the pamphlet we have discussed today and look on page 4, column 3.	9
Teacher:	For tomorrow, please prepare a two or three sentence description of a book you would like to write or read.	9

STRUCTURING—PAUSE OR SILENCE

Teacher Code   *Student Code*

0   *Structure—Pause or Silence*   10
           Absence of verbalizations utilized to pro-
           mote the sequence planned.

The silence structuring behaviors are *not* immediately part of the teaching-learning situation except as these behaviors affect the strategy; they are used to allow thought or action.

EXAMPLES OF STRUCTURING—SILENCE

		Code
Teacher:	Please don't answer without thinking first.	9
Student:	Pause.	0
Teacher:	The books on that table are *not* to be touched.	1
Teacher:	Pause.	0

Practice Opportunities

Now, complete the practice drills that follow. They provide an opportunity to check understanding of categories and functions as verbal behaviors. (Answer keys are available in the Appendix.)

DIFFERENTIATION DRILL A

Differentiation requires classification of questions as knowledge or comprehension, application, analysis, synthesis, or evaluation. Knowledge type questions are classified as restricted thinking questions (2 or 12) and other type questions are classified as expanded thinking questions (3 or 13). Classify these questions first using Bloom's classifications, then using the ETC categories 2/12 or 3/13.

Bloom (1956) *Knowledge–Other*	*ETC Category* *2/12 or 3/13*	*Questions or Statements*
———	———	1. Teacher: Can you name a plant which is a parasite?
———	———	2. Teacher: Joe, give us some ideas about how to prepare a chart listing parasites, regions where they grow, etc.?
———	———	3. Student: Do you think our experiment with product X indicates that it is effective as a parasite control?
———	———	4. Teacher: How would you analyze the data collected in our experiment?
———	———	5. Teacher: Do you think mistletoe would be a parasite if we use our definition?
———	———	6. Student: What do you mean when you say "haustoria?"
———	———	7. Student: I've heard that some ancient peoples worshiped mistletoe—can you tell us about that?
———	———	8. Teacher: Describe the appearance of common mistletoe?
———	———	9. Teacher: Can you think of some ways that mistletoe seeds are spread?

DIFFERENTIATION DRILL B

Classify these responses using Bloom's classifications and using the
ETC categories 4/14 or 5/15.

Bloom (1956) Knowledge-Other	ETC Category 4/14 or 5/15	Responses
————	————	1. Teacher: Name three types of evergreen trees. Student: Juniper, Cedar, Fir
————	————	2. Teacher: Susan, what do you know about starfish? Student: I read that scientists have discovered each piece of a cut-up starfish, if it's big enough, will grow into a whole new animal.
————	————	3. Student: Please explain what you mean by pentagon? Teacher: A pentagon is a five-sided polygon.
————	————	4. Teacher: How would you interpret this rainfall chart? Student: The legend is not quite clear to me, but I think according to the chart the average rainfall in June in Atlanta is four inches, in Birmingham, three inches, etc.
————	————	5. Student: Do you think that the "Jackson Times" usually provides accurate news accounts? Teacher: No, I can give several specific incidents of gross error—I know—I was there.
————	————	6. Teacher: Can you think of an easy way to multiply 98 by 25? Student: First you multiply 100 by 25 and then subtract 50 from the product.
————	————	7. Teacher: What do you think the city council should do about the garbage collectors strike? Student: I think the council should agree to meet the union demands so the men would go back to work.
————	————	8. Teacher: How does an eiderdown duck look? Student: The female adult is brown; the males have black bellies and white backs.

DIFFERENTIATION DRILL C

Classify the following verbal behaviors as behaviors that maintain (6/16), extend (7/17), or terminate (8/18) the level of participation.

ETC Category
6/16, 7/17, 8/18   *Verbal Behavior*

1. Preceding cognitive level: restricted thinking
   Teacher: Can you tell us when Jackson was President?

2. Preceding cognitive level: Restricted thinking
   Teacher: If you were a congressman, how would you have voted and why?

3. Preceding cognitive level: Expanded thinking
   Student: Explain how your plan might be implemented.

4. Preceding cognitive level: Expanded thinking
   Student: I think we have spent too much time talking about the form of the report; let's discuss the content.

5. Preceding cognitive level: Restricted thinking
   Teacher: Can you suggest some ways to use the facts we have gathered?

6. Preceding cognitive level: Expanded thinking
   Teacher: Your reports on rock collecting were very interesting and now I would like to try to interest you in another hobby—pottery making.

7. Preceding cognitive level: Restricted thinking
   Student: If x = 3, then $x^2 = 9$.

8. Preceding cognitive level: Expanded thinking
   Student: But how do you feel about the dress code?

Collecting information with the ETC requires two fundamental acts: understanding the functions and categories of function described by the classification scheme (Table 4.1); and observing and recording the behaviors as they occur.

The process of understanding is facilitated through study of the functions —presenting, questioning, answering, reacting, and structuring—and their substantive descriptions (pp. 97–109). For example, the reader might study the function "reacting" described on pp. 102–106, and come to the conclusion that reacting behaviors can be used to describe those verbal acts that are employed by teachers or students to maintain the cognitive level, to raise the verbal behavior in taxonomic level, or to terminate the verbal sequence through some technique of closure. Further, he might determine that, to be most useful, reacting verbal behaviors must be limited by definition to those verbalizations functioning as maintainers, extenders, or terminators that are preceded by a questioning function and a responding or answering function.[3] In other words, to be coded as reacting (6/16, 7/17, or 8/18), the verbal behavior in question would, by definition, be preceded by an answering behavior. This does not presuppose other "by definition" applications of reacting codes, but instead attempts to delimit the observational procedure for a given purpose—such as a study of content level following responding or answering behaviors.

Evidence of understanding can then be ascertained by completing practice drills in which reacting behaviors of the three specified types—maintaining, extending, and terminating—are to be identified (pp. 102–106). Further practice on live or simulated data can be easily arranged by taping sequences of question-answer reaction in classrooms or by practice coding television programs that include such sequences. It is the opinion of the authors that this particular function—reacting—is of such significance to warrant separate practice until accuracy is mastered.

Collection Procedures [4]

The observe-record procedures, although relatively simple to describe, do necessitate a good bit of practice on the part of a "would-be" observer. As far as the actual observation is concerned, there are three main approaches that are of considerable utility in the average school setting:

1. The observer can arrange to visit live situations and code verbal interactions as they happen.
2. Audio tapes of self-taught sequences or other-taught lessons can be prepared, and are usually a maximum of thirty minutes per taping.
3. Videotaping of self-taught or other-taught instructional segments is now possible with the half-inch equipment that is available in many school settings.

At this time, available evidence indicates that at least ten to twelve hours are needed in actual practice coding, working with criterion scores, to develop acceptable accuracy. There are reports by those using systematic observation in research activities suggesting fifty hours of closely supervised study and practice. It has been the authors' experience that

---

[3] It has previously been noted that at least two viable approaches to coding 6/16, 7/17, and 8/18 are available to the ETC user and should be selected on the basis of the observer's objectives in application. (See p. 102.)

[4] Criterion scores should be available for comparative purposes. To prepare criterion scores implies expertness in recognizing and coding the identified verbal behaviors. The criterion score provides a record of expert opinion on the behaviors in question.

more than half the teachers spending ten to twelve hours in coding practice—including audio tapes and micro-teaching scripts—become reason-
ably accurate (.60 or better) for self-analysis purposes.[5]

Recording in the ETC is comprised of the basic acts of classifying mentally and according to function the verbal behaviors as they occur and
writing the category codes in sequence. Thus, a continuous record of
actual sequence is maintained and is available for careful assessment.
Generally, once a taped record is secured, the observer can accomplish
the coding at individual leisure. When an observer views the classroom
situation live, the important considerations are to disrupt the classroom
as little as possible and to situate oneself so that coding is possible. Considerations such as observer comfort, both of body and mind, availability
of the necessary equipment, and the space in which to use the equipment
should not be overlooked.

The only equipment essential to recording is a pencil or pen. However,
for convenience, two collection forms are illustrated. The first (Figure 4.1),
much like the form suggested for the Reciprocal Category System in
Chapter 3, consists of columns of blanks. Since there is no time element
involved in the ETC data collection, there are more recording spaces to
make maximum use of paper. A standard size (8½ x 11) is recommended
so that a loose leaf notebook can be maintained for a simple file system.
The second suggested form, much like the approach used by Parsons
(1968) in *Guided Self Analysis* and Flanders in a 1970 AERA position
paper, is similar to the chronology approach in historical descriptions.
This procedure allows the observer to view simultaneously the usage
trends of various combinations of categories. (See Figure 4.2.)

Beginning at the left, each function can be coded by simply checking
(✔) the appropriate box. This procedure is best used to study either the
instructor (as illustrated) or the student. If the observer wishes to use this
approach for coding both simultaneously, it is suggested that a check (✔)
or checks (✔ s) be used to designate who did what with the ✔ representing the instructor and the ✔ s representing the student. Various applications can easily be determined. For situations in which the observer
is recording by function only—presenting, questioning, answering, reacting, structuring—using the ✔/✔ s approach, the form suggested in
Figure 4.3 is illustrative. Other modifications will come to mind as the
system is applied. For most basic uses, the columns suggested in Figure
4.1 are sufficient and provide a complete record from which summary
charts or records can be developed.

[5] Jeannine N. Webb, Ernest L. Bentley, and R. Robert Rentz, "Observation as a
Methodology" (read at AERA, Minneapolis, 1970).

Figure 4.1

OBSERVATION RECORD SHEET—ETC

Observer _____   Completion Time _____

Observed _____   Subject Area _____

Number of Observation _____   Topic_____

Beginning Time_____   Planned Strategy _____

	1	2	3	4	5	6	7	8	9	10	11	12	13	14	15	16
1	—	—	—	—	—	—	—	—	—	—	—	—	—	—	—	—
2	—	—	—	—	—	—	—	—	—	—	—	—	—	—	—	—
3	—	—	—	—	—	—	—	—	—	—	—	—	—	—	—	—
4	—	—	—	—	—	—	—	—	—	—	—	—	—	—	—	—
5	—	—	—	—	—	—	—	—	—	—	—	—	—	—	—	—
6	—	—	—	—	—	—	—	—	—	—	—	—	—	—	—	—
7	—	—	—	—	—	—	—	—	—	—	—	—	—	—	—	—
8	—	—	—	—	—	—	—	—	—	—	—	—	—	—	—	—
9	—	—	—	—	—	—	—	—	—	—	—	—	—	—	—	—
10	—	—	—	—	—	—	—	—	—	—	—	—	—	—	—	—
11	—	—	—	—	—	—	—	—	—	—	—	—	—	—	—	—
12	—	—	—	—	—	—	—	—	—	—	—	—	—	—	—	—
13	—	—	—	—	—	—	—	—	—	—	—	—	—	—	—	—
14	—	—	—	—	—	—	—	—	—	—	—	—	—	—	—	—
15	—	—	—	—	—	—	—	—	—	—	—	—	—	—	—	—
16	—	—	—	—	—	—	—	—	—	—	—	—	—	—	—	—
17	—	—	—	—	—	—	—	—	—	—	—	—	—	—	—	—
18	—	—	—	—	—	—	—	—	—	—	—	—	—	—	—	—
19	—	—	—	—	—	—	—	—	—	—	—	—	—	—	—	—
20	—	—	—	—	—	—	—	—	—	—	—	—	—	—	—	—
21	—	—	—	—	—	—	—	—	—	—	—	—	—	—	—	—
22	—	—	—	—	—	—	—	—	—	—	—	—	—	—	—	—
23	—	—	—	—	—	—	—	—	—	—	—	—	—	—	—	—
24	—	—	—	—	—	—	—	—	—	—	—	—	—	—	—	—
25	—	—	—	—	—	—	—	—	—	—	—	—	—	—	—	—
26	—	—	—	—	—	—	—	—	—	—	—	—	—	—	—	—
27	—	—	—	—	—	—	—	—	—	—	—	—	—	—	—	—
28	—	—	—	—	—	—	—	—	—	—	—	—	—	—	—	—
29	—	—	—	—	—	—	—	—	—	—	—	—	—	—	—	—
30	—	—	—	—	—	—	—	—	—	—	—	—	—	—	—	—
31	—	—	—	—	—	—	—	—	—	—	—	—	—	—	—	—
32	—	—	—	—	—	—	—	—	—	—	—	—	—	—	—	—
33	—	—	—	—	—	—	—	—	—	—	—	—	—	—	—	—
34	—	—	—	—	—	—	—	—	—	—	—	—	—	—	—	—
35	—	—	—	—	—	—	—	—	—	—	—	—	—	—	—	—
36	—	—	—	—	—	—	—	—	—	—	—	—	—	—	—	—
37	—	—	—	—	—	—	—	—	—	—	—	—	—	—	—	—
38	—	—	—	—	—	—	—	—	—	—	—	—	—	—	—	—

Figure 4.2

VERTICAL OBSERVATION RECORD A–ETC

Observer _____ Completion Time _____

Observed _____ Subject Area _____

Number of Observation _____ Topic _____

Beginning Time _____ Planned Strategy _____

Category
Number

0													
1													
2													
3													
4													
5													
6													
7													
8													
9													

In summary, collection procedures are accomplished by learning the categories, observing an instructional segment, and recording the verbal behavior in sequence by function or by category. Rules governing specifics of recording were presented as functional guidelines.

Additional guiding principles are:

1. *Use the appropriate category symbol for each category.* A thorough understanding and memorization of these categories is necessary.

2. *Place a dash when the behavior is not classifiable according to the system.* If the verbal behavior is not aptly classified by any of the categories, simply skip the appropriate number of spaces.

Figure 4.3

VERTICAL OBSERVATION RECORD B—ETC

Observer _____   Completion Time _____

Observed _____   Subject Area _____

Number of Observations _____   Topic _____

Beginning Time _____   Planned Strategy _____

Functions:

Presenting											
Questioning											
Answering											
Reacting											
Structuring											

3. *Circle the code of any irrelevant behaviors.* When verbal behaviors that are irrelevant to the general discussion occur, they can be coded and then circled to provide evidence about staying with the subject or plan.

Successful study of the functions and performance on the Differentiation Drills should already be a fact. Now that a working knowledge of the ETC functions and categories is apparent, the reader is ready to try a practice coding exercise of an actual classroom sequence. Although it is quite different to code live behaviors that are lost if not quickly identified and recorded, the practice script approach is not unlike that of an individual teacher taping a segment of instruction and playing it back to listen to verbal interchanges that may have been missed.

Practice Script

The script that follows is a seventh grade mathematics lesson.[6] The teacher

[6] Appendix includes the answer code for the script with a commentary on selected behavior codes.

attempts to develop for her pupils a better understanding of inductive reasoning using the discovery learning approach. She guides the pupils to actually discover several general principles for themselves using the inductive method. As the teacher leads her pupils to the first discovery, she is quite specific in her directions—her purpose being to help her pupils develop the organizational skills needed for successful inductive reasoning. After they have completed the first exercise, teacher directions become less frequent and less detailed, thus allowing the pupils freedom to organize ideas for themselves. Specific objectives include: discovery that the number of triangles into which a polygon may be divided is two less than the number of sides of the polygon $[A = n - 2]$; discovery that the sum of the measures of the angles of a polygon is equal to 180 degrees times the number of triangles into which the polygon may be divided $[X = 180 (n - 2)]$; discovery that the measure of each angle of a regular polygon may be found by dividing the total measures of the angles by the number of sides of the polygon $[Y = 180 (n - 2)/n]$.

Interaction	*Codes*
Teacher: Today you will need to have your pencil and paper, your protractor, and your polygon models handy as we will be using those materials as we make other discoveries about polygons. Please get out these materials.	_____ (1)
Pause.	_____ (2)
John, do you remember some characteristics of a polygon?	_____ (3)
John: A polygon contains line segments and it is a closed figure.	_____ (4)
Teacher: That's correct. Who can give another characteristic? Jean?	_____ (5)
Jean: A polygon has only two dimensions even though our models are three-dimensional. And, also a polygon has sides and angles that may be measured.	_____ (6)
Teacher: Good. Have you ever seen a polygon with only two sides?	_____ (7)
Norma: No, it's impossible for a polygon to have only two sides. There must be at least three.	_____ (8)
Teacher: Right, Norma. What name do we use for a three-sided polygon?	_____ (9)
Norma: Triangle.	_____ (10)
Teacher: That's right. Let's make a list of names for polygons that we have discussed. Do this on your paper now. Make your list look like this so you will have room to do some other things on your paper too. (Shows a transparency as an example.)	_____ (11) _____ (12)

	Interaction (cont.)	*Codes*
	Pause.	_____ (13)
	Molly, will you read your list and tell us how many sides each one has?	_____ (14)
Molly:	Triangle, three; quadrilateral, four; pentagon, five; hexagon, 6; I forgot the name of a seven-sided polygon.	_____ (15) _____ (16)
Class:	Heptagon.	_____ (17)
Molly:	Oh, yes, now I remember. Octagon, eight; nonagon, nine; and decagon, ten.	_____ (18) _____ (19)
Teacher:	That's good. Now beside each item on your list, sketch a picture of that type polygon.	_____ (20) _____ (21)
	Pause.	_____ (22)
Teacher:	Did the picture you sketched for a quadrilateral have four sides with equal measures and four angles with equal measures, Jim?	_____ (23)
Jim:	No.	_____ (24)
Teacher:	Jim, what about the cardboard polygon models I gave you yesterday; did they have equal sides and equal angles?	_____ (25)
Jim:	Yes.	_____ (26)
Teacher:	Yes.	_____ (27)
	Class, now use your regular polygon models to draw regular polygon models of each item on your list.	_____ (28)
	Pause.	_____ (29)
	Everyone finished?	_____ (30)
Class:	Yes.	_____ (31)
Teacher:	Beginning with the quadrilateral, choose one vertex and draw as many diagonals as possible.	_____ (32)
	Pause.	_____ (33)
	How many triangles were formed?	_____ (34)
Class:	Two	_____ (35)
Teacher:	Ok, now do the same thing with the other polygon sketches, and count the triangles formed in each case.	_____ (36)
	Pause.	_____ (37)
	Sid, what did you find out?	_____ (38)
Sid:	For the pentagon, I got three triangles, four for the hexagon, five for the heptagon, six for the octagon, and so on.	_____ (39)
Teacher:	Sid said "and so on." I think he's got the scheme! Sid, suppose you had a polygon with fifty sides; how many triangles would be formed?	_____ (40) _____ (41)

	Interaction (cont.)	*Codes*

Sid: Forty-eight.   _____ (42)

Teacher: Right. Suppose I had a polygon with n sides and had drawn diagonals from the vertices, how many triangles would be formed?   _____ (43)

Sid: Two less than whatever n is.   _____ (44)

Teacher: Now, Sid, let's be sophisticated. Give us a mathematical formula.   _____ (45)

Sid: Oh, well, how about $n - 2$?   _____ (46)

Teacher: Good.   _____ (47)

Recently we talked about two types of reasoning. They were called inductive reasoning and deductive reasoning. Which type did you use to find the formula?   _____ (48)   _____ (49)

Class: Inductive.   _____ (50)

Teacher: That's correct. Yesterday, we used our protractors and measured the angles of several triangles. Here again, we used inductive reasoning and decided that the sum of the measures of the angles on a triangle is 180 degrees. Many of you will take a course in a few years called Plane Geometry, and in that course you will use deductive reasoning to prove that this is true.   _____ (51)

Now, I have a new problem for you. Using the facts that the sum of the measures of the angles of a triangle is 180 degrees and the fact that you just discovered about diagonals of a polygon, find out how to find the sum of measures of the angles of any polygon and try to write a formula.   _____ (52)   _____ (53)

Pause.   _____ (54)

Sally, did you forget that you have a problem to solve?   _____ (55)

Sally: No.   _____ (56)

Pause.   _____ (57)

Teacher: John, what is the sum of the measures of the angles of a pentagon?   _____ (58)

John: 510 degrees.   _____ (59)

Glenn: No. It's 540.   _____ (60)

Susan: I got 510 also.   _____ (61)

Teacher: No, Susan. Glenn got the correct answer.   _____ (62)

Glenn, did you write a formula?   _____ (63)

Glenn: Yes.   _____ (64)

I took the other formula we wrote to find the number of triangles and multiplied it by 180 degrees because all of the angles of each triangle added to-

Interaction (cont.)	*Codes*

	gether would be the same measure as all the angles of the polygon. Well, it's hard to explain.	_____ (65)
	May I show you on the board?	_____ (66)
Teacher:	Yes.	_____ (67)
Glenn:	(Demonstrates by making drawings). This angle is equal to the sum of the measures of these three, and this one is equal to the sum of the measures of these two and so on. So, I wrote this formula: $180 (n - 2)$.	_____ (68) _____ (69)
Teacher:	Good. Glenn used this formula to determine that the sum of the measures of the angles of a pentagon is 540 degrees.	_____ (70)
	If this pentagon is a regular pentagon, what is the measure of each angle?	_____ (71)
	Pause.	_____ (72)
Susan:	108.	_____ (73)
Teacher:	Use your protractor to measure an angle of your regular polygon model.	_____ (74)
	Pause.	_____ (75)
	Is Susan's answer correct?	_____ (76)
Class:	Yes.	_____ (77)
Teacher:	Write a formula to use in finding the measure of each angle of a regular polygon.	_____ (78)
	Pause.	_____ (79)
John:	Ok, Charlie. Keep quiet so I can think.	_____ (80)
Teacher:	Who has found a formula? Jean?	_____ (81)
Jean:	$\dfrac{180 (n - 2)}{n}$	_____ (82)
Teacher:	Good.	_____ (83)
	Now I've thought of a good problem for homework. I want to put tiles on my bathroom floor. I plan to use regular polygons. Your problem is to tell me which regular polygons I will be able to use.	_____ (84)
Teacher:	Now, remember, I don't want any holes in my floor. Also remember that the sum of the measures of the angles about a point is 360 degrees.	_____ (85)

Preparation Procedures

Following collection of data on selected instructional situations there are useful procedures that make it possible to gain information from the recorded information. They involve summarizing the data in such a manner that inferences and conclusions in data interpretation can be made quickly and evidently apparent. Three techniques are included for use—

tabulation, computation, and branching. The reader will discover additional quantifying techniques with considerable usefulness in local application.

Tabulations

Counting the number of codes for each category provides a way of summing and thus, viewing the relative distribution of verbal behaviors among
the categories. Two useful approaches are simple counting and recording
in a format such as that illustrated in Figure 4.6 and entering the data
in a summary chart such as that illustrated in Figure 4.7. When using the
raw tabulation form, the reader will observe that he can study irrelevant
behaviors by category simply by utilizing a slash and by reporting in the
upper left corner relevant behaviors for a particular category with the
irrelevant behaviors relegated to the lower half.

Counting and recording in the suggested format makes comparisons of
gross raw data totals posisble. It is possible to see by the "eye-balling"
technique which categories tend to contain the largest numbers of inci-
dence. A caution is probably unnecessary but the data preparer should
remember that unless he chooses a time or a time-process recording procedure, the totals represent only how many times such a behavior occurred.
When a time element is included, such as the RCS, it is additionally possible to roughly estimate the amount of instructional time spent in certain
behavior categories. When the time-only (record every three seconds as
in Flanders' interaction analysis) recording approach is implemented,
close estimates of actual time per category should be obtainable, simply
by multiplying the total number of incidents of any category by three.

Figure 4.4 indicates summaries of each possible action per category
and additionally includes exceptions such as non-coded segments (those
that the system does not assess) and non-strategy related comments.
Dashes indicate several behaviors the system does not code and circles
around codes identify non-related comments that may have been included
in the verbal interchange.

The summary chart exhibited in Figure 4.5 is based on the matrix
approach espoused in the RCS discussion. However, it is included for
utility in spotting types of interchange occurring—teacher-student, student-
teacher, etc.—and not as a sequence study approach. The procedure for
tallying or entering the data into the chart is practically the same as for
the RCS. Data are grouped in pairs as illustrated below:

$$
\begin{array}{c}
\lceil\ 2 \\
\lfloor_{14\rceil} \\
\quad\lceil_{6\rfloor}
\end{array}
$$

Figure 4.4

RAW DATA TABULATION FORM

Category	1	2	3	4	5	6	7	8	9	0	11	12	13	14	15	16	17	18	19	10	T_r	-	T_i	T
Incidences																								
% of T_r																								
% of T																								

Key

T_r: total relevant behaviors
-: behaviors not measured by the ETC
T_i: total irrelevant behaviors (circled codes)
T: total recorded behaviors

121

Figure 4.5

Summary Chart of Interchange: ETC

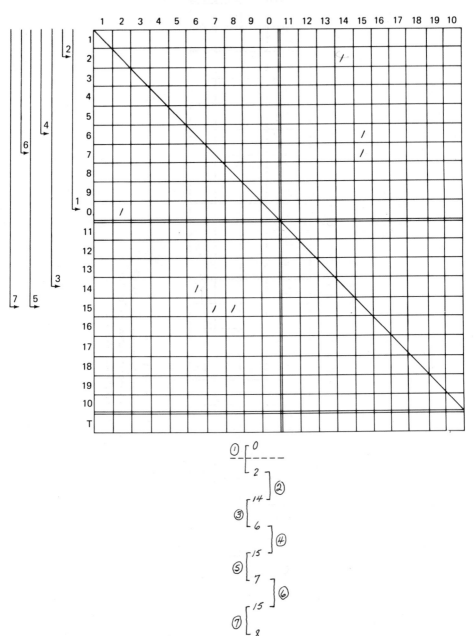

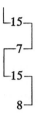

However, the first code must be treated as if it followed another be-havior in order to begin tallying. This is quite an arbitrary decision based on expediency.

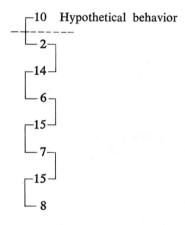

These data or codes should be entered by going down the left side, finding the first code in the pair, and then across the right until the appropriate number for the column is reached. A tally is, then, placed in the cell that is located on the row of the first code in the column of the second code. Figure 4.5 illustrates the procedure. For purposes of the Summary Chart of Interchange, non-codeable behaviors are ignored. Irrelevant behaviors, codes that are circled, can be plotted in the nor-mal fashion. Quadrant One (I) reveals the instructor verbal behaviors alone; Quadrant Two (II) demonstrates student-after-instructor behaviors; Quadrant Three (III) summarizes student-before-instructor behaviors; and Quadrant Four (IV) reviews student interchange.

Computations

Percentages and ratios are useful in determining relative concentration of activity in any classroom episode or strategy sequence. Category percent-ages of the recorded functions, of individual categories, and of recorded deviations such as non-related material are computed by dividing the total number of incidents recorded into the individual totals.

To compute percentage of a function, divide as follows:

$$\text{Percentage of function} = \frac{\text{Total codes of a function}}{\text{Total verbal behaviors recorded}}$$

If there are thirty codes on the data sheet recorded for teacher questions (both 2 and 3) and there is a total of 150 codes (0/10 through 9/19), the computation would appear as follows:

$$\frac{\text{Total of teacher questions}}{\text{Total incidences recorded}} = \frac{30}{150} = .20 = 20\%$$

In this example, 20% of all recorded verbal acts were teacher questions.

To compute the percentage of a specified category, divide the total in any category (Figure 4.6) by the total recorded codes or incidences. Thus, to compute the percent of teacher questions in the lower cognitive levels, divide the number of Category 2 codes by the total recorded Category 2 and 3 verbal functions.

$$\frac{\text{Category total of lower order teacher questions (2)}}{\text{Category total of teacher questions (2 and 3)}}$$

This yields the percent of all questions asked that were designed to elicit knowledge-responses.

Users of the ETC can and will ascertain the percentages of greatest usefulness, the desirability of using raw data for gross comparisons through visual inspection, and/or the advisability of computing ratios to illustrate various relationships. Some suggested ratios will clarify the procedure and the practitioner can define others that are appropriate to the local application.

Ratios that may be of concern to the ETC user include:

(a) $\dfrac{\text{Teacher}}{\text{Student}} = \dfrac{0 - 9}{10 - 19}$

(b) $\dfrac{\text{Lower order student response}}{\text{Higher order student response}} = \dfrac{\text{Total for category 14}}{\text{Total for category 15}}$

(c) $\dfrac{\text{Teacher extending reactions (7)}}{\text{Teacher reacting behaviors (6, 7, 8)}} = \dfrac{\text{Total for category 7}}{\text{Total for categories 6, 7, 8}}$

Since the procedure is the same as that discussed in the RCS, computations of examples are omitted. It should be noted, for non-mathematical readers, that the usefulness of the system is not the ability to compute. Rather, it resides in the value for strategy planning and execution which can be assessed through systematic observation—here, the ETC.

Branching

The technique known in chemistry as flow charts and in math and the computer sciences as branching, uses the principle of the family tree or genealogical record. Its usefulness is the visual display of antecedents and consequents in strategy sequence. The instructor might hypothesize, for example, that the use of a Category 2 behavior leads to the students' Category 14 responses, but that the subsequent use by the teacher of a Category 7 behavior could raise the level of activity in taxonomic terms. Thus, the branching record would appear like this:

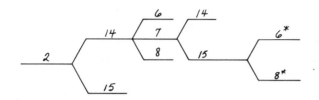

* Since the preceding category was a higher cognitive level (15) the only two re-acting alternatives are to maintain (6) or to terminate (8).

Similarly, the total number of instances in which a sequence occurs can be summarized on a multipurpose branching chart. The usefulness in planning, as a projective viewing mechanism and then for subsequent study of actual recorded verbal sequences, should be apparent. (See Figure 4.6.) Hypothetical and actual comparisons lend themselves to the concept of "awarenes and control" espoused consistently in this publication.

Practice Opportunities

Following this cursory view of several types of data preparation—tabulation, computation, and branching—practice opportunities provide a quick check of understanding level. The coded verbal behaviors, from the practice classroom script, are summarized on a data collection sheet for use in these exercises. Follow the previously studied instructions for tabulation, computation, or branching and apply the procedures in the solution of the drill problems. Use the data summarized in Figure 4.7 for this set of exercises. Answer Keys are available in the Appendix.

These exercises should assist the serious student in identifying weaknesses in the preparation areas. The following section—Data Interpretation, page 131—is largely dependent on such arranging of data into interpretable form.

Figure 4.6

MULTIPURPOSE BRANCHING CHART

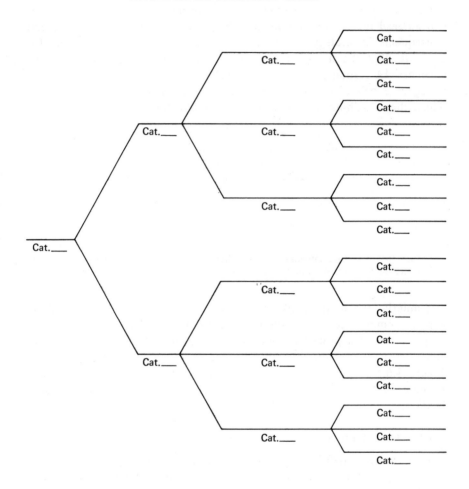

1. Identify the frequency of occurrence for each category by counting on the observation record sheet (Figure 4.7) and insert the totals in the correct columns on the raw data tabulation form (Figure 4.8).

Figure 4.7

OBSERVATION RECORD SHEET: ETC

Observer _____   Completion Time _____

Observed _____   Subject Area _____

Number of Observation _____ Topic_____

Beginning Time_____   Planned Strategy _____

	1	2	3	4	5	6	7	8	9	10	11	12	13	14	15	16
1	9	14	5													
2	0	1	9													
3	2	7	0													
4	14	15	19													
5	6	6	4													
6	14	15	15													
7	7	6	8													
8	15	15	9													
9	6	8	1													
10	14	1														
11	8	3														
12	9	15														
13	0	1														
14	2	8														
15	14	9														
16	11	0														
17	14	(2)														
18	1	(4)														
19	14	10														
20	8	3														
21	9	15														
22	0	15														
23	2	15														
24	14	1														
25	6	6														
26	14	14														
27	8	11														
28	9	19														
29	0	9														
30	9	10														
31	19	15														
32	9	1														
33	0	6														
34	2	0														
35	14	15														
36	6	9														
37	0	0														
38	6	6														

Figure 4.8

RAW DATA TABULATION FORM

Category	1	2	3	4	5	6	7	8	9	0	11	12	13	14	15	16	17	18	19	10	T_r	-	T_i	T
Incidences																								
% of T_r																								
% of T																								

Key

T_r: total relevant behaviors
-: behaviors not measured by the ETC
T_i: total irrelevant behaviors (circled codes)
T: total recorded behaviors

2. Plot the Summary Chart of Interchange by bracketing the data in Figure 4.7 and entering the pairs in the chart provided in Figure 4.9. Then, obtain totals for each column by adding down the columns and enter these figures as appropriate totals. (Don't forget to use a hypothetical beginning code (10).)

Figure 4.9

SUMMARY CHART OF INTERCHANGE

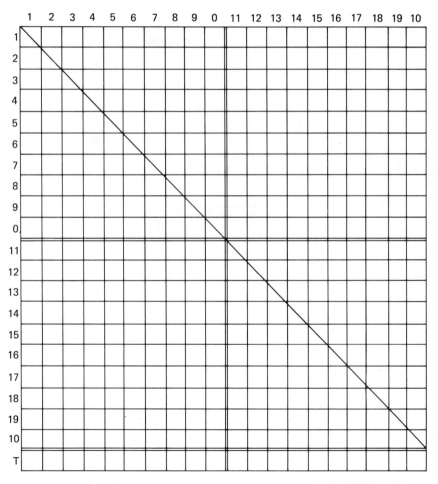

Grand
Total

COMPUTATION DRILL

Compute the following category percentages and ratios based
on the data summaries completed:

  a. Category 2
  b. Category 14
c. Teacher/ratio for all functions/Student
d. Restricted Question—Teacher/Expanded Question—Teacher
e. "Extending" Reacting—Teacher/All Reacting (6, 7, & 8)—Teacher

BRANCHING DRILLS

Fill in the actual number of behaviors for each category identified
on the branching examples following.

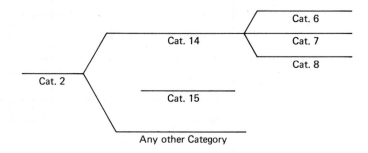

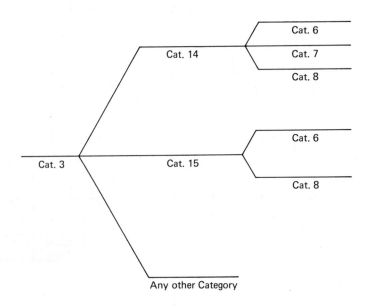

Three general themes are suggested, relevant to usage of ETC data: visual inspection of the coded sequence and prepared forms; consideration of computed percentages and ratios; and comparative viewing of planned and actual verbal behaviors or of actual behaviors over time.

Visual Inspection

Raw data or codes recorded on the observation form can be quite informative in relation to actual patterns or sequences. In order to prepare comparative charts, the data must be inspected, and often the charts provide quantitative evidence of phenomena known to the inspector. For example, such items as irrelevant contributions and non-codeable behaviors will be easily identified in either absence or presence. Repetitions of patterns or series of behaviors in sequence will also be in evidence.

However, inspection of organized data will save time and will reduce the probability of erroneous generalizations based on inaccurate visual inspection. Tabulation activities, presented as counting and as summarizing, result in frequencies that make it relatively simple to estimate or compute information (such as, category emphasis in terms of percentages, or to ascertain the dominant types of interchange). Summary Chart of Interchange—ETC quadrants—reveal the direction and quantity of interchange.

Knowledge of the relative percent of functions (% of T_r, % of T_i, etc.) is useful in planning modifications of previously planned and taught instructional segments. Emphasis planned for Categories 3 and 15 will be evident, when achieved. Other choices of strategy will have similar visibility. Most applications based on processed and interpreted data are directly related to awareness factors—factors leading to the decision of acceptable or non-acceptable strategy, acceptable or non-acceptable quality in the cognitive efforts, and acceptable or non-acceptable levels of participation.

To illustrate the emphasis of visual inspection, the data from a previously coded classroom script are presented in Figure 4.10. Student lower-cognitive answers (Category 14), those identified as a result of restricted thinking, occur with the same frequency as student upper-cognitive responses (Category 15). Teacher maintaining (Category 6) occurs more frequently than Closure (Category 8) or Extending (Category 7)—10 times versus 6 and 2 respectively.

To extend the example, the same data as plotted in Figure 4.11—the Summary Chart of Interchange—are present.

Figure 4.10
Raw Data Tabulation Form

Category	1	2	3	4	5	6	7	8	9	0	11	12	13	14	15	16	17	18	19	10	T_r	-	T_i	T
Incidences	7	4	2	1	1	10	2	6	11	10	2	0	0	11	11	0	0	0	3	2	83	0	2	85
% of T_r	8	5	2	1	1	12	2	7	13	12	2	0	0	13	13	0	0	0	4	2	-			99%
% of T	8	5	2	1	1	12	2	7	13	12	2	0	0	13	13	0	0	0	4	2			2	99%

Key

T_r: total relevant behaviors
-: behaviors not measured by the ETC
T_i: total irrelevant behaviors (circled codes)
T: total recorded behaviors

132

Figure 4.11

SUMMARY CHART OF INTERCHANGE—ETC

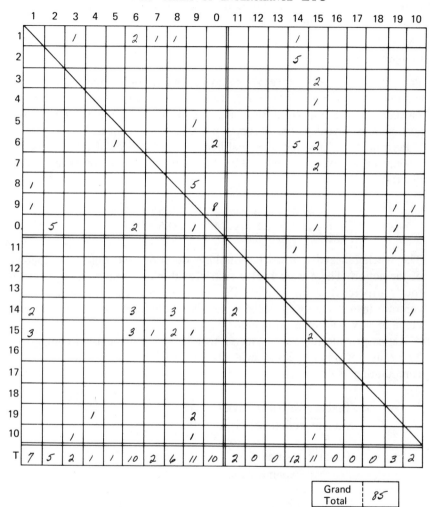

The largest concentrations of interchange are teacher to teacher and student to teacher (Quadrants I and III). The teacher quadrant contains thirty-two tallies; the teacher-student quadrant twenty-two; the student-teacher quadrant twenty-three; and the student quadrant eight. Since the purpose of the lesson was guided discovery, such a range could be considered a successful implementation of planned strategy.

The value of visual inspection is amply demonstrated, and the discussion of profile comparisons simply extends the view. It is now apparent that interpretation refers to teacher judgments based on quantified verbal behaviors that have been coded for just such a purpose. The tool is not evaluative (other than describing discrete activities), but yields data upon which responsible judgments may be made.

Computed Information

Percentages of types of verbal behavior and ratios comparing significant variables are computed according to procedures discussed in the section on data preparation. Here, the interest is in what the relative size or proportion may reveal to the observer as he assesses collected data.

Percentages of a specified verbal behavior are indices of relative concentration in a given function. The following examples of computations illustrate:

$$\% \text{ of Category } 2 = 5/85 = 5\%$$
$$\% \text{ of Category } 14 = 12/85 = 14\%$$

The teacher asked a restricted-thinking question five times, five percent of the action. There were twelve restricted-thinking responses by students, fourteen percent of the activity. Depending on the teacher's intent to concentrate in a category, a decision can be made about successful achievement of any part of a strategy.

Ratios provide the alert observer with simple statements of comparison. The range of possibilities is evidenced by three examples from the same computation drill:

$$\frac{\text{Teacher verbal behavior}}{\text{Student verbal behavior}} = \frac{55}{30} = 1.83$$

$$\frac{\text{Teacher restricted-thinking questions}}{\text{Teacher expanded-thinking questions}} = \frac{5}{2} = 2.5$$

$$\frac{\text{Teacher extending reactions}}{\text{Total of teacher reactions}} = \frac{2}{18} = .111$$

Each time a student contribution occurred, 1.8 teacher verbal behaviors were employed. The teacher used more restricted-thinking questions than expanded-thinking at the rate of 2.5 to 1. Only a small proportion of the reacting functions were to extend or raise the level of verbal response solicited from the students. (However, if the discussion was already operating in the higher taxonomical levels, most reacting behaviors would be expected to be maintainers.)

As expressed previously, decisions about the appropriateness of these comparative figures are dependent on the teacher plan (objectives and strategy). More sophisticated ratios (such as the 2–14–7 sequence/ 3–15–6 sequence) can be designed as the observer becomes familiar with the system and its operation.

Profile Comparisons

Three profile comparison techniques are evident in the preceding discussions of tabulation, computation, and branching. This commentary is intended to highlight the advisability of looking at the types of actual verbal behaviors that transpire in the instructional setting and comparing the apparent stratagem with that planned (based on previously stated performance objectives).

Figure 4.4, the Raw Data Tabulation Form—ETC, contains information to be used in developing daily or lesson profiles so that longitudinal study is possible. If an instructor is striving for the use of more Category 3, 15, and 7 behaviors (higher order teacher questions, higher order student answers and extending teacher verbal statements), charts or tables similar to the example in Figure 4.12 are possibilities. Relative percentages and other aspects of importance can be graphically depicted. Any number of lessons or instances can be displayed by column and by categories of function, or the functions can be assigned as the rows.

Figure 4.5, the Summary Chart of Interchange—ETC, can be used in

Figure 4.12

PROFILE COMPARISONS—ETC

Categories Compared	1st	2nd	3rd	4th	5th	6th	No. of Lesson
2							
12							
3							
13							
4							
14							
5							
15							

a similar manner. By maintaining this type record over time, it is possible to visually inspect the grouping of interchange and to make decisions about the appropriateness of particular strategies in terms of the kinds of participation desired. (To be able to ascertain the degree of involvement in student-student participation requires a coding technique that differentiates the number of individual students contributing, and may be more easily acomplished on the Observation Record Sheet—ETC.)

Branching provides another means of establishing profiles for examining planned and actual strategies. Should the strategy require the teacher to deal with student responses by using only Category 8 (closure or termination) to see what happens to student reaction and participation over time, the hypothetical alternatives could be noted. Figure 4.13 is such a hypothetical statement. What actually occurs in the recorded observation can then be identified from the data collection form and displayed in the same manner. Actual totals of the types of student behavior are possible if deemed relevant and important.

Figure 4.13

HYPOTHETICAL BRANCHING STATEMENT

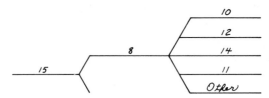

Again, the actual data of an earlier exercise are presented to illustrate the use of branching to maintain a visual record of actual patterns or sequence. In this example, the sequence is primarily 2–14–6 (Figure 4.14).

Figure 4.14

BRANCHING EXAMPLE

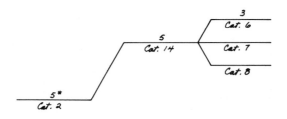

* Includes irrelevant as well as relevant 2s.

Other ways of comparing profiles will become evident as the system is applied. The works of Parsons (1968) and of Flanders (1970) provide additional useful approaches.

Summary Reflection

An experimental concept in systematic observation—Equivalent Talk Categories—has been presented in considerable detail. Based conceptually on extensive first-hand experience in developing training materials, in training teachers to use criterion measures in the RCS, and on extensive review of work by Hughes (1959), Smith (1960), Taba (1966), Bellack (1966), and Parsons (1968), this model is proposed as a way to operationalize much that has been suggested in the area of cognitive strategy. The procedures employed have involved description of the underpinnings of the ETC system, presentation of the categories and functional guidelines for coding the functions described by the categories, provision for coding experience, practice in skill development, and introduction to interpretive implications. Precision that results from utilization can be developed as observers learn to collect data by defining toward discretion.

For the beginning observer, the ETC offers certain advantages:

1. It serves as an organized frame of reference for viewing and describing actual classroom interaction.
2. It provides a set of variables for use in planning teaching strategies related to cognitive level of content.
3. It acts as a feedback source of instructional segments related to strategies, participation, and quality of content.
4. It describes, in application, variables as they are sequenced, thus providing data for judgment and modification.
5. It leads to a keen awareness of what is happening, so that training in the system is a major contribution to individual comprehension of classroom action.

It can be used in observing, in planning, in practicing, and in assessing. In it is the value of learning how systematic observation, as a concept, can lead to improved instruction.

The greatest difference in the RCS and the ETC is the concentration of the ETC on quality of content and strategical maneuvers to accomplish increased attention to more complex cognitive levels of intellectual activity. As the chapter on strategy will indicate, there is no attempt to deny the importance of affective considerations. Rather, the ETC is focused on cognitive level and instructional strategy in such a way that an individual teacher will find it possible to plan practically for simultaneous development. Multidimensionality as a classroom phenomenon demands a multiplicity of assessment-modification approaches.

5

Instructional
Strategy
Building

Classroom learning has been described as an interaction among teacher, student, and content, consisting of three steps:

1. Developing objectives
2. Planning and executing instruction
3. Measuring and assessing results.

Smith's definition of teaching as a "system of actions intended to induce learning" does support this posture. If one accepts the definition of an instructional situation as one in which learning takes place, the question arises of how to facilitate this learning. As the definition implies, the first step entails determining the objectives; the second step, planning and executing the instruction; and the third step, measuring and assessing the results of that instruction. As affirmed in the first chapter, the focus of this work is the planning and execution of the actual instruction—planning the instructional strategy, and making it work, to be more specific.

Strategy, in *Toward a Theory of Teaching,* refers to "a pattern of acts that serves to attain certain outcomes and to guard against certain others" (Smith, in Bellack, et al, 1963). The instructional situation itself is composed of two sets of factors:

1. One set that the *agent* (teacher) can not control—size of classroom, number of students.
2. One set that the agent can modify, with respect to the desired results—assignments, ways of forming questions.

It is the set of factors that the agent can control that this book addresses; it is this set of factors to which the teacher can apply instructional strategies. The approach suggested here is one in which the teacher uses the awareness and control developed through systematic observation to plan instructional strategies. The two observational systems introduced in this book—the RCS and the ETC—aim at two important areas that the teacher can control: the socio-emotional classroom climate and the learning stimuli. Both systems present a way to view and analyze functions of the teaching-learning act. The RCS focuses on functions that are directly related to the climate of the classroom: warming, cooling, accepting, correcting, presenting, clarifying, and questioning and responding. The ETC also looks at the functions of presenting, questioning, and responding, but with a slightly different emphasis. The ETC is designed to view verbal functions as they interact to *maintain, expand,* or *close* the cognitive interaction or participation.

The authors propose that for learning to be facilitated, two basic conditions must be met:

1. A positive socio-emotional classroom climate, in which the student feels comfortable and is motivated to learn, must exist.
2. The instructional agent (teacher) must manipulate and control the learning stimuli and the quality of the verbal statements (cognitive level) in ways that will result in maximum student learning.

Therefore, the awareness and control fostered by the RCS and the ETC are immediately applicable to planning instructional strategies.

To introduce the concepts of an instructional strategy and a function as they are related, it is necessary to review the six different operations necessary for effective teaching:

1. Identification and separation of the basic elements that characterize and comprise any given instructional-learning situation.
2. Conceptualization and interrelation of these interacting elements.
3. Selection and formulation of teaching strategies that will effect maximum student learning in a wide variety of instructional-learning situations.
4. Developing and sharpening suitable skills in order to translate planned instructional strategies into effective practice in the classroom.
5. Obtaining reliable and meaningful feedback describing the quality of teaching performance.
6. Modification and revision of teaching behavior to improve future instruction.

The first two operations are facilitated by the RCS and the ETC. "Select and formulate teaching strategies that will effect maximum student learning . . ." follows logically in sequential order of operation and is dependent upon the "identification and separation of the basic elements that characterize any given instructional-learning situation," and the "conceptualization and interrelationship of these interacting elements."

An instructional strategy is a purposefully conceived and determined plan of action. Ideally, the strategy is designed to facilitate a particular kind of learning, in a given situation and in terms of a specific learning objective. The strategy is selected for use *after* a comprehensive assessment of the specific situation and *prior to* the actual instructional act. The operations of assessing the situation and selecting the instructional strategy represent the "professional expertise" that the teacher brings to the instructional setting.

An instructional strategy consists of several parts. Bellack *et al.* (1966) describe "teaching cycles" that begin with initiating maneuvers (structuring or soliciting) that are followed by reflexive moves—responding and reacting. Their four pedagogical moves—structuring, soliciting, responding, and reacting—are classified in terms of pedagogical functions. While these "teaching cycles" are not teaching strategies in and of themselves, they are the *substance* of which teaching strategies are made. A complete teaching strategy would include not only the "teaching cycles" or pedagogical functions to be utilized, but also the way that these smaller portions of the strategy are to be combined to reach a predetermined goal.

When used in the context of this book, a function is a specific teacher or student behavior, as defined by a category, item, or an observational system. To be more specific, each of the categories of the RCS (p. 39) and those of the ETC (p. 88) represents observable functions. It is the sequential linking of these functions—for the express purpose of facilitating or meeting a specific learning objective—that constitutes the instructional strategy.

Functions, Strategies, and Planning

By their nature, functions operationalize strategies, and because they are stated in behavioral, observable terms, functions also describe what the teacher and/or student is doing in a given situation. Because functions and, therefore, entire strategies are observable, the teacher is in a position to state instructional plans in written strategy form in terms of separate, specific functions. In turn, he can implement his plans in the instructional setting, obtain a taped video or audio recording of his performance, and play back the recording for study and analysis. During playback, the teacher can collect observational data through the use of one or more observational systems—in this case the RCS and the ETC. The teacher then has available performance data, describing what actually occurred, that he can compare with what was planned. This comparison will reveal:

1. The appropriateness of the selected strategy.
2. The skill of the teacher in *carrying out* the strategy in a live situation.

An instructional strategy may be compared to a football game plan. Prior to the game, as much information as possible concerning the upcoming game is secured—playing styles of individual players; plays that are normally run by the opposition; whether or not it is a home game; likely weather conditions of the game day; and physical condition of the players (injuries, illnesses), etc. All of these factors, and many others, have a bearing on the outcome of the game. Scouting reports are read over and over. Game films are run, re-run, backed-up, and run again. After hours of study and thought, the game plan is framed. Crucial decisions have been made by a professional—the coach—who has put into the plan his very best professional expertise, representing his best thinking and wisest judgments in view of the information that was available to him. Once the team takes the field,—fully aware of the game plan and committed to its execution—the fate of the game is essentially dependent upon the playing skill of the individual players.

In the classroom, the teacher plays the role of the coach. He assesses the upcoming situation carefully and secures as much descriptive information as possible. "What is the nature of the learner?" "What are the objectives to be learned?" "What materials are available?" "How do these learners, objectives, and materials relate to and complement the purposes the community holds to be vital?" After due consideration, the teacher selects the strategy that, in his professional judgment, will best suit the given situation.

Once the instructional strategy is determined and put into operation, its successful outcome, in terms of student learning, is essentially contingent upon the instructional skill of the teacher. At the operational level, carrying out instructional strategies requires the teacher to have special skills that are slightly different from those needed to make professional decisions. However, strategy execution is not necessarily the end of the matter. The instructional act is usually demonstrated in observable behaviors that can be studied and evaluated. To be most effective, however, the teacher needs to evaluate the effectiveness of his total instructional skill. He needs to determine, by valid and reliable means, the appropriateness of both the instructional strategies selected and their execution. Once again, the usefulness of the observation systems comes into play.

The Process of Strategy Building

Major considerations of the teacher taking a step-by-step look at the process of strategy building would be:

1. The educational philosophy of the institution—system, school, community—in which he operates.
2. The objectives established for the learning situation.
3. The learning theory to which the teacher subscribes or considers appropriate for the situation.
4. The functions that are most appropriate for a strategy or plan of action for the situation.
5. The observation and feedback plans to assess the effectiveness of the planned strategy.
6. The modification or improvement of the strategy in terms of feedback.

Philosophy and Objectives. The educational philosophy under which the teacher operates is, essentially, the point of departure for a teacher. It is on this philosophy that the general and specific objectives must be based. While there are ways of influencing and establishing this philosophy, that is not the point in question here. Rather, this allusion to the underlying philosophy of education is simply a recognition of the fact that objectives cannot be developed in the absence of an overall framework.

Again, the objectives of the learning situation are a necessary prerequisite to the planning of instructional strategies. Strategy building begins when objective formulation ends; as the objectives are formulated on the basis of the educational philosophy, the strategy is developed to meet the specific objectives.

Learning Theory. The whole concept of learning theory comes into focus as one begins to select functions and develop strategies to achieve certain educational goals. While, to some extent, inclusive of the areas of affective and psychomotor development, learning theory basically rests on the view of intellectual development that the theorist holds. There are two *basic* views of cognition—that held by the behavioristic and neo-behavioristic theorists, and that of the cognitive theorists. The most striking difference between these two views of learning is that one focuses on behavior as the evidence of cognitive growth, while the other focuses on perception as the most significant aspect of cognitive development. Two major views of learning that fit neither the behavioristic nor the cognitive camp are the computer model of cognitive functioning and the developmental theory of Jean Piaget.

The authors of this book present this view of the learning theory, not as an acceptance or rejection of any one position, but rather, as a frame of reference from which to develop strategies for the teaching-learning process. Either before or after formulating the objectives for a teaching-learning situation, the teacher must choose an approach to reaching that objective—the learning theory—and develop a plan—the strategy—based on that approach.

The Behavioristic–Neo-behavioristic Approach to Learning

The publicly observable responses and their environmental instigators serve as the focus for the behavioristic–neo-behavioristic approach to learning. The most fundamental kinds of learning found in this approach are those of operant conditioning, rote verbal learning, discriminator learning, and instrumental learning. Early American psychologists, such as William James and John Dewey sought to discover the *functions* of behavioral events like learning and thinking, rather than simply the composition of these events. These early thinkers believed that the nervous system played a central role in the connection of sense impressions and behavior. The key word was *action*. From this idea grew the behavioristic approach to learning, supported by the work of Pavlov, Thorndike, Skinner, Watson, and many other behaviorists. The key reality of the behavioristic and neo-behavioristic approach is that learning is viewed as a matter of establishing individual associations—conditioned responses—firmly based in the nervous system.

The Cognitive Approach to Learning

The cognitive theory of learning focuses primarily on organized and differentiated experience as it is involved in perception and thinking. Major cognitive theorists—Bruner, Gagné, and Ausubel—purport that the long-term objective of education is the learner's acquisition of clear, stable, and organized bodies of knowledge. According to the cognitive theorists, these bodies of knowledge, "once acquired, constitute in their own right the most significant independent variable influencing the meaningful learning and retention of new subject matter material." This school of thought suggests two means of controlling meaningful learning:

1. By showing concern for the unifying concepts and principles—the "structure" of a discipline.
2. By employing suitable principles and ordering the internal logic and organization of the subject matter.

Ausubel (1968) maintains that the "acquisition of new meanings is thus held to be coexistent with meaningful learning, a process that is considered qualitatively different from rote learning in terms of the non-arbitrary and substantive relatability of what is to be learned to existing ideas in cognitive structure."

Bruner (1962) proposes that problem-solving or discovery is the approach "necessary for 'real possession' of knowledge," and that this approach "has certain unique motivational advantages, organizes knowledge effectively for later use, and promotes long-term retention."

From Bruner's Viewpoint. The question—What shall we teach and to what end?—focuses the attention of the teacher not only on the material to be covered in a classroom or instructional situation, but also on a much more critical element—that of the approach to be used. In addition to the pleasure of learning and growing intellectually, Bruner (1956) indicates that learning should, as its first object, serve the learner in the future. He, then, proposes an approach to learning that involves the development of problem solving, discovery, and concept building techniques, and further proposes four major concerns in determining teaching strategies:

1. The role of structure in the instructional setting.
2. The student's readiness for learning.
3. The nature of intuition or the intellectual technique of arriving at plausible, but tentative, foundations without going through the analytical steps by which the ensuing conclusions would be found to be valid or invalid.
4. The desire to learn and how this desire may be stimulated.

By structure, Bruner is referring to the most fundamental understanding of the underlying principles, that give form to a subject, that can be achieved. "Teaching specific topics or skills without making clear their context in the broader, fundamental sense is uneconomical and fruitless. Knowledge that one has learned without sufficient structure is knowledge that is likely to be forgotten."

He further maintains that any subject can be taught effectively in some intellectually honest form, to any child, at any stage of development. This hypothesis states that the first representations can later be made more powerful and precise more easily, by virtue of early learning.

In Bruner's view, the act of learning is composed of three elements: the acquisition of new information, the transformation of this information, and the evaluation of both the information and the transformation. The pattern of decisions affecting the acquisition, retention, and utilization of information has the following objectives:

1. To insure that the concept will be attained after the minimum number of encounters with relevant instances.

2. To insure that a concept will be attained, regardless of the number of instances one must test prior to attainment.
3. To minimize the amount of strain on inference and memory capacity, while insuring that a concept will be attained.
4. To minimize the number of wrong categorizations prior to attaining a concept.

General education, according to Bruner, does best to aim at being generic education—training people to be good guessers, and stimulating the ability to go beyond the information given, to probable reconstructions of other events. Going beyond the information given by utilizing inference, learning the redundancy of the environment, learning a certain formal schemata that may be fitted to or may be used to organize arrays of diverse information (coding), and theorizing are the vital elements in this kind of education.

From Gagné's Viewpoint (1965).   While Gagné is traditionally viewed as a cognitive theorist, his approach to the idea of learning is somewhat more inclusive and conditional than the insight or Gestalt version of the cognitive view. He identifies the varieties of learning—including the behaviorally-oriented as well as the cognitively-oriented—and then gives account of conditions that govern the learning process itself. He describes eight types of learning with which the teacher has to deal in planning instructional strategies:

1. *Signal Learning.* In signal learning, the conditioned response is the outcome. Two forms of stimulation must occur almost simultaneously:
   a. the stimulus that produces the desired reaction
   b. the stimulus that provides the signal.
   Stimulus responses are characterized by the fact that they are *general, diffuse, emotional reactions.*
2. *Stimulus-Response Learning.* Precise movements of the skeletal muscles responding to specific stimuli or combinations of stimuli make up this kind of learning. An important element in the general stimulus-response variety of learning is that of reward and reinforcement. The general conditions of stimulus-response learning are (a) gradual learning of this act, (b) as it continues, increased precision of the response.
3. *Chaining.* The chaining variety of learning involves the connecting of two or more previously learned stimulus-responses. It is necessary that the individual links in the chain be previously established; each link must be contiguous with the next and the following one; chaining occurs on a single occasion, when the two previous conditions are met.
4. *Verbal Association.* Verbal association is a subvariety of chaining, and is most closely associated with the cognitive objectives.

The chain—verbally associated—is composed of highly individual-
istic internal parts of the chain. Such a chain involves
a. knowing what the initial element is
b. connecting this initial element with another element
c. coding the connection
d. reproducing this chain in a sequence.

5. *Multiple Discrimination.* The fact that what has been learned
and stored is subject to being weakened or obliterated by other
activities is important to multiple discrimination. While the basic
nature of the learning process is not changed by adding things
to learn, forgetting does occur. The basic mechanism for forgetting, the process of interference, is, therefore, a prominent characteristic of the learning of multiple discriminations. The matter
of reducing or preventing interference can be crucial to learning
multiple discriminations. Multiple discrimination can be called
rote learning in that it does require memory. Interference must
be overcome if retention is to be assured in multiple discrimination.

6. *Concept Learning.* The neural processes of representation are
necessary for concept learning to occur. "Learning a concept
means learning to respond to stimuli in terms of abstracted properties like 'color,' 'shape,' 'position,' 'number,' as opposed to concrete physical properties like specific wavelengths or particular
intensities."

Concept learning is fostered by the following conditions:

a. The stimulus portion of the chain must have been previously
learned.
b. A *variety* of stimulus situations, incorporating the conceptual
property to be learned, must be presented in order that this
discrimination can occur.
c. Because the discrimination process must occur in a variety
of different stimulus situations, the learning of a brand new
concept may be a *gradual* process.

7. *Principle Learning.* A principle is a chain of two or more concepts—a relationship between concepts. The learning of principles
appears to be accompanied by these conditions:
a. The involved concepts must have been previously learned.
b. After the first condition has been fulfilled, the process of
chaining is a simple matter—generally by verbally stating.
c. When the first two conditions are present, the learning of a
principle takes place on a single occasion.

8. *Problem Solving.* By thinking, man has the capability of combin-
ing the principles he has already learned into a great variety of
novel higher-order principles. Therefore, by using principles already known to him, he learns to solve problems and create new
solutions. Certain conditions are apparently essential for this
problem solving:
a. The learner must identify the essential features of the response
that will be the solution, *before* he arrives at it.

    b. The recalled principles are combined; a new principle emerges and it is learned.

    c. Relevant principles, that have been previously learned, should be recalled.

    d. There may be many individual steps involved in problem solving. While the entire act may take some time, it appears that the solution is arrived at suddenly.[1]

Regardless of the view or views of learning held by the teacher, they must, to a large extent, determine the functions used in building an instructional strategy. A simple, behavioristic stimulus-response approach to teaching something like sums in arithmetic would certainly require a different combination of functions than would an instructional strategy for developing concepts.

Functions for Strategy Building.   Taba and Elkins (1966) treat the types of instructional strategies in terms of planning learning sequences. Based on a thorough knowledge of what the students know and can do, the teacher must:

    1. select sequences of instruction,

    2. translate knowledge about students into motivational devices, and

    3. make abstractions concrete.

It is this selection of sequences that is crucial to strategy building.

The premise that awareness and control of the instructional situation makes possible the planning, executing, observing, modifying, and re-executing of effective instructional strategies revolves around the concept of systematic observation. Two specific systems have been presented: the RCS, which focuses on the socio-emotional climate of the classroom, and the ETC which concentrates on the cognitive learning-stimuli. Therefore, the functions made observable by these two systems are the most meaningful ones with which to deal.

The RCS presents nine functions that can be used in designing a strategy to develop a positive—or negative—socio-emotional climate. These functions are:

—Warming	—Questioning
—Accepting	—Responding
—Clarifying	—Initiating

---

[1] Robert M. Gagné's "Eight Types of Learning" as listed on pp. 58–59 in *The Conditions of Learning* by Robert M. Gagné. (Descriptive summaries by Richard L. Ober.) Copyright © by Holt, Rinehart & Winston, Inc. Used by permission of Holt, Rinehart & Winston, Inc.

—Directing   —Cooling
—Correcting

By choosing from these functions, into which practically all of the verbal interaction can be categorized, the teacher can plan strategies to accomplish objectives related to climate.

From a cognitive, content viewpoint, the ETC functions make it possible to design strategies that either maintain, expand, or close the level of cognitive process. The functions made observable by the ETC are:

—Presenting   —Reacting
—Questioning   —Structuring
—Responding

Again, by choosing from these functions, the teacher can plan strategies that can accomplish the instructional objectives.

Illustrative Strategies

While both the RCS and the ETC make observation of cognitive activity possible, the RCS is specifically designed to focus on socio-emotional aspects of the learning situation and the ETC on the quality of cognitive interaction. The RCS, for example, provides categories for both questioning and responding—functions directly related to cognitive interaction— just as the ETC does. Where the systems differ and complement each other lies at this very point. The RCS makes possible specific observation of warming-cooling behaviors, as well as negative and positive reinforcement. The ETC concentrates on those functions that relate directly to effecting changes in the level of cognitive interchange. The awareness of and ability to isolate the teaching-learning functions illustrated by the RCS and the ETC makes it possible to develop teaching strategies both from the socio-emotional and the cognitive viewpoint.

The strategies developed by using the RCS and ETC functions may be large and global or they may be limited, specific strategies. A drill strategy, for example, would contain only two or three categories of behavior, while a guided-discovery strategy might utilize the whole range of behaviors. The following examples illustrate strategies developed using the functions isolated by the RCS and the ETC.

Illustrative strategies include:

—Stimulus-Response Strategy—RCS and ETC
—Strategies Designed to Affect Climate—RCS

—Strategies Designed to Affect Cognitive Level—ETC

—Guided-Discovery Strategy—RCS and ETC

Stimulus-Response Strategy.   The objective of the lesson is, for example, to review the vowel and consonant sounds in English. The appropriate learning theory is a simple conditioned response. The reward or reinforcement is verbal acceptance. Under these conditions, a strategy for this lesson would look something like this:

Function	Interaction	RCS Category
Questioning	What are the vowels?	4 or 14
Response	A, E, I, O, U and sometimes Y.	15 or 5
Acceptance	Right!	2 or 12
Question	What is an example of the Y sound?	4 or 14
Response	The word dyad.	15 or 5
Acceptance	OK.	2 or 12

The same drill strategy in ETC terms would be:

Function	Interaction	Category
Question—limited	What are the vowels?	2 or 12
Response—limited	A, E, I, O, U and sometimes Y.	4 or 14
Closure	Right!	8 or 18
Question—limited	What is an example of the Y sound?	2 or 12
Response—limited	The word dyad.	4 or 14
Closure	OK.	8 or 18

Strategies Designed to Affect Climate.   The RCS functions lend themselves to planning strategies which directly affect the climate of the classroom. Following are examples of climate strategies planned with the RCS.

WARMING STRATEGY—RCS

Function	Interaction	RCS Category
Warming	"I'm really glad to turn back your papers this time. You all did so well. Nearly everyone got all of the questions correct. It's a pleasure to grade a set of papers like this."	1 (9 seconds)

COOLING STRATEGY—RCS

Function	Interaction	RCS Category
Cooling	"I'm ashamed of you people. You really did a poor job on this test. Apparently you didn't study. I certainly hope that you never perform like this again. I would suggest that you start to study."	9 (9 seconds)

POSITIVE REINFORCEMENT STRATEGY—RCS

Function	Interaction	RCS Category
Questioning	"What is the square root of 64?"	4
Responding	"Eight."	15
Accepting	"Right."	2

NEGATIVE REINFORCEMENT STRATEGY—RCS

Function	Interaction	RCS Category
Correcting	"If you miss this problem, John, you'll have to re-work the whole list of problems.	8
Questioning	"Now, what is the valence of silver?"	4
Responding	"Plus one."	15
Accepting	"OK."	2
Initiating	"I'm sure glad that you don't have to work all of those problems again."	6

ASSESSMENT OF STUDENT FEELINGS—RCS

Function	Interaction	RCS Category
Warming	"I gather that this may be a bit strange to some of you.	1
Questioning	"What troubles you, Sue?"	4
Initiating	"Well, I don't like to think about little children being punished for something they can't help."	16
Clarifying	"Why do you feel this way?"	3
Initiating	"It just doesn't seem right, that's all. They're innocent, helpless. It seems like their parents should be the ones to be punished."	16
Questioning	"Do any of the rest of you feel this way?"	4

Strategies Designed to Affect Cognitive Level. The ETC system lends itself to developing strategies directly related to the cognitive level of the classroom interchange. Following are examples of cognitive strategies planned with the ETC.

RESTRICTED QUESTIONING-RESPONDING STRATEGY

Function	Interaction	ETC Category
Informing	"Today we shall continue our study of vowels."	1
Questioning	"What are the vowels?"	2
Responding	"A, E, I, O, U, and sometimes Y."	14

EXPANDED QUESTIONING-RESPONDING STRATEGY

Function	Interaction	ETC Category
Informing	"Today we shall continue our discussion of vowels and consonants."	1
Questioning	"What do those two words make you think of, Susie?"	3
Responding	"Sounds—round sounds and square sounds."	15

STRUCTURING OF ACTIVITIES STRATEGY

Function	Interaction	ETC Category
Informing	"Today we shall continue our discussion of vowels and consonants."	1
Structuring	"I want you to put aside all your books. Keep out a pencil or pen and a piece of paper.	9
	Pause.	0
	"Now, think about the word vowel and what it means and draw something on your paper that represents that meaning.	9
	Pause.	0
	"Now, push aside your paper and think of a sound that represents the meaning of vowel."	9

Each of these strategies—the two kinds of questioning and responding and the structuring—serves a the basis for the development of strategies leading to cognitive development. To these basic introductory or stage setting strategies is added the function of reacting—either to maintain, extend, or terminate. The following examples of reacting strategies illustrate the way that the reacting function develops the complete strategy.

REACTING TO MAINTAIN STRATEGY [1]

Function	Interaction	ETC Code
Responding	"A, E, I, O, U, and sometimes Y."	14
Reacting	"What are the consonants?"	6
Responding	"All other letters of the alphabet."	14

[1] The point in reacting here is to maintain the level of cognitive interaction—in this case, the lower level of knowledge or memory. The function of reacting to maintain may also be used to maintain higher levels of interaction.

REACTING TO EXTEND STRATEGY

Function	Interaction	ETC Code
Responding	"A, E, I, O, U, and sometimes Y."	14
Reacting	"What comes to mind when you hear sounds like A, E, I, O, and U?"	7
Responding	"Music notes."	15
Reacting	"What kind of music notes?"	6
Responding	"Do, re, me, fa, so . . ."	14
Reacting	"What does each of those notes have in common that makes you think of vowels?"	7
Responding	"They each contain a vowel."	15

REACTING TO TERMINATE STRATEGY [1]

Function	Interaction	ETC Code
Responding	"A, E, I, O, U, and sometimes Y."	14
Reacting	"Now that we know the vowels, let's move on to something else."	8

[1] The role of the reacting to terminate function is that of closing one discussion and moving to another.

RCS and ETC Strategy for Guided Discovery Lesson. Many objectives need to be approached from both the climate and learning stimuli viewpoint. The RCS strategy for this lesson concentrates on the use of direction, questions, and acceptance to create a positive environment for the discovery.

THE RCS STRATEGY

Function	Interaction	RCS Category
Direction (Teacher)	Put the red clip on the terminal marked plus and the green clip on the minus terminal.	7
Silence	Pause.	10
Question	Now, which way does the meter hand swing, Joe?	4
Response (Student)	To the right.	15
Acceptance Direction (Teacher)	OK. Now, reverse the clips on the terminals.	2 7
Silence	Pause.	10
Question	Which way does it swing now, Joe?	4
Response (Student)	To the left.	15
Question (Teacher)	What do you make of this change?	4
Initiation (Student)	Well, I guess maybe the poles of the meter change when the battery terminals are changed.	16
Acceptance (Teacher)	Good.	2

The ETC strategy for this lesson concentrates on the use of structuring, questioning, and reacting functions to lead the student to discovery.

THE ETC STRATEGY

Function	Interaction	ETC Category
Structuring (Teacher)	Put the red clip on the terminal marked plus and the green clip on the minus terminal.	9
	Pause.	0
Questioning	Now, which way does the meter hand swing, Joe?	2
Responding (Student)	To the right.	14
Structuring (Teacher)	OK. Now, reverse the clips on the terminals.	1 9
	Pause.	0
Questioning (Teacher)	Which way does it swing now, Joe?	6

Function	Interaction (cont.)	ETC Category
Responding (Student)	To the left.	14
Reacting (Teacher)	What do you make of this change?	7
Responding (Student)	Well, I guess maybe the poles of the meter change when the battery terminals are changed.	15
(Teacher)	Good.	1

Simulated Instructional Strategy Development

From these examples of simple strategies designed around RCS functions to affect the climate and around ETC functions to affect the cognitive level of the interchange, the use of systematic observation in strategy planning comes into view. While there are overlapping functions—questioning, responding, initiating or presenting—each system makes a decided contribution. A full scale development of a strategy based on a real objective and a specific learning theory illustrates this point.

Philosophy: A Guided Discovery Lesson on π (Pi)

The philosophical position supporting these instructional sequences is Bruner's contention that ". . . education does best to aim at being generic education, training people to be good guessers," stimulating the ability to go beyond the information given to probable reconstructions of other events.

Objective. The general objective of the following instructional sequence is to develop the concept of π (Pi).

Learning Theory. The learning theory on which this learning sequence is based is Gagné's sixth type of learning—concept learning. The stimulus portion of the chain has been previously learned; that is, previously learned facts or ideas serve as the base of the concept development. Several different functions will be used as stimuli.

Functions. In developing a strategy to achieve the objective set forth for this instructional sequence, the teacher must select the appropriate functions to be used. Based on the awareness and control fostered by the RCS and the ETC, selections can be made of functions to establish the learning climate and reach the cognitive goal.

The functions selected for this guided discovery approach to learning the concept of π (pi) are as follows:

RCS: Directing
       Questioning
       Responding
       Initiating
       Accepting

ETC: Structuring
       Questioning
       Reacting
       Responding

The teacher, after selecting the functions plans the ways in which these functions, will be utilized.

Observation and Feedback.   After executing the planned strategy, the teacher uses the RCS and the ETC to observe what actually happened. The script of the instructional sequence on the concept of π (pi) follows as it was observed by the teacher using the RCS and the ETC. Analyses follow for each system based on the prescribed procedures (Figures 5.1 and 5.2).

		RCS	ETC
Teacher:	Today, we're going to do something a little bit different. Usually I tell you what I want you to learn. Today you are going to discover it for yourselves. I'm going to tell you to do certain things and then ask you questions about what you've done and then we'll see what we have learned.	(1) _6_ (2) _6_ (3) _6_ (4) _6_ (5) _6_ (6) _6_	_∠_ (1)
	But before we get started, let's each get out a sheet of paper—scrap paper will do. Do that now. Get out a pencil and a piece of scrap paper.	(7) _7_ (8) _7_ (9) _7_	_9_ (2)
	Pause.	(10) _10_	_0_ (3)
	The concept that I want you to learn today has to do with the wooden circle that each of you has and the tape measures that are on the desks in front of you—like the one Al has tied around his neck.	(11) _6_ (12) _6_ (13) _1_ (14) _10_	_∠_ (4)
	Class laughs.		_=_ (5)
	I want you to take a look around the room and notice that your wooden circle is not necessarily the same size as your neighbor's circle. Look around and determine that now.	(15) _7_ (16) _7_ (17) _10_	_9_ (6)
	Pause.	(18) _6_	_0_ (7)

| | | *RCS* | *ETC* |
| | | *(cont.)* | *(cont.)* |

	Some of the circles are the same size, but nine chances out of ten your circle is not the same size as your neighbor's.	(19) _6_	_1_ (8)
	Pause.		_0_ (9)
Teacher:	OK, now take a look at your tape measure. What is the smallest part of an inch we can measure with these tapes? Joe?	(20) _7_ (21) _4_ (22) _15_	_9_ (10) _2_ (11)
Joe:	One-fourth.	(23) _3_	_14_ (12)
Teacher:	Are you sure about that, Joe?	(24) _15_	_6_ (13)
Joe:	Oh, I'm wrong. We can measure one-eighth of an inch.	(25) _2_	_14_ (14)
Teacher:	Right! These tape measures are marked off in one-eighth inch units so we can measure to the nearest one-eighth inch. OK, we are going to use the tape measure to measure the circles that each of you has. First, measure the circumference of your circle and write it down on your paper in decimal form.	(26) _3_ (27) _6_ (28) _7_ (29) _10_	_1_ (15) _9_ (16)
	Pause—silence.	(30) _10_	_0_ (17)
Beth:	I forgot, what is the circumference of a circle?	(31) _14_	_12_ (18)
Rod:	The distance around.	(32) _15_	_14_ (19)
Teacher:	Right. The distance around.	(33) _2_	_1_ (20)
	Pause.	(34) _3_	_0_ (21)
	Be sure to write the circumference in decimal form.	(35) _6_	_9_ (22)
Al:	What do you mean "Decimal form?"	(36) _13_	_12_ (23)
Teacher:	Well, instead of writing a whole number and a fraction, you write a number, a decimal point, and the decimal equivalent of the fraction.	(37) _5_ (38) _5_	_4_ (24)
Al:	Oh, I remember, we used the decimal equivalent chart to change fractions to decimals.	(39) _16_	_16_ (25)
Teacher:	Right. For instance, if your circle measured seven and three-eighths inches, you would write seven, decimal point, three, seven, five. Be sure, class members, to use the decimal equivalent chart above the blackboard to convert your decimals to fractions.	(40) _2_ (41) _3_ (42) _3_	_1_ (26)
		(43) _7_	_9_ (27)
	Pause; class snickers.	(44) _10_ (45) _10_	_0_ (28)
Teacher:	Did I say it the other way? Yes, I mean fraction to decimal. Thank you, that's the first mistake I've made this month.	(46) _3_ (47) _6_ (48) _2_ (49) _1_	_1_ (29)

		RCS (cont.)	*ETC* (cont.)
	Class laughs.	(50) 10	— (30)
	Pause.	(51) 10	0 (31)
	Has everyone measured the circumference and written it down?	(52) 4	2 (43)
	Pause.	(53) 10	0 (33)
	OK. Fine! Now measure the diameter—of course you know that's the distance across— the distance around is the circumference and the distance across is the diameter.	(54) 2 (55) 7 (56) 6 (57) 6	1 (34) 9 (35)
	Pause.	(58) 10	0 (36)
Teacher:	Write down the diameter in decimal form like the circumference.	(59) 7	9 (37)
	Pause.	(60) 10 (61) 10	0 (38)
	Has everyone measured the diameter?	(62) 4	2 (39)
	Pause.	(63) 10	0 (40)
	OK! Now, divide the circumference by the diameter.	(64) 7	9 (41)
	Pause.	(65) 10	0 (42)
Joe:	I don't understand. What do you mean?	(66) 13	13 (43)
Teacher:	You mean you don't understand what to divide by what?	(67) 3	6 (44)
Joe:	Yeah.	(68) 15	14 (45)
Teacher:	OK. What did you get for the circumference?	(69) 2 (70) 4	7 (46)
Joe:	Seven, point, eight, eight.	(71) 15	15 (47)
Teacher:	OK. What did you get for the diameter?	(72) 2 (73) 4	7 (48)
Joe:	Two, point, five, zero.	(74) 15	15 (49)
Teacher:	Now, divide the seven, point, eight, eight by the two, point, five, zero.	(75) 7	7 (50)
Joe:	Oh, I see. I didn't know which was which.	(76) 12 (77) 16	15 (51)
Teacher:	Remember class, divide the distance *around* by the distance *across*.	(78) 7	1 (52)
	Pause.	(79) 10	0 (53)
Beth:	How far should we carry it out?	(80) 14	12 (54)
Teacher:	Good question. Carry it out to the nearest hundredth. Who knows how to get the nearest hundredth?	(81) 2 (82) 7 (83) 4	1 (55) 4 (56) 2 (57)
	Pause.	(84) 10	0 (58)

	RCS (cont.)	ETC (cont.)

Bill: I believe you carry it out three decimal places and cross off the last. If it's five or greater you add one to the second place.

(85) *16*
(86) *16* *14* (59)

Teacher: Right! That's good, Bill. Carry it out to the

(87) *2* *1* (60)
(88) *1*

nearest hundredth. Otherwise you could go on dividing all night. That's not necessary.

(89) *7*
(90) *1* *9* (61)

Class laughs.

(91) *10* *−* (62)

Pause.

(92) *10* *0* (63)
(93) *10*

Is everyone finished?

(94) *4* *2* (64)

Pause.

(95) *10* *0* (65)

OK—good   Now, let's write some of your answers here on the board and see what we have. What did you get Al?

(96) *2* *1* (66)
(97) *7* *3* (67)
(98) *4*

Al: Three and thirteen hundredths.

(99) *15* *15* (68)

Teacher: OK. Beth, what did you get?

(100) *2* *6* (69)
(101) *4*

Beth: Three, point, one, seven.

(102) *15* *15* (70)

Teacher: OK—Joe?

(103) *4* *6* (71)

Joe: Six and sixty-two hundredths.

(104) *15* *15* (72)

Teacher: You divided wrong, Joe. Try it again. Sue, what is your answer?

(105) *8* *1* (73)
(106) *7* *9* (74)
(107) *4* *6* (75)

Sue: Three and thirteen hundredths.

(108) *15* *15* (76)

Teacher: OK—Bill?

(109) *4* *6* (77)

Bill: Thirty-one and forty-one hundredths.

(110) *15* *15* (78)

Teacher: You misplaced the decimal point. Check it again, Bill. Beth?

(111) *8* *1* (79)
(112) *7* *9* (80)
(113) *4* *6* (81)

Beth: Three, point, one, five.

(114) *15* *15* (82)

Teacher: OK, Joe?

(115) *4* *6* (83)

Joe: I did divide wrong. Now I get three and twelve hundredths.

(116) *15* *11* (84)
(117) *15* *14* (85)

Teacher: That's better, Joe. Bill, did you get your answer straightened out?

(118) *2* *1* (86)
(119) *4* *6* (87)

Bill: Yeah. Three, point, one, four.

(120) *15* *15* (88)
(121) *15*

Teacher: OK. Good. Well, that should be enough to get what we want to learn today. Let's take a look at the answers on the board.

(122) *2*
(123) *6* *8* (89)
(124) *6* *9* (90)

Pause.

(125) *10* *0* (91)

	RCS *(cont.)*	ETC *(cont.)*

Notice anything unusual about them?	(126) _4_ _3_	(92)
Pause.	(127) _10_ _0_	(93)

Joe: Well, they all came out to three and a little
over.   (128) _16_ _15_ (94)

Teacher: Right. In other words, regardless of the size (129) _2_
of the circle, when you divided the circumfer- (130) _3_
ence by the diameter, the answer came out to (131) _3_
be three and a little over.   (132) _3_

This is the concept that I wanted you to learn
today. The concept is called "pi." I'll write (133) _6_
it on the board.   (134) _6_ _1_ (95)
                                             (135) _10_
Pause. Write it on the board.   (136) _6_ _0_ (96)
p–i, Pi. Mathematicians have calculated
pi by very accurate means and they find that
it always comes out to be three, point, one (137) _6_
four, one, six and so on. Of course, we usually (138) _6_
only use it to the nearest hundredth—three,
point, one, four.   (139) _6_ _1_ (97)

Beth: You mean that no matter how big or how
small the circle, pi is always three, point, one,
four?   (140) _13_ _12_ (98)

Teacher: That's right!   (141) _5_ _4_ (99)

Al: You mean that if we divided the distance
around the earth by the distance through it,
we would still get three, point, one four?   (142) _14_ _16_ (100)
                                             (143) _14_

Teacher: Let's try and see. Anybody know how far it (144) _3_ _9_ (101)
is around the earth?   (145) _4_ _6_ (102)

Ann: A little over 22,000 miles, I believe. (146) _15_ _14_ (103)

Teacher: OK. And what is the earth's diameter? (147) _2_ _6_ (104)
                                             (148) _4_

Ann: Around 7,000 miles.   (149) _15_ _14_ (105)

Teacher: OK. Now divide 22,000 by 7,000.   (150) _2_ _9_ (106)
                                             (151) _7_

Pause.   (152) _10_ _0_ (107)
Be sure to place the decimal point correctly. (153) _7_ _9_ (108)
Pause.   (154) _10_ _0_ (109)
Carry it out to the nearest hundredth.   (155) _7_ _9_ (110)
Pause.   (156) _10_ _0_ (111)
What did you get, Joe?   (157) _4_ _7_ (112)

Joe: Three, point, one, four.   (158) _15_ _15_ (113)

	RCS *(cont.)*	ETC *(cont.)*

Teacher: That's the figure that I gave you for pi,
isn't it Joe? (159) _4_ _8_ (114)

Joe: Yeah. How 'bout that! (160) _11_ _18_ (115)

Class laughs. (161) _10_ __ (116)

Figure 5.1

RCS DATA COLLECTION FORM

	1	2	3	4	5	6	7	8	9	10
1.	10	7	2	10	14	2	15	13	11	
2.	6	4	3	10	2	4	15	5	10	
3.	6	15	3	4	7	15	2	14		
4.	6	3	7	10	4	4	6	14		
5.	6	15	10	7	10	15	6	3		
6.	6	2	10	10	16	8	10	4		
7.	6	3	3	13	16	7	4	15		
8.	7	6	6	3	2	4	10	2		
9.	7	7	2	15	1	15	16	4		
10.	7	10	1	2	7	4	2	15		
11.	10	10	10	4	1	15	3	2		
12.	6	14	10	15	10	8	3	7		
13.	6	15	4	2	10	7	3	10		
14.	1	2	10	4	10	4	6	7		
15.	10	3	2	15	4	15	6	10		
16.	7	6	7	7	10	4	10	7		
17.	7	13	6	12	2	15	6	10		
18.	10	5	6	16	7	15	6	4		
19.	6	5	10	7	4	2	6	15		
20.	6	16	7	10	15	4	6	4		

Discussion of the RCS Data

A cursory scanning of the matrix leads to several observations. First, both
the overall teacher and overall student talk are rather "flexible" as evidenced by the total number of cells occupied in the entire matrix (57 of
the 361 cells have a loading). Second, the talk is distributed among the

Figure 5.2

RCS MATRIX

Situation _____ Date _____ Name _____

	1	2	3	4	5	6	7	8	9	11	12	13	14	15	16	17	18	19	10	T
1							I												III	4
2	II		IIII	THH		I	IIII													16
3			III	I		IIII	I							II						11
4										I				THH II THH II					THH	20
5					I								I		I					3
6	I	I				THH III	III					II							III	23
7	I			THH		I	III				I								THH THH	21
8							II													2
9																				0
11																			I	1
12															I					1
13			I		II															3
14		I	I										I	I						4
15		IIII THH	I	IIII			I	II						II						19
16		IIII					I								I					5
17																				0
18																				0
19																				0
10		II	I	THH		IIII	THH					I	II		II				THH	28
T	4	16	11	20	3	23	21	2	0	1	1	3	4	19	5	0	0	0	28	161
%	2.48	9.93	6.83	12.42	1.86	14.28	13.04	1.24		.62	.62	1.86	2.48	11.80	3.10	0	0	0	17.39	91.34

162

four sub-matrices as demonstrated by the total number of cells occupied in each (20 loaded cells in the teacher-teacher sub-matrix, 7 in the teacher-student, 11 in the student-teacher, and 5 in the student-student). Third, the preponderance of total talk was concentrated in the teacher-teacher sub-matrix as evidenced both by the total number of cells occupied (20) and the loadings in the teacher-teacher sub-matrix cells (56 tallies).

Given the teaching plan previously proposed—discovery of a concept—the types of patterns to be expected are in evidence. The 7–10–4 sequence provides needed instruction, allows for silence or confusion as the instructions are followed, and uses leading questions to get to the desired content goal. The 4–15–4 and 4–15–8 patterns give indication of question—reinforcement strategy.

Other observations related to previously presented skills of preparation and interpretation can be made:

1. Generally, the teacher was "warm" in his talk as shown by the total amount of category 1 (2.48%). Although not out of line with the other 18 category totals, 2.48% is as great or greater than might be expected to be observed in the average classroom.

2. There was considerable use of category 2—9.93%. In terms of distribution, nine times the teacher reinforced a student response to a narrow question (the 15–2 cell) and three times he reinforced a student initiation (the 16–2 cell).

3. There was less use of Category 6 (14.28%) than might be expected in the average classroom. Often the total use of Category 6 equals 30 to 35 percent.

4. There was a much greater use of Category 7 (13.04%) than might be expected. On ten occasions, Category 7 (giving directions) was followed by Category 10 (silence or confusion) as indicated in the 7–10 cell.

5. The category with the greatest total use was Category 10—17.29%. The use of Category 10 was distributed with silence or confusion following teacher directions (Category 7) ten times as shown in the 7–10 cell and Category 10 followed by Category 10 on six occasions (the 10–10 cell).

6. The teacher asked a narrow question fourteen times as evidenced in the 4–15 cell. In contrast, not a single broad question was asked by the teacher (and then answered immediately by the student) as indicated by no loading in the 4–16 cell.

7. Twice (or for 6 seconds) a student either asked for clarification or extended the idea or contribution of another (Category 13) following lecture (Category 6) as evidenced by the loading of two in the 6–13 cell; once a student used Category 13 following silence or confusion as shown in the 10–13 cell.

Application of data preparation skills reveals that 161 total responses were tallied. These were apportioned among the sub-matrices as follows:

Teacher-Teacher (I: 1–9 followed by 1–9 = 56; Teacher-Student (II: 1–9 followed by 11–19) = 22; Student-Teacher (III: 11–19 followed by 1–9) = 27; Student-Student (IV: 11–19 followed by 11–19) — 6. (No Category 10s are counted in summing sub-matrices, thus, 111 tallies are represented. Twenty-eight coded behaviors were 10s and 22 coded behaviors followed a 10, making it impossible on the matrix to ascertain to which sub-matrix the loadings should be assigned.) Category comparisons of interest reveal:

Teacher Warm-Cool	Cat. 1/Cat. 9	4/0
Teacher Accepts-Corrects	Cat. 2/Cat. 8	16/2
Teacher Amplify-Elicit	Cat. 3/Cat. 4	11/20
Teacher Lecture/Direct	Cat. 6/Cat. 7	23/21
Student Answers Narrow-Broad	Cat. 15/Cat. 16	19/5

The teacher/student ratio for all tallies (100/33) is 3.33. Other ratio comparisons may be computed as desired.

These are a few of the obvious observations that can be made when analyzing a plotted matrix. Theoretically, each of the 361 cells could be considered and studied. However, such an exhaustive analysis would probably represent a waste of time and would turn up little information relevant or significant to the overall effectiveness of the teacher's verbal behavior. When analyzing and interpreting a plotted matrix, one usually looks for information of the following order:

1. Total use of each of the nineteen categories.
2. Distribution of loadings *among* and *within* each of the four submatrices.
3. Distribution of the teacher's use of Category 2 by scanning the second column.
4. Distribution of the teacher's use of Category 3 by scanning the third column. More specifically, the frequency with which the teacher amplified a student response (the 15–3 cell) and/or amplified a student initiation (the 16–3 cell).
5. The number of narrow questions asked by the teacher, answered immediately by a student (the 4–15 cell), as compared to the number of broad teacher questions (the 4–16 cell).
6. The distribution of Category 10 by scanning the tenth column and the tenth row.
7. A comparison of the teacher's use of Category 1 (warming) and his use of Category 9 (cooling) by scanning columns one and nine, and rows one and nine.
8. The overall flexibility of the lesson by calculating the total number of cells with a loading and the total number of loaded cells within each of the four sub-matrices.

When interpreting a plotted matrix, it should be remembered that the loadings of a particular cell and the loaded cell of a matrix show what occurred during a given lesson or segment of classroom interaction. The data *do not* reflect, in themselves, the effectiveness of the teacher's behavior. Judgments related to teacher effectiveness cannot be made reliably unless one can relate them to other information, such as the nature of the learning objective(s) under consideration, the age of the students, the instructional strategy(ies) originally selected by the teacher, whether or not the learning objective(s) was reached, and the cognitive level of the students prior to the lesson.

Perhaps the most significant advantage of feedback in the form of observational data (plotted matrix) is to the teacher himself. He knows what he planned to do in a given lesson, and he knows why he chose that particular technique. With the observational data describing what he actually did, the teacher can analyze the relationship between what he planned to do and what actually happened. Considerations of this sort are extremely valuable to a teacher when he is attempting to improve his own teaching behavior.

Discussion—ETC

From the Observation Record Sheet (Figure 5.3), the recorded incidents total 116. Of these, four behaviors were not measured by the system as revealed by the dash in blanks (1–5), (1–30), (2–24) and (4–2) pp. 156–161. There were no irrelevant behaviors—there are no circled codes.

The largest concentrations of teacher functions, evident both on the Summary Chart of Interchange (Figure 5.4) and the Raw Data Tabulation Form (Figure 5.5) were structure of learning activities (category 9 occurred 17 times), Present Information (Category 1 was recorded 17 times), Structure by Pause or Silence (Category 0 was coded 22 times), and React to Maintain (Category 6 occurred 11 times). Student verbal behaviors as functions or most prevalent categories were Respond-Expanded thinking (Category 15 was noted 13 times) and Respond-Restricted thinking (Category 14 was coded 8 times).

Patterns expected in a discovery approach or guided inquiry include the 9–0–1–9–2, 2–14–6–14, 3–15–6–15, 6–14–7–15, and 7–15–8. These are evident from the Observation Record Sheet (Figure 5.3). Instructions in the form of structuring verbal behaviors; pauses for thinking, silent activity or reflection; presenting information or input and questions were utilized. Further, both Restricted and Expanded questions were used to lead to cognitive recognition of the concept of π (pi) (Category 2s and Category 3s) with the implementation of maintaining and extending comments (Category 6s and Category 7s) as facilitation. Discovery of the concept resulted in Termination of Participation (8/18).

Figure 5.3

Observation Record Sheet—ETC

Observer _____   Completion Time _____
Observed _____   Subject Area _____
Number of Observation _____   Topic_____
Beginning Time_____   Planned Strategy _____

	1	2	3	4	5	6	7	8	9	10	11	12	13	14	15	16
1	1	2	6	18												
2	9	0	15	-												
3	0	9	1													
4	1	0	9													
5	-	13	6													
6	9	6	15													
7	0	14	6													
8	1	7	11													
9	0	15	15													
10	9	7	1													
11	2	15	6													
12	14	7	15													
13	6	15	8													
14	14	1	9													
15	1	0	0													
16	9	12	3													
17	0	1	0													
18	12	4	15													
19	14	2	1													
20	1	0	0													
21	0	14	1													
22	9	1	12													
23	12	9	4													
24	14	-	16													
25	16	0	9													
26	1	2	6													
27	9	0	14													
28	0	1	6													
29	1	3	14													
30	-	15	9													
31	0	6	0													
32	2	15	9													
33	0	6	0													
34	1	15	9													
35	9	1	0													
36	0	9	7													
37	9	6	15													
38	0	15	8													

Figure 5.4

SUMMARY CHART OF INTERCHANGE

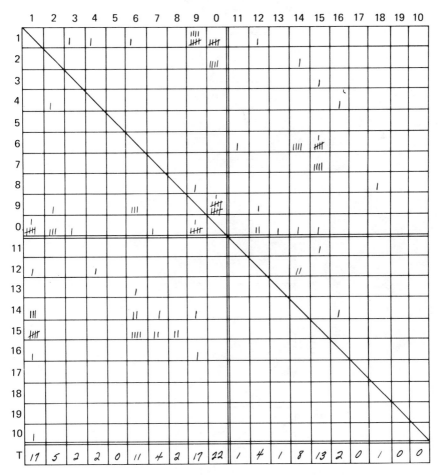

Ninety-seven percent of the behaviors coded 112/116 were relevant to the lesson planned. Eighty-two of the behaviors were attributed to the teacher with thirty assigned student codes (10–19). The Teacher-Student ratio can be stated as 2.73 82/30. The 1/9 ratio is 1.0 17/17 and the 14/15 ratio is .62 8/13. Since this was not an effort to promote discussion but to lead students to conceptualization of an idea, the ratios and patterns tend to support the teacher's strategy.

Two noticeable differences in the RCS coding and the ETC coding

Figure 5.5

Raw Data Tabulation Form

Category	1	2	3	4	5	6	7	8	9	0	11	12	13	14	15	16	17	18	19	10	T_r	-	T_i	T
Incidences	17	5	2	2	0	11	4	2	17	22	1	4	1	8	13	2	0	1	0	0	112	4	0	116
% of T_r	15	4	2	2	0	10	4	2	15	20	1	4	1	7	12	2	0	1	0	0	100%			
% of T	15	4	2	4	0	10	3	2	15	19	1	3	1	7	11	1	0	1	0	0	97%	3%		100%

Key

T_r: total relevant behaviors

-: behaviors not measured by the ETC

T_i: total irrelevant behaviors (circled codes)

T: total recorded behaviors

168

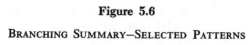

Figure 5.6

BRANCHING SUMMARY—SELECTED PATTERNS

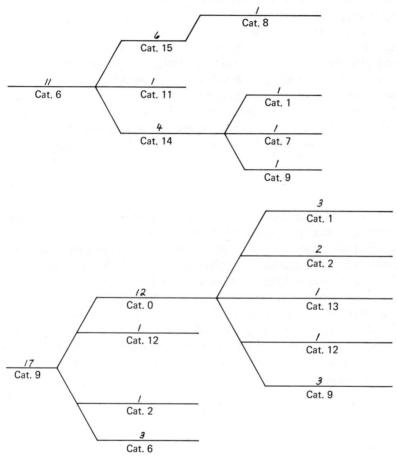

are the total number of recorded codes and the coding of accepting-correcting feedback in the ETC as the Present Information Category (ETC codes 1/11). Although student willingness to participate provides an index to classroom environment, the ETC makes no effort to scrutinize the socio-emotional variables encompassed by RCS categories 1/11, 2/12, 8/18 and 9/19. The two systems applied to a selected strategy complement and supplement information available when only one system is applied.

Modification

Inspection of the raw data on the summary observation forms (Figures 5.1 and 5.3), evidences that, in the previous example, the strategies were successfully carried out. Sequences illustrative of the selected strategies are visibly apparent even in a brief look. At other times, the success will be relatively less obvious. In such cases, careful treatment of the data for analysis purposes is desirable.

Following data preparation—matrix plotting and profile comparisons—judgments can be made on the relative success of implemented strategy versus planned strategy. It is quite possible that practice exercises such as those included in Chapter 6 will be useful in developing *awareness* of actual classroom or instructional practice into *control*. Three types of activities that seem to be appropriate when additional practice is desired are the use of protocol materials, experience in sensitivity training based awareness skills, and participation in video or audio taped simulation.

Conclusion

The concept of instructional strategy is introduced as a way to organize the functions that comprised the teaching-learning situation. It is established that strategies can not be developed in a vacuum—they must relate to philosophy of education, objectives in a given setting, applicable facets of learning theory, and the actual instructional methodology.

Awareness and control are reported to be fostered by systematic observation. Particularly, planning and practicing strategies with subsequent self-analysis are suggested as ways of leading to improved instruction in the elements of socio-emotional climate and learning stimuli (content). Chapter 6 offers methods of refinement and modification, once a strategy has been assessed.

6

Modification
and
In-Practice Uses

For some time now, researchers have searched for teacher effectiveness. Ventures in these directions have included studies designed to investigate how learning might be related to such variables as the total amount of light in the classroom, barometric readings on particular days, the grouping patterns of students, and the length of a class period. In the majority of these studies, findings can be summed up in three words—"no significant findings." Although factors of this sort are a part of the classroom and probably have direct influence on particular individuals in the classroom, they do not seem to have a direct bearing on the learning that is facilitated in the instructional-learning situation; they are not "cause-and-effect" relationships as far as actual learning is concerned.

Systematic observation provides a means for focusing on the variables that are interacting in the dynamics of the instructional-learning situation. Systematic observation looks explicitly at the process of facilitating learning. It yields information that allows the teacher to observe teaching behavior—that of others as well as his own—in terms that can be related to student learning. Two systems have been presented in Chapters Three and Four and ways of applying the learned concepts have been suggested.

Recently, attention has been focused on practice techniques that are applicable in pre-service or field experience and that provide organized trial-modification routines. One of the older of these techniques, simulation, is well known for its application in fields such as flight training, driver training and in war games. The in-basket technique and, more currently, protocol materials have used many of the same concepts. The most recent outgrowth is in micro-teaching and micro-simulation. These methodologies have in common the capability of constructive failure. Additionally, they are promising means of reducing initially the total number of variables impinging on a person, situation, or particular interaction until rudimentary understandings and management skills are consolidated. Conditions can then be altered to increase the difficulty level in competence trials or practice opportunities to become as realistic as desired.

The purpose in this work is not to pursue these techniques in detail. Each is the subject of varying numbers of theoretical and practical expositions in the professional literature of several fields—business, industry, and education, for example. Rather, the reader has been alerted to the techniques and approaches because of their suitability, individually and in combination, to do the following:

1. Make possible guided experience in learning and using systematic observation
2. Make possible intensive, focused experiential opportunities in critical teaching problems
3. Make possible self-analysis of teaching behavior
4. Make possible modification and alteration of teaching strategies in an unfettered problem-solving situation without fear of failure and censure.

Lifelike learning situations that join theory and practice are suggested, based on the forthcoming principles. Although the combinations of laboratory experience presented in the ensuing discussion may not be readily recognizable to the purist in the techniques already identified, they do represent combinations of theory and practice that have been successfully used in earlier systematic observation applications.

A series of exercises presented in this chapter, is designed especially to help the teacher in observing and studying the instructional-learning situation. Exercises are outlined for observing classroom situations and for practicing teaching in controlled, laboratory situations. Provisions are made in each exercise for feedback data that will enable the teacher (observer) to describe what he has seen in meaningful terms. In turn, he can analyze and study this information in order to gain new insights into the role of teacher and how to become more effective.

Practice Techniques

The exercises have several features that render them applicable to both the laboratory and the live classroom setting: the "multidimensional" approach; micro-simulation; and video and/or audio recordings.

The *multidimensional approach* uses more than one observational system in a given situation. Several observers, each using a different observational system, observe the same situation simultaneously. The advantage of this approach is that more total data are obtained describing a wider variety of variable kinds. The RCS and the ETC are used as the observational systems in this chapter as the means for securing data describing the socio-emotional climate of the classroom and the nature of the content or learning stimuli that are present for the learner.

Consider again the analogy between the football coach and the teacher as described in Chapter 5. After the game plan is drafted and the game actually begins, the outcome is essentially determined by the skill of the individual players; not entirely, however, because during the game, the coach continues to make professional judgments even as the variables and conditions of the situation fluctuate. Some of these decisions might be more influential on the outcome of the game than those made in the pre-game plan.

The judgments made by the coach during the game are made in terms of the feedback that he receives from his observers stationed strategically throughout the stadium. From these individual data collectors, he receives a variety of vital pieces of information: the left linebacker is keying off of the flanker back; the fullback is a split-second off on his timing; the safety man is pulling in too tight on the long pass plays. Each bit of information is considered in terms of others and judged accordingly. From such considerations, the coach makes critical judgments—professional judgments—regarding how the game should be played. In effect, the pre-game plan is altered and modified in terms of the new, incoming data.

Keep in mind that the coach does not usually make a judgment as a result of considering only one piece of information. For instance, he cannot direct the strategy of the linebackers unless he knows the sequence and formations of the opposition's offensive plays. Since one kind of information is related to another, he secures as much of as many kinds of information as possible.

The same holds true in teaching. As a teacher progresses through the lesson, he needs to secure feedback describing "how he's doing." He needs to secure as much feedback as possible from as many sources as possible. Was the goal reached? Did the the students feel comfortable? Did they see the learning as being relevant and useful? Who did most of the talking? What kind? What kinds of questions did students raise? How did the teacher react to the questions? These and other questions call for real, objective answers if a teacher expects to improve his instructional effectiveness. These answers require feedback.

The term *micro-simulation* means that when compared to a typical classroom instructional situation, the micro-simulation is (1) shorter in terms of time, (2) narrower in scope, and (3) conducted in a laboratory setting using peers as the student subjects. Several advantages can be gained from this approach. (1) It is more convenient in the pre-intern stages of development to conduct exercises of this sort in a campus laboratory where participants can meet and work together without having to travel. (2) Participants are afforded the opportunity to play two different roles—both teacher and student rather than teacher only. (3) Each participant has the opportunity to observe each of his peers teach. Consequently, there are additional opportunities to observe and evaluate the instructional act. (4) It is easier to control certain variables of the situation in a laboratory setting than in an actual classroom. Room facilities, materials, and equipment can be more easily secured and provided from a common local resource center, thus eliminating the transportation of such items out into the field. However, this is not to suggest that micro-simulation should entirely replace internship teaching experiences in an actual classroom setting. Micro-simulation experiences, as described here, are probably of greatest value at the beginning stages of teacher preparation or as a means for introducing and practicing new techniques and skills. (5) A college instructor (resource person) is easily accessible for immediate consultation. This permits the advantage of the student immediately receiving both expert advice and suggestions of the instructor.

In all but two of these perpared exercises, the instructional performance is recorded for replay either on *video or audio tape*. This allows the student to view or hear his performance as many times as he wishes. It also allows him to hear or see himself in action. With the advantage of a video recording, nonverbal behaviors are made available. Experiences involving these kinds of feedback reveal insights that would rarely be detected by another observer and, that would, therefore, escape the attention of the teacher. This is probably one of the most dramatic and meaningful forms of feedback—to see one's self in action.

Synthesis of Exercises

Five exercises are described in this series: the "One-Way, Two-Way"; In Field Classroom Observation; Two-minute Micro-simulation; Five-minute Micro-simulation; and Fifteen-minute Micro-simulation.

One-Way, Two-Way Communication Demonstration. The One-Way, Two-Way exercise is designed to demonstrate two different patterns of classroom communication. The one-way pattern of communication is all teacher talk with the verbal communications all going one way—from teacher to student. In contrast, the two-way pattern provides for verbal interaction between teacher and student as well as student and student. Various data are obtained, treated, and studied in order to gain insights into how the socio-emotional climate and cognitive learning are related within the classroom setting. A detailed procedure is incorporated in the Appendix; the exercise requires approximately one hour to complete.

Two reasons for using this exercise are: the teacher has observed self-taught instructional segments and determined that consistently a very large percentage of the verbal behavior in the classroom is teacher talk; and to illustrate that two-way communication is superior to one-way communication. Assuming a reason such as the above, a practical means of investigating the attributes of one-way and two-way communication is to participate in an exercise that involves both types of communication in performing similar tasks. A group of five individuals is recommended.

This demonstration is divided into two segments; the first being one in which all verbal communication is done by the individual who serves as instructor. The instructor is seated with his back to the other members of the group. These members are to be instructed to draw an arrangement of geometric figures, in this case five rectangles. (See Figure 6.1.) The

Figure 6.1

Rectangle Arrangement 1

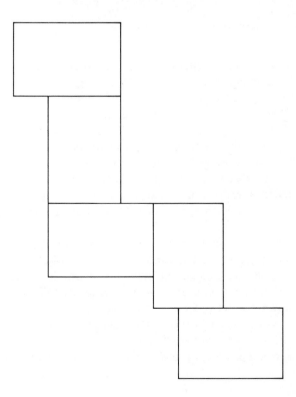

group members may ask no questions as the instructions are given. When the instructions are completed, the drawings are collected and the group participants complete a reaction form concerning "feelings." The five-part rating scale ranges from "very uncomfortable and frustrated" to "comfortable and sure." (See Figure 6.2.) The participants are also asked how

Figure 6.2

FEEDBACK FORM

One way communication

In regard to my feelings concerning reproducing the rectangles correctly, I feel:

1	2	3	4	5
Very uncomfortable and frustrated		Somewhat comfortable and somewhat sure though perhaps a bit frustrated		Comfortable and sure

I think that I correctly reproduced_____rectangles.

many figures (rectangles, squares, etc.) they drew correctly, and the reaction forms are collected.

The second segment of this demonstration involves the same group of participants with the same individual serving as instructor. He instructs the group in a face-to-face situation, allows question from participants, and permits discussion among group members. Participants may ask questions or make comments for the purpose of clarifying instruction and facilitating the task at hand. The task for this segment is another set of geometric figures arranged in a sequence of equal difficulty. (See Figure 6.3.) The same procedures apply to collecting drawings and rating reaction forms.

Information is tabulated on a chart like the one illustrated in Figure 6.4. The findings generally substantiate what one would suspect. Participants predict a higher number of accurate figures in situation two (the two-way) and report a greater degree of comfort. The average number of figures drawn correctly does, in fact, increase.

Results of participation in these two exercises should be convincing evidence that the socio-emotional climate is more conducive to achievement when two-way communication exists, and content goals are achieved at a higher level.

Figure 6.3

RECTANGLE ARRANGEMENT 2
(FOR USE WHEN GIVING INSTRUCTIONS IN
FACE-TO-FACE SETTING; TWO-WAY)

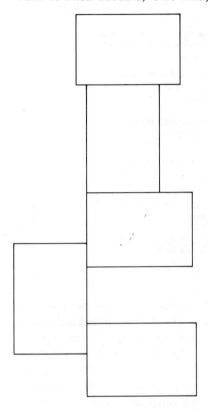

Live Classroom Observation Exercises. Classroom Observation Exercises provide the student with an opportunity to observe a live classroom using two different observational systems—the RCS and the ETC. In addition, analysis and evaluation of these two kinds of data will assist the observer to see more clearly the interaction between the socio-emotional and the content (learning stimuli) variables of the instructional-learning situation as they are identified through the two sets of data.

Two approaches for planning and conducting live classroom observations are described here. The first, Plan 1, is designed for a single individual, and Plan 2 is designed for a pair or team of observers. Regardless of whether Plan 1 or Plan 2 is used, proper arrangements should be made prior to the actual classroom visit.

The teacher should be contacted ahead of time and permission to visit

Figure 6.4

RECORDING TABLE
(TO BE PLACED EITHER ON BLACKBOARD OR ON OVERHEAD OVERLAY)

	Situation 1	Situation 2
1. Average number of rectangles drawn correctly as predicted by students		
2. Average number of rectangles drawn correctly as predicted by teacher		
3. Average number of rectangles drawn correctly		
4. Degree of comfort experienced by students		
5. Degree of comfort experienced by teacher		
6. Total time required		

should be secured. The classroom teacher should be briefed regarding the purpose of the visit. He should understand that the observers will be collecting data using an observational system. Perhaps a brief description of what is meant by systematic observation will be in order if he is not aware of its purpose and use. He should be assured that these data and any evaluation of them will be kept strictly confidential as far as his colleagues, supervisors, and superiors are concerned. He is only permitting you to observe to gain practice in the use of observational systems and for the opportunity to gain further insight into the whole field of teaching.

Procedures can be summarized from material presented already in this book:

1. Arrange properly with the teacher for the visits.
2. Arrive at the classroom and get situated before the class begins.
3. Collect data using both observational systems.
4. Treat, analyze, and evaluate data.
5. Consider the questions that are listed on pages 181–82.

It is usually suggested that observers visit classrooms in pairs or small teams (three or four). The team approach offers two advantages; first, it permits the use of two different observational systems by two observers simultaneously, and second, data from two systems collected simultaneously provide interesting comparisons when the data are analyzed and studied. This point is discussed in Plan 2.

The observer (trained to use both the RCS and the ETC) visits the classroom with data collection sheets for both systems, or a supply of lined paper for collecting data. Either prior to or immediately after the observational period, the observer should secure from the observed teacher a statement and description of the objectives for the lesson. In addition, he should obtain information describing the grade level of the class, average age of the students, sex distribution, socio-economic background, racial distribution, and so on. A suggested format for securing this information is shown in Figure 6.5. Additional data may be added as the situation requires.

The observer situates himself in a position that permits him to view and listen clearly to the interaction of the instructional-learning situation. He should spend a few minutes getting acclimated to the setting (i.e., allow

Figure 6.5

DATA DESCRIBING OBSERVED CLASSROOM SITUATION

Date: _____

Teacher: _____

School: _____

Subject: _____

Grade level: _____

General lesson objective: _____

Specific lesson objective(s), if different from general: _____

Average student age: _____

Sex distribution: Male_____ Female_____

Average socio-economic background: _____

Racial distribution: _____

Comments_____

Observer: _____

time for the students to get used to him, and allow the learning activities to get underway). Then he should begin by collecting data for a three to five minute period using either the RCS or the ETC. He should have some indication, however, as to the estimated length of the lesson to be observed in order to gauge his time appropriately. After collecting data for three to five minutes using one of the two systems, the observer collects data for a second three to five minute period using the other observational system. He continues to collect data for three to five minute periods, alternating systems until the lesson is completed.

As he collects data, the observer should mark each three to five minute period in the proper collection sequence so that he can "fit" the lesson together when he analyzes the data.

When the lesson is completed, the observer should note anything concerning the lesson and the classroom setting that might he considered relevant. He might even conduct a short interview with the teacher to get an idea of how the teacher felt during the lesson. Did he feel that he had achieved his goal(s)? Did he feel that he had held the attention of the students? What would he plan to do differently if he were to teach the lesson again? Questions of this sort often provide new insights for the observer. Experiences in live classrooms tend to stimulate ideas concerning the different approaches and techniques that might be used when the observer assumes the role of the teacher.

After the observation and the short interview, the observer retires to a convenient place to complete the treatment of the data. RCS data should be plotted in a matrix for closer study. ETC data should be treated as outlined in Chapter 4.

With the treated data in hand, the observer can analyze and evaluate the total performance. In evaluating the observed performance, the questions and points of consideration listed at the end of this exercise (page 181) should be used as a point of departure.

Plan 2 is similar to Plan 1 except a pair or team of observers visits the classroom rather than an individual. Because more observers will be in the classroom, arrangements should be made accordingly, in order to avoid disturbing the normal activities of the class. Chairs should be provided and arranged before the class begins. The observers should arrive before the class begins, in order to be situated when the learning activities start.

As in Plan 1, observers should obtain general data describing the lesson to be observed (i.e., general and/or specific objectives, subject, grade level, background of the students, etc.).

The data collection for Plan 2 is similar to Plan 1 except each observer of a pair (or team) uses a different observational system. One team member collects data using the RCS, while the other team member collects data using the ETC. If more than two observers are operating as a team, then half of the observers use the RCS and the other half use the ETC. All observers should begin collecting data at the same time. If one observer stops collecting data for one reason or another, all observers should also stop. Data should be collected for at least twenty minutes and preferably longer if the class continues for more than twenty minutes.

After data collection is completed, observers note any relevant infomation that will be valuable when data are analyzed and discussed. A short interview with the teacher as described in Plan 1 is also desirable. This can evolve into an interesting discussion since several individuals will be involved. It might be better if the teacher and observers move to another room in order to carry on the discussion in the absence of the students.

After data collection and an interview with the teacher, the observers should treat the raw data (tabulate, plot, etc.). Following data treatment, the data should be analyzed and an evaluation made of the overall teaching performance. Questions at the end of this section are appropriate for guiding the course of a group discussion of the teaching performance.

Questions for Consideration

The following questions are suggested for consideration following the collection, treatment, and analysis of data describing a live instructional-learning situation. If the individual is working alone, he should consider these questions either by himself or with a fellow student who has been involved in a similar experience. The observer may wish to prepare a written résumé of his experience organized around these points for consideration or he may choose to discuss some or all of them with his instructor. Another suggested technique is to arrange for a group of observers (perhaps an entire class) to meet and discuss their individual experiences as classroom observers.

Questions of this type should be considered by the observer:

1. Were the objectives for the class met (regardless of whether or not the teacher *thought* they were met)?
2. What are the reasons for your answer to Question 1?
3. What techniques and/or behaviors demonstrated by the teacher were most effective? unique? least effective? completely out of line?
4. In terms of the RCS and ETC data collected, were the instructional strategies selected by the teacher appropriate for facilitating the learning set forth in the objective(s)?
5. Defend the answer to Question 4 by referring to specific RCS and/or ETC data that were collected.
6. How do the RCS data and the ETC data compare in terms of interrelationships?

7. Was the socio-emotional climate generally warm, neutral, or cool as shown by the RCS data? Was the climate conducive to the facilitation of learning in that particular situation?

8. Was the content (learning stimuli) generally appropriate as shown by the ETC data?

9. What suggestions could be made to the teacher regarding the effectiveness of his overall performance?

10. What suggestions could be offered to the teacher for his future improvement?

Evaluation for this exercise is in terms of the opinions and ideas of individual participating student observers. It might be appropriate and helpful to organize and conduct a general group discussion involving several pairs or teams of observers for the purpose of sharing insights and ideas.

Two-Minute Micro-simulation. This exercise provides an opportunity to plan a lesson in which behavior is controlled according to a predetermined listing of either RCS or ETC category/item descriptions. A short two to five minute lesson of a predetermined listing of either RCS or ETC category/item descriptions. (See Table 6.1) or a combination of the two are taught in small groups of five or six. Each participant teaches a lesson while one of the group plays the role of an observer and the remaining members are students. The Two-minute Micro-simulation experience is specifically designed to give experience in (1) planning a short lesson using a sequential ordering of categories from an observational system, and (2) collecting data using that system.

Procedures are presented in detail in Appendix B but can be summarized briefly as follows :

1. Take a strip of paper upon which appears a sequential listing of either RCS or ETC category/item descriptions (Table 6.1). Plan a short lesson, built around any subject, in terms of the listings on the strip of paper.

2. Arrange in circular fashion in groups of five or six, then teach a lesson while one of the group serves as observer and the remaining group members play student roles.

3. After each presentation, the observed data collected by the group observers are to be compared with the original data listing used by the teacher of that particular lesson.

4. A short discussion should be conducted among individuals of the group.

5. Follow the above procedures until each group member has taught his lesson.

Analysis and evaluation of individual teaching performances should be discussed by the group members. Constructive criticism, suggestions for

Table 6.1

SAMPLE LISTING OF DATA FOR
TWO-MINUTE MICRO-SIMULATION

RCS	ETC
7	1
7	1
10	2
10	14
7	6
7	14
10	16
10	14
7	7
7	15
10	6
10	15
4	8
15	0
2	0
4	2
15	15
2	9
4	14
15	7
2	15
1	17
6	15
6	8
4	9
16	
2	
7	

improvement, reinforcement of appropriate behaviors, comments, and the like should be offered openly. The discussion portion of this exercise is vital and meaningful to the teacher and to the student role players. Major concerns in such a discussion include comparison of the two sets of data (predetermined script and that collected by observers); achievement of lesson goals; and control of teaching behavior as evidenced by the collected data. The practical experience of planning a teaching strategy based on selected observation system categories should demonstrate the realistic nature of the exercise. Additionally, this particular exercise is one of the better ways of learning data collection.

The Five-minute Micro-simulation exercise is designed to give the student laboratory experience in planning and executing either one or two instructional strategies in a controlled situation. For example, the exercise might be a drill session, a short guided discovery lesson, or a short lesson for the purpose of diagnosing the students' level of understanding. The student states the purpose of the lesson (learning objective), selects the strategy that he plans to use, and prepares a sequential listing of the observational categories or items that will demonstrate the selected strategy. Then he teaches the lesson to several peers while it is recorded on a video or audio tape. Then he plays back the tape, collects observational data, and compares these with the data listed originally to describe the strategy to be demonstrated. An analysis of these data enables the student to evaluate the effectiveness of his performance and to make suggestions for future improvement. An optional variation of this exercise is a revision and re-execution of the same lesson for the purpose of improvement.

The Five-minute Micro-simulation. In this exercise, the learner will have an opportunity to teach a short lesson in which he demonstrates his ability to control his behavior in terms of a predetermined instructional strategy of his choice. The instructional strategy is comprised of one or more functions, described in either the RCS categories or ETC items, properly ordered according to the instructional strategy being demonstrated. The purpose of this exercise is to provide the teacher with an opportunity to control his teaching behavior according to a predetermined pattern of behaviors set forth in terms of an observational system (the RCS or the ETC).

The performance is to be recorded on video tape (audio tape is satisfactory if video equipment is not available). By replaying the video tape, the student is able to collect observational data using either the RCS or the ETC, depending upon the given strategy(ies). A comparison of the observational data with the categories or items that describe the strategy will reveal the teacher's ability to control his own behavior.

This exercise should be conducted in a laboratory that will accommodate five or six students. Any materials or equipment required to demonstrate the instructional strategy should be available (i.e., blackboard, overhead projector, overlays, filmstrips, projector, etc.). Video or audio recording equipment is required to record the performance.

Procedures can be generally described in the following eight points:

1. Select an instructional strategy for demonstration.
2. State the strategy in terms of either RCS categories or ETC items.
3. Plan a lesson that will demonstrate ability to control behavior in terms of the selected instructional strategy.
4. Arrange the laboratory properly for the demonstration. See that equipment and materials are in order and operating.

5. Teach the lesson to four or five student peers while a video or audio recording is made.
6. Play back the recording and collect observational data using either the RCS or the ETC.
7. Compare the observed performance data with those stated in Step 2.
8. Evaluate the quality of the performance with the assistance of a peer partner and/or the instructor.

The quality (effectiveness) of the performance should be determined by analyzing and discussing the data and overall performance with a partner and/or the instructor. If the performance is judged unsatisfactory, the student should repeat the entire exercise until he reaches criteria.

Planning the Lesson

An instructional strategy that represents a skill or technique that will serve to expand and strengthen the observer's available repertoire of behavioral competencies should be selected. The selected strategy should be written in pattern form as shown in the sample strategies that follow.

SOME SAMPLE INSTRUCTIONAL STRATEGIES IN RCS PATTERN FORM
(TO BE USED IN THE FIVE-MINUTE MICRO-SIMULATION)

1. The "drill" pattern: 4–15–2, 4–15–2 . . .
2. The "clarification of an idea" pattern: 16–3–16, 16–3–16 . . . or 15–3–15, 15–3–15 . . . or 14–3–14 . . . (the idea here is to use Category 3 as extensively as possible)
3. The "guided discovery" pattern: 7–10, 7–10 . . . (giving directions and allowing time for the student to comply) or 4–16–3– 16 . . . 4–15–3–15 . . . ("drawing information from the student" in order to bring him to an understanding . . .)
4. The "warming" pattern: 1–6 . . . 6–1 . . . 4–15–1 . . . 4– 16–1 . . . 14–1 (the obvious and varied use of Category one —warming)
5. The "question-with-a-question" pattern: 14–4 . . . 13–4 . . . 16–4 (the following of a student question or contribution with another question; closely resembles the "clarification of an idea" pattern above in #2)
6. The "positive reinforcement" pattern: 4–15–2 . . . 4–16–2 . . . 14–2 . . . 13–2 . . . 16–2 (reinforcing all desirable student verbal behavior)

Note: These are several suggested patterns. The student should feel free to design patterns of his own and/or combine two or more patterns into a multi-strategy.

SOME SAMPLE INSTRUCTIONAL STRATEGIES IN ETC PATTERN FORM
(TO BE USED IN THE FIVE-MINUTE MICRO-SIMULATION)

1. The "drill" pattern: 2–4–6 (maintain cognitive level)
                          2–4–7 (extend cognitive level)
2. The "guided discovery" pattern: 1–9–0
   (giving information, directions, and time for the student to think
   and respond)
3. The "extended reaction" pattern: 2–14–7
   (Following a restricted response, the teacher reacts to extend the
   level.)
4. The "maintained reaction" pattern: 2–14–6
                                         3–15–6
   (Following a response—either restricted or expanded, the teacher
   reacts to maintain the level.)
5. The "structure with directions" pattern: 1–9–14
                                               1–9–15
   (The teacher structures the learning situation with directions)
6. The "structure with silence" pattern: 1–0–14
   (The key to this pattern is the use of   1–0–15
   silence to structure the learning   9–0–14
   situation.)   9–0–15

Pick a topic of some familiarity and plan a short lesson that requires four
to eight minutes to present. The lesson plan should include one learning objective stated in behavioral terms (i.e., an observable behavior, the conditions under which the learning is to be measured, how well the learner must
perform in order to be judged "acceptable"), the instructional strategy that
is to be demonstrated, and the procedures for measuring the learning.

Teaching the Lesson

This exercise is conducted in groups of four to six students in which one
teaches the lesson, one collects observational data (using the RCS or the
ETC), and the remaining group members assume student roles. Each
teaching performance is recorded on video tape.

Following the instructional phase of the lesson, video recording is
stopped while the teacher and the students complete the *Student Feedback
Form* (Figure 6.6) and the *Teacher Feedback Form* (Figure 6.7). These
data are collected and held for future reference.

Upon completing the feedback forms, the video recorder is started again
and a group discussion/critique of the instructional performance is conducted and recorded. The discussion should be open and frank. Constructive criticism, suggestions for improvement, and comments regarding the

Figure 6.6

STUDENT FEEDBACK FORM

Teacher _____

1. I felt that I learned (or would have learned had I not already known the content):

```
1              2              3              4              5
|_____|_____|_____|_____|
Almost nothing              Some              A great deal
```

2. In regard to my interest in the lesson, I was:

```
1              2              3              4              5
|_____|_____|_____|_____|
Not very interested         Somewhat          Very
at all                      interested        interested
```

3. In regard to my feelings in involvement during the lesson, I felt:

```
1              2              3              4              5
|_____|_____|_____|_____|
Little or no            Involved some of      Involved most
involvement             the time              of the time
```

Figure 6.7

TEACHER FEEDBACK FORM

Teacher _____

1. I felt that I facilitated learning as follows:

```
1              2              3              4              5
|_____|_____|_____|_____|
Almost no learning    Some learning    A great deal of learning
```

2. In regard to student interest in the lesson, I felt they were:

```
1              2              3              4              5
|_____|_____|_____|_____|
Not very interested     Somewhat interested    Very interested
at all
```

3. In regard to student feelings of involvement during the lesson, I felt that they experienced:

```
1              2              3              4              5
|_____|_____|_____|_____|
Little or no involvement    Involved some of the    Involved most of the
                            time                    time
```

overall presentation should be presented to help the teacher to improve. This recording should be replayed to provide another form of feedback for the teacher.

Analyzing the Data

When the lesson is completed and all data secured, the observer-teacher is ready to analyze the data and evaluate his teaching performance. The following raw data should be available for analysis:

1. The video recording of the performance
2. The Student Feedback Forms
3. The Teacher Feedback Form
4. The video recording of the discussion/critique

The video recording of the presentation should be played back while the teacher and a peer partner collect observational data using the observational system that is appropriate to the selected strategy (either the RCS or the ETC). The two observers should compare data. If discrepancies in recorded observations are found, the tape should resolve all disagreements concerning the data that describe the teaching performance. It may be necessary to consult the instructor to resolve disagreements of this sort.

From the Student Feedback Forms the teacher should calculate an average rating for each of the three dimensions included in the form—learning, interest, and involvement. The total ratings for all students on a single dimension is calculated; this total rating is divided by the number of student raters involved to produce the average rating for that particular dimension. The average student rating for the Student Feedback Form is recorded along with the teacher's rating of the Teacher's Feedback Form, and all data held for future reference.

The video recording of the discussion/critique should be replayed while the teacher makes notes concerning the criticisms, suggestions, and comments that were offered by the group members. These notes are kept for final evaluation.

With all the data in hand, the teacher is ready to conduct a final evaluation of the overall performance. The following considerations should be made and a short written report made of each:

1. *How well did the observational data (RCS or ETC) compare with the category or item listing of the instructional strategy that was demonstrated?*

   The observational data that was collected during playback should be compared closely with the strategy description that was selected to be demonstrated. Do the observational data show that strategy was used? How and where did the teacher deviate from the strategy and/or original plan? What was the cause of this deviation? Was the strategy appropriate to the learning objective that had been stated in the lesson plan?

2. *How did the students and the teacher feel during and about the performance?*

Compare the data secured from the Student Feedback Forms and the Teacher Feedback Form by placing both ratings—the student's average and the teacher's—on a single continuum for each of the three dimensions of learning, interest, and involvement. Were there any wide discrepancies? If so, what might have caused them? Which perception, the teacher's or the students', is most likely to be the valid one? (This should be discussed in detail.) What can the teacher do in the future to accommodate for this sort of discrepancy?

3. *What were the criticisms, suggestions, and comments of the group members?*

From the notes taken from the playback of the discussion/critique, an evaluation should be made of the total performance. What things did the teacher do well? What things did he do poorly? Are these criticisms valid or are they subjective? What specific suggestions are offered by the group members for future improvement? What would you do differently if you were to teach a lesson of this sort again?

The written report prepared above should be read by and discussed with one's partner and the instructor. They will have additional comments and insights to offer that will prove to be of help.

Teach—Reteach Option

In the event the lesson presentation was of less than acceptable quality, the student should repeat the exercise. The lesson should be replanned, retaught, reanalyzed, and reevaluated according to the same procedures described above. This presentation might be planned around a different topic and different learning objective(s), but the strategy should probably be the same. This will allow the student an opportunity to "redeem" himself and demonstrate that he can, in fact, master that particular strategy.

If the performance is judged as having been acceptable, the teacher may wish to plan and teach another lesson according to the procedures outlined above. This lesson might incorporate either the same objectives and a different strategy or a different objective and the same strategy. Either of these plans will allow the student to see how the same objective and/or strategy can be employed in two different kinds of situations. It will help to demonstrate the importance of variety and flexibility in teaching.

The format described in the two paragraphs above is called the "teach-reteach" approach and is quite useful in early training exercises and for the purpose of introducing a new strategy. It is useful, since the total performance time is less than fifteen minutes and a number of students can be accommodated daily by limited video equipment.

The "Fifteen–Minute Micro–simulation." Slightly different from the five-minute micro-simulation, the fifteen-minute micro-simulation is a complete lesson in miniature. An entire lesson is to be planned: state objectives, develop a testing instrument, and select the instructional strategy(ies) that are to be used, then teach the lesson in a micro-simulation setting while the performance is recorded either on video or on audio tape. Following instruction, secure various data describing the overall performance (i.e., observational data from playback, individual feedback on feelings during instruction, test results, etc.). Analyze these data and evaluate the performance by writing a critique according to the included format.

This exercise "puts it all together." It resembles as closely as possible the complete lesson as typically planned, taught, and evaluated in the regular classroom. The student gets an opportunity to see himself in action and to observe his own teaching behavior using both the RCS and the ETC. The purpose of this exercise is to provide an opportunity to combine all of the elements of planning and teaching a lesson under conditions which will allow a thorough, comprehensive analysis and evaluation of the total performance.

The facility should be large enough to accommodate from six to twelve students and should have any equipment required (i.e., blackboard, overhead projector, filmstrip projector, etc.). Video or audio facilities should be provided in order to record the teaching performance.

The exercise is divided into four sections for convenience—planning the lesson, teaching it, analyzing it, and preparing the written critique. Each section is discussed in detail.

Planning the Lesson

The student should select a topic with which he is well acquainted and feels comfortable. Probably this will be from his major or minor field, but the topic can be from any subject as long as it appeals to the student.

The student should select and state at least one objective in behavioral terms (i.e., describe an observable behavior, explain the conditions under which the behavior is to be performed, and the procedures by which the learning is to be measured). More than one objective may be stated, but the teacher should take care to prepare a lesson that will require at least fifteen, but not more than twenty minutes.

In accord with the basic philosophy of behavioral objectives, a testing instrument—neither extensive nor lengthy—should be prepared that will measure the learning in terms of the behavioral objective(s) that have been stated above. (A copy of the testing instrument should be prepared for each individual in the group.)

The student should, then, carefully select the instructional strategies that he judges will be most effective in facilitating the learning described in the objective(s). For example, will he use lecture, discussion, lecture-discussion, guided discovery, drill, etc.? This is the most important phase of the planning process. Because the instructional strategy(ies) selected by the student will determine many of the other aspects of the lesson, care should be taken in their selection.

Model (planned) observational data should be generated and recorded in regular form for the RCS and the ETC. The student has several options from which to choose when generating model data as follows:

1. Record raw data in regular form for the RCS for the full predicted amount of time. These data should be predicted in terms of what the student expects to take place. He will end up with approximately fifteen to twenty minutes of model data that he can plot in a blank RCS matrix according to the directions given in Chapter 3. ETC data should be generated according to the same process and listed in model form.

2. Record raw data in regular form for the RCS as outlined in 1 above, but record only five minutes of data rather than twenty. Then plot the five minutes of data in a blank RCS matrix. After plotting the data, multiply the loading in each occupied cell by four to secure the cell loading that would be plotted for twenty minutes of data.

3. Record raw data in regular form for both the RCS and the ETC outlined in 1 above. However, rather than plotting in a matrix, write down each of the strategy patterns that will be used in regular form, using RCS and ETC categories (i.e., "4–15–2," "7–10–17," "3–16–3," etc.) Then estimate the number of times that each pattern will be generated during the actual presentation.

Note: Be sure to prepare sufficient copies of all handouts and resource materials so that each individual member of the group will have his own copy. Also, be sure to secure all materials and equipment necessary for one's presentation (overhead projectors, overlays, filmstrips, projectors, grease pencils, books, etc.).

Teaching the Lesson

Arrange the room to accommodate the learning experiences that you have planned. Set up any necessary equipment; lay out all materials that are to be used. Be sure that the video camera operator is ready for the lesson to begin.

Before the actual lesson and before the camera begins to record, orient the group members. Explain the nature of the lesson; subject, topic, objectives (if appropriate), grade level, socio-economic background of the students they are to roleplay, the background material that they are expected to know in order to succeed in the lesson, etc. Proper orientation of the group members insures a more successful performance.

Begin the lesson while being recorded on video tape and complete the lesson as planned. During the teaching performance, the instructor and/or your partner should observe the performance and make written observations concerning 1) voice, 2) apparent ease with which the teacher handles himself, 3) use of materials and/or equipment, 4) empathy demonstrated to the students, and 5) any other relevant comments. Hold these as a part of the data to be analyzed later.

At the close of the teaching performance stop the camera, distribute the *Student Feedback Forms* (shown on page 187), and ask each student to complete one, indicating how they felt during the lesson in terms of interest, learning, and involvement. As the students are completing their forms, the teacher should complete his copy of the *Teacher Feedback Form* (Figure 6.7). Hold these data for analysis later.

Following the completion of the feedback forms, distribute the testing instruments and request that the students complete them. Students should react to the testing instrument according to the student roles that they have been assigned to play. Even though they might have known the information before it was presented, they are to respond to the testing instrument in terms of this question: "If I didn't know the information before the lesson, would I know it now as a result of this lesson?" They should be instructed to respond to the test in these terms—purposely missing an item if appropriate to their student role. In the event that the testing procedures involve some form of measurement other than a pencil-paper instrument, conduct them accordingly, recording the students' performance in proper form to be held for future reference.

After collecting the evaluation instruments, or recording student performance in terms of some other measuring procedure, re-start the video camera to record a group discussion of the performance. Group members should offer any comments they feel are appropriate. Constructive criticism, suggestions for improvement, and alternate techniques are all appropriate and helpful. This recorded discussion/critique will be replayed and analyzed later as a part of the analysis and critique.

Analysis of the Data

At this point in the exercise, the following kinds of raw data should be available for treatment and analysis:

1. The learning objective(s) that were stated at the beginning
2. The selected instructional strategies and the model RCS and ETC data
3. The testing instrument
4. The video recording that will provide:
   a. actual RCS data
   b. actual ETC data
   c. information from the recorded discussion/critique
   d. the nonverbal behavior of the teacher during his performance
5. *Student Feedback Forms*
6. *Teacher Feedback Forms*
7. Completed testing instruments
8. The evaluation by the partner and/or instructor

The data listed above in 4, 5, and 7 must be treated before they can be added to the others for final consideration and evaluation.

In order to obtain RCS and ETC data describing the performance, the video recording should be played back while both the teacher and his partner collect data. Both sets of collected data should be compared and any discrepancies should be resolved by replaying a given section of the recording to determine the proper interpretation.

The raw RCS and ETC data should be treated for final study and analysis after collection. The RCS data should be plotted in a blank RCS matrix. In turn, the actual RCS data should be plotted in another blank matrix, along with the model RCS data that was generated and recorded in the planning phase. Figure 6.8 on page 194 shows how these data should appear when both sets are plotted in the same matrix. Each cell having either model and/or actual data should be divided diagonally as shown in the figure. Model RCS data should be shown in one of the triangular shaped cell halves, recorded in one color and the actual RCS data should be recorded in the other triangular cell half in another color. If a cell or a cell half is not loaded, do not draw a diagonal line through it. By entering both the model and the actual data in the same matrix, the observer is permitted a clearer view of what was planned and what occurred in terms of RCS data.

The ETC data should be treated similarly. Both sets of data—the model and the actual—should be reported on the same reporting form as shown in Figure 6.8. Hold both sets of treated data (the RCS and the ETC) for future reference in the critique section.

After completing the treatment and final reporting of the RCS and ETC data, replay the discussion/critique section of the video recording. Note comments, criticism, suggestions, reactions, etc. concerning the discussion of the performance and hold these for future reference.

From the data recorded on the Student Feedback Forms, calculate the

Figure 6.8

MODEL AND ACTUAL DATA REPORTING

Situation_____ Date_____ Name_____

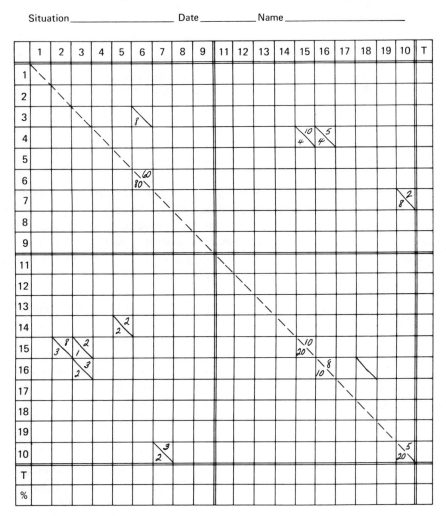

average rating for each of the three dimensions—interest, learning, and involvement as reported. (Total the ratings for a given dimension for all of the forms and divide the total by the number of individuals submitting forms; this will yield the average for that dimension. Do this for each of the three dimensions.) Hold these data along with the others for final analysis and evaluation.

Grade the tests and determine how many items were completed correctly. Hold these data for future reference.

Preparation of the Written Critique

Before beginning the preparation of the written critique, study all of the data that are listed on page 193 under "Analysis of the Data." These data will provide the information that is needed to prepare the written critique. The written critique can be prepared according to the format and special instructions included in the Appendix.

"Control" Variations for the Fifteen-Minute Micro-simulation

To demonstrate a specific control technique, the student might plan a lesson with one of the following restrictions:

1. Using no more than five percent of Category 6 (teacher initiated information, lecture), as measured by the RCS. This will restrict the amount of teacher initiation and require use of other techniques to present information.

2. Using no more than one percent of Category 2 (teacher acceptance), measured by the RCS. This will demonstrate that the use of Category 2 ends discussion. The idea here is that by *not* using Category 2, the teacher is attempting to draw out and develop discussion.

3. Using a minimum twenty percent each of Categories 7 and 10 (giving directions and silence), as measured by the RCS. The purpose of this control is to demonstrate how a teacher can present a concept through the guided discovery approach. The students are told to do something and then given time to do it. The alternating intervals of giving directions and silence should be short (perhaps no longer than 20–30 seconds) in order to keep the pace moving.

4. Using no more than ten percent combined teacher talk as measured by the RCS. This control requires the teacher to incorporate strategies that stimulate and promote student talk (Category 10 is not included when calculating the total teacher talk). The teacher will have to control his own verbal behavior very carefully and skillfully to make best possible use of the small amount of total talk allowed him.

Exercises Revisited

Five exercises have been summarized in sufficient detail to make possible extended practice in live and simulated conditions. As techniques useful to the observer intent on awareness and control, these exercises utilize broadly based principles from simulation, micro-teaching, the in-basket technique, protocol materials, and sensitivity training. As the need for practice in modification becomes evident, these five exercises should prove their worth again and again:

—One-Way Two-Way Communication
—Live Classroom Observation
—Two-Minute Micro-simulation
—Five-Minute Micro-simulation
—Fifteen-Minute Micro-simulation

Systematic Observation: A Tool for Strategy and Self-Evaluation

Classroom activity includes teaching of thinking skills—teaching kids how to think is what it is all about. In teaching youngsters how to deal with cognitive and affective concerns, the instructor employs himself, content, and procedural strategies in conjunction with student capabilities and dispositions. Systematic observations offer a means of recording classroom sequences as they occur in such a form that teaching strategies can be replayed to identify strengths and weaknesses. Organized modification becomes probable as intended and actual behaviors are placed in juxtaposition. Much as a successful coach devises a workable Saturday afternoon game plan, individual teachers can tailor strategies based on comprehensive feedback.

Medley and Mitzel (1963) stated that observations of classroom behavior are seldom included in research studies because:

—Observations are expensive of time, money, and skill.
—Observations constitute invasions of privacy resented and restricted by teachers and administrators.
—Observers in a classroom are disturbing and cause possibility of atypical behavior.
—Observational procedures as a major study methodology have not increased knowledge about teaching and learning.
—Observation is usually deleted so a larger sample can be studied.

Although these researchers' interest in the problem was admittedly research-oriented while the major interest of this publication is self-investigation, self-analysis, or self-evaluation, these hypothetical or real problems are revealing when basic contributions and potential of observational approaches are considered.

A point to be clearly established is that the use of systematic observation as a technique of self-evaluation, in and of itself, overcomes many of the stated problems. The authors have introduced systematic observation techniques [1] to hundreds of classroom teachers, principals, and other professionals, as well as to pre-service teaching prospects, and have confirmed that "time, money, and skill" are, in a relative sense, very cheap.[2] The estimate of fifty hours for the preparation of a researcher is quite possibly a conservative estimate. On the other hand, in two-day training sessions, non-selective groups of teachers have learned the RCS well enough that sixty percent or more have agreement ratings with experts of .60 or better.[3] Several agree at .70 and greater. One hundred heterogenously grouped participants recently instructed simultaneously by one trainer performed at the above stated levels when compared with criterion measures prepared by "experts." At an expenditure of eleven to twelve hours of instructional time by participants, two days of expert help, and with prepared teaching materials costing approximately $5.00 per person, approximately two-thirds of these teachers and principals were ready, in terms of established criterion measures, to begin objective study of themselves in the home classroom with confidence that other similarly trained observers would identify the same teaching-learning sequences were they present as observers.

There is no invasion of privacy when the teacher uses tape recorders to gain audio records of what is happening in his classes. In the privacy of his classroom, with the knowledge that only he and those he chooses will ever have access to the taped sessions, there is no reason to feel apprehensive about applying systematic observation approaches to personal teaching strategies and sequences. Pressures associated with the "outside agent," should a teacher choose to be videotaped, are minimized in the self-observation plan. Medley and Mitzel (1963) reported that even with live observers in the classroom, teachers and administrators cooperate enthusiastically when apprised of the value of observations and planned utility in the research studies. Recently, Baum reported on New York City's use of videotaping in conjunction with self-analysis applications of systematic observation and commented that teachers look forward to "their time" on taping schedules.[4]

It is difficult to observe unobserved behaviors. The chance that behaviors

---

[1] Primarily these have included Ober's RCS, Brown's Florida Taxonomy of Cognitive Behaviors, and the ETC, though depth exposure to Flanders' Interaction Analysis and Parson's Guided Self-Analysis are included in the author's preparation and experience.

[2] Unpublished monograph by Bentley, E. and E. Miller, *Teacher Evaluation: A Personal Responsibility* and "Observation as a Methodology," Jeannine Webb, Ernest L. Bentley, and R. Robert Rentz, a paper presented to AERA, 1970.

[3] Paper presented by Webb, Bentley, and Rentz.

[4] Guided self-analysis conference, Grand Rapids, Michigan, November 11, 12, 13, 1969.

are not really typical when outside observers or tape recorders are present seems inconsequential if one assumes that knowledge of teaching strategies and student involvement under observation is better than a total absence of knowledge about how teachers and students interact. Again, with the emphasis on self-evaluation and analysis, this concern is certainly minimized.

Two very real concerns should be posed, however. First, there is a demand in self-evaluation procedure for intellectual and personal honesty that can often be most difficult in situations of self-confrontation, such as when classifying your own teaching as it becomes evident that what was planned and intended is not always what happens. Defensiveness should dissipate as satisfaction is gained when progress becomes evident. A major strength in using systematic observation procedures is that the visibility of intended and actual behaviors makes possible *awareness* and *control*.

Once one knows what is actually occurring, the choices are simple— satisfaction with results; mild cognitive dissonance,[5] as the anticipated and actual results do not quite measure up to expectations; and considerable dissatisfaction and cognitive dissonance. Complete lack of acceptability is a rare phenomenon and probably just as well that it is—some hope must be felt or total frustration results.

A second, and perhaps greater, potential problem is the assumption that overall teacher effectiveness can be expected through modified teacher strategies without conscious attention to other instructional roles involved in improved strategies. For example, the comparison of intent and actual teaching strategies depends to a great degree on lesson preparation—particularly the outcomes anticipated. The actual teaching strategy may achieve the desired outcomes even though it is not exactly what the teacher planned. Thus, there are aspects to be considered related to effectiveness of implementation of the strategy itself, and effects upon students.

Instructional personnel historically have been somewhat ill-prepared in stating specified performance goals of improved thinking, and in assessing other factual information. It is not sufficient simply to teach systematic observation techniques to teachers and expect them to view, analyze, modify, and become more effective without providing educational or in-service opportunities to do additional work on instructional objectives; to investigate human growth and development factors related to thinking, behaving, and learning; to assess student progress based on behaviors desired and taught, rather than factual information alone; and to experience human relations principles basic in teaching-learning interactions. Knowledge of student capabilities, content, and the planned treatment must grow simultaneously as the interactions are systematically examined and analyzed, and as the treatment is modified.

[5] Dissonance refers to the state of dissatisfaction induced through the knowledge that what is actually taking place is *not* what was planned or thought to be occurring.

Observational systems attempt to answer the following questions:

—Does the planned teaching strategy operate effectively in relation to stated behavioral changes desired?

—What knowledge can be gained about individual teacher influence on classroom actions?

—How do students perceive teacher behaviors?

—How much control is the teacher able to exert over his own behavior in the classroom?

—Will modified teaching strategies result in changed student behavior?

Rather than tell what *should* be going on in the classroom, a well-constructed observation system tells what *is* going on in the classroom. Individual teachers become more sensitive to their own behavior and their understanding of how it effects the classroom and the individual students. They accept the responsibility for self-improvement by systematically investigating their own teaching.

Dynamics for change operate in at least two areas. First, as teachers see achievement of the instructional practices they desire by bringing actual in line with intent, they strive for additional evidence and change. Second, when the changes aimed at reduction of inconsistencies or dissonance are not rapidly effective, more experimentation will result.

Self-evaluation is chosen rather than "outside agent" or supervisory evaluation because of the belief, supported by substantial evidence in sociology and psychology, that self-analysis is a greater influence for change. It eliminates the opportunity to rationalize the results an outside observer might report. Rather, it employs self-confrontation and self-study in a systematic objective fashion.

A New York City evaluation report on systematic observation included the following informal conclusions:

1. Teachers expressed continuing awareness of changes in their own perception of self.

2. Teachers expressed awareness of changes in their perceptions of pupil behaviors.

3. Teachers began to discuss openly the inadequacies of their teaching practices with regard to developing their pupils' thinking skills.

4. Teachers began to reconceptualize "discipline problems," and to speak of the relationship between classroom teaching and discipline.

5. Teachers expressed surprise at the extent of the changes in themselves in talking, thinking and thus, in their teaching. They began

to see that these changes were favorably reflected in pupil behavior and learning.

While the definition of observation systems as tools that have been developed for the purposes of identifying, classifying, quantifying, and analyzing
specific classroom behaviors, has an imposing and statistical sound, the
development of skills in using the systems is not a difficult task.

The authors feel that the major strengths of observation systems as techniques of self-evaluation are that (1) they provide a common set of organ-
izers, a vocabulary that can be used both by the theoretician and the
teacher, (2) they provide for increased awareness of the different elements
of classroom behavior and interaction, and (3) they tend to bring to attention alternative patterns, methodological approaches, or teaching skills that
may effect desired goals.

Appendix

Keys to Drills [1]

DIFFERENTIATION DRILL, PAGE 54

M, C, D or E	5/15 or 6/16	Questions
D	6	1. Teacher
M	15	2. Student
M	5	3. Teacher
E	6	4. Teacher
D	16	5. Student
C	5	6. Teacher
C	5	7. Teacher

DIFFERENTIATION DRILL, PAGE 48

C or D	5/15 or 6/16	Verbal Responses
D	16	1. Student
C	5	2. Teacher
C	15	3. Student
C	5	4. Teacher
D	16	5. Student
D	6	6. Teacher

RECOGNITION DRILL, PAGE 51

Category Number	Keyword in Category Definition
1. 1	warms
2. 5	responds (convergent)
3. 14	elicits

[1] Keys to drills are not strictly in chronological order.

RECOGNITION DRILL (*cont.*)

Category	Number	Keyword in Category Definition
4.	10	silence or confusion
5.	2	accepts
6.	19	cools
7.	18	corrects
8.	15	responds (convergent)
9.	16	initiates (divergent response)
10.	8	corrects
11.	17	directs
12.	6	initiates
13.	12	accepts
14.	3	amplifies or clarifies
15.	11	warms
16.	4	elicits
17.	7	directs
18.	9	cools

DATA COLLECTION DRILL, PAGES 54–58: DATA COLLECTION FORM

	1	2	3	4	5	6	7	8	9	10
1.	10	4	6	13	16	3	4			
2.	7	15	4	13	3	4	10			
3.	7	4	15	4	3	15				
4.	6	15	6	15	4	2				
5.	4	4	4	10	16	6				
6.	7	15	13	16	16	4				
7.	15	2	6	16	16	15				
8.	15	3	4	16	16	18				
9.	15	16	18	3	4	2				
10.	15	6	10	6	14	4				
11.	15	16	16	16	16	6				
12.	1	3	13	3	16	4				
13.	1	4	13	6	16	15				
14.	6	15	18	16	16	6				
15.	6	4	13	16	2	4				
16.	4	15	13	16	6	15				
17.	15	2	2	18	6	4				
18.	2	6	4	2	6	6				
19.	6	4	15	16	4	6				
20.	6	6	12	16	16	4				

CATEGORY IDENTIFICATION DRILL, PAGE 53

1.	10	10.	13
2.	7	11.	18
3.	8	12.	4
4.	14	13.	11
5.	3	14.	5
6.	15	15.	1
7.	2	16.	17
8.	16	17.	6
9.	19	18.	12

COMPARATIVE CATEGORY RATIO DRILL, PAGE 71

—Accept/Correct for Teachers = 3.5
—Warm/Cool for Teacher = 8.0
—Direct/Divergent for Students = 1.3
—Teacher/Student = 2.8

DATA INTERPRETATION DRILL, PAGES 74–75

1. 4–4/16–16
2. 12
3. Teacher-Teacher
4. 6
5. None
6. 8
7. 19
8. 3
9. 115

DIFFERENTIATION DRILL A, PAGE 108

1. K, 2
2. O, 3
3. O, 13
4. O, 3
5. O, 3
6. K, 12
7. O, 13
8. K, 2
9. O, 3

Data Interpretation: Page 78: Data Collection Form

	1	2	3	4	5	6	7	8	9	10
1.	10	6	16	4	16					
2.	6	6	4	15	16					
3.	6	7	15	2	12					
4.	6	10	2	4	16					
5.	6	10	4	15	10					
6.	6	7	4	2						
7.	4	7	10	6						
8.	15	10	4	6						
9.	2	10	4	6						
10.	4	18	10	6						
11.	15	18	6	6						
12.	2	1	6	6						
13.	6	1	6	6						
14.	6	6	6	6						
15.	6	6	6	6						
16.	7	7	6	10						
17.	7	7	6	10						
18.	10	10	4	10						
19.	10	16	4	16						
20.	14	16	4	16						

Differentiation Drill B, Page 109

1. K, 14
2. K, 14
3. K, 4
4. O, 15
5. O, 5
6. O, 15
7. O, 15
8. K, 14

Differentiation Drill C, Page 110

1. 6
2. 7
3. 16
4. 18

5. 7
6. 8
7. 17
8. 16

KEY TO SCRIPT, PAGE 116: OBSERVATION RECORD SHEET—ETC

Observer _____   Completion Time _____
Observed _____   Subject Area _____
Number of Observation _____   Topic_____
Beginning Time_____   Planned Strategy _____

	1	2	3	4	5	6	7	8	9	10	11	12	13	14	15	16
1	9	14	5													
2	0	1	9													
3	2	7	0													
4	14	15	19													
5	6	6	4													
6	14	15	15													
7	7	6	8													
8	15	15	9													
9	6	8	1													
10	14	1														
11	8	3														
12	9	15														
13	0	1														
14	2	8														
15	14	9														
16	11	0														
17	14	②														
18	1	⑭														
19	14	10														
20	8	3														
21	9	15														
22	0	15														
23	2	15														
24	14	1														
25	6	6														
26	14	14														
27	8	11														
28	9	19														
29	0	9														
30	9	10														
31	19	15														
32	9	1														
33	0	6														
34	2	0														
35	14	15														
36	6	9														
37	0	0														
38	6	6														

Comments on Selected Codes

1.   <u>9</u>   These comments are made by the teacher for the purpose of structuring the learning activity. A direction is also given here.

2.   <u>0</u>   The pause is teacher-initiated to allow pupils time to comply with directions. A considerable number of pauses or silences is to be expected in a discovery lesson.

3.   <u>2</u>   It appears that this question asks John to recall characteristics of a polygon that were discussed in a preceding lesson.

4. <u>14</u>   The student relies on memory to recall facts previously learned—restricted thinking.

7.   <u>7</u>   The teacher attempts to raise the level of participation by having the pupil apply several principles to arrive at a conclusion—expanded thinking.

8. <u>15</u>   The pupil's answer is recorded as Category 15 since the correct principles were applied to reach the desired conclusion.

9.   <u>6</u>   The teacher encourages the continuation of the discussion—a maintaining behavior.

11.   <u>8</u>   The teacher terminates the discussion here and turns to a structuring behavior.

16. <u>11</u>   This is an unsolicited comment not directly related to the solicited response, but an impromptu comment simply explaining that she does not remember the answer.

17. <u>14</u>   Though the previous behavior was not structured in the form of a question, this pupil reacts to the comment by supplying the correct answer—again, a recall from a previous experience.

18.   <u>1</u>   The pupil presents unsolicited information before continuing her response.

30.   <u>9</u>   The teacher question here is recorded as Category 9 since the next phase of the lesson will be structured one way for a "no" response and

31. <u>19</u>   another for "yes" response. As the teacher will depend on the class answer, their response will structure the learning situation. (Category 19.)

38.   <u>6</u>   The student has been instructed to proceed through several processes, applying certain principles in an attempt to arrive at a conclusion—one that the student himself has discovered. The teacher is calling for a response that involves the same idea as previous question (code 33)—thus maintaining the cognitive level.

40.   <u>1</u>   The teacher simply gives information here but then proceeds directly

41.   <u>7</u>   with a question intended to raise the level of participation—she is guiding the pupils toward a generalization.

42. <u>15</u>   Once the pupil has made his discovery, the specific answers may be generated by application of a rule or procedure—expanded thinking.

45. __6__ The teacher desires to continue the higher level of participation by leading the pupil to state his discovery in a general form, so that it may be accepted as a general rule and may be used to compute the answer for any number of sides. This calls for him to consider his individual cases and write a precise statement applicable to any case through use of the inductive method—thus maintaining the level.

46. __15__ The pupil is definitely "on the right track," but the teacher encourages him to continue his level of participation by being more concise and precise in making his general statement.

51. __1__ This sequence of sentences summarizes some previous information gathered by the class.

(55.) __2__ The teacher directs her comment to a specific individual—a reminder that the student's behavior is not the desired one. This comment is in the form of a question but is not directly related to the idea being discussed—the code is circled.

59. __14__ ⎫
60. __11__ ⎬ These are specific responses—not all in agreement—that are
61. __19__ ⎭ responses to the teacher's question.

68. __10__ Note that this is a pause initiated by a student.

69. __15__ This response is coded as a final response (Category 15) to the teacher's question, "Glenn, did you write a formula?" (The response (code 65) began by his giving information intended to show his answer was correct and therefore was coded as on 11.)

77. __15__ While the question calls for a yes or no response only, the correct response "yes" requires use of higher levels cognitive processes than memory and this response should be coded as an expanded thinking (Category 15) response.

80. __10__ The student attempts to structure the learning situation by bringing about the silence needed.

84. __9__ The teacher structuring the learning situation by making an assignment.

Computation Drill, Page 130

1. 5%
2. 13%
3. $\frac{55}{30} = 1.83$
4. $\frac{12}{11} = 1.09$
5. $\frac{2}{18} = .111$

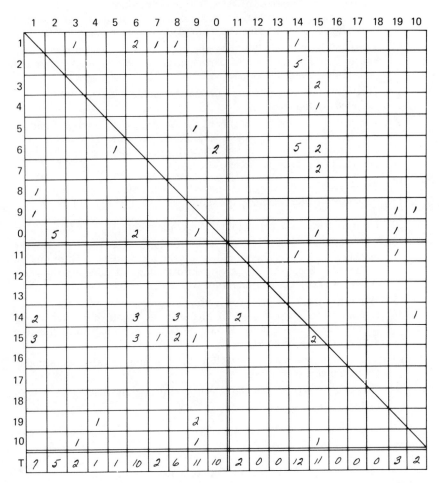

Grand Total

Key to Tabulation Drill, Page 127
Raw Data Tabulation Form

Category	1	2	3	4	5	6	7	8	9	0	11	12	13	14	15	16	17	18	19	10	T_r	-	T_i	T
Incidences	7	4	2	1	1	10	2	6	11	10	2	0	0	11	11	0	0	0	3	2	83	0	2	85
% of T_r	8	5	2	1	1	12	2	7	13	12	2	0	0	13	13	0	0	0	4	2	100%	-	1	97%
% of T	8	5	2	1	1	12	2	7	13	12	2	0	0	13	13	0	0	0	4	2	98		2	99%

Key

T_r: total relevant behaviors
-: behaviors not measured by the ETC
T_i: total irrelevant behaviors (circled codes)
T: total recorded behaviors

209

KEY TO BRANCHING DRILLS, PAGE 130

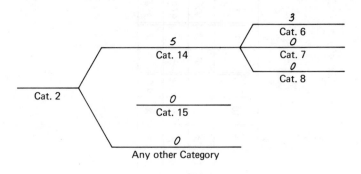

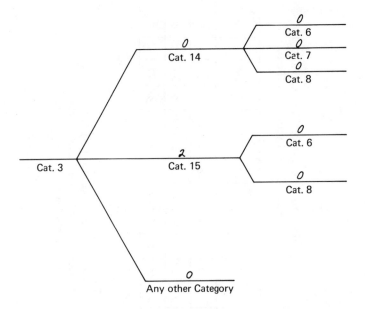

PROCEDURES FOR SITUATION 1 (ONE-WAY COMMUNICATION)

Step 1. Prior to meeting the students face-to-face, you are to set up a tape recorder and record for reply your instructions to the students for drawing the five rectangles as shown in *Rectangle Arrangement 1 for Situation 1* (shown on page 175). Dictate your instructions to the students for drawing the rectangles *only* once. *Do not give the taping of instructions more than once.* It is important that you follow this instruction rigidly. Hold these recorded instructions for use in the next step.

RECTANGLE ARRANGEMENT 1 FOR SITUATION 1
(TO BE USED WHEN TAPING INSTRUCTIONS ONE-WAY)

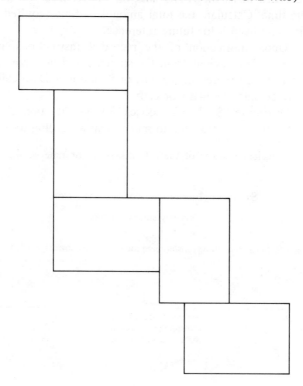

Step 2. When you meet the students face-to-face in Situation 1, advise them as follows:

a. You have recorded some instructions for drawing rectangles. In a moment you will play the recording.

b. The students are to follow your instructions as closely as possible.

c. Once it is started, the recorder will not be shut off until the end of the recorded instructions is reached.

d. The students may not ask either you or another student a question or make any comments either while the recording is in progress or until after all papers are collected. *Absolute quiet is required during the playback of the recorded instructions. Also, they are not to use any kind of arm gestures, "sky drawing," etc. in order to facilitate the drawing of the rectangles.*

Step 3. Provide each student with a piece of paper with "Situation 1" written at the top (to be prepared ahead of time). Instruct the students to write their names on the paper.

Step 4.   Note and write down the *starting* time and turn on the recorder. Play the recorded instructions and shut off the recorder. Note and record the *finishing* time. Calculate the total amount of time required for playing the recording and keep it for future reference.

Step 5.   Upon completion of the recorded instructions, immediately collect the rectangle drawings from the students and hold for future reference. These drawings represent the part of Situation 1 Data called "Actual Number of Rectangles Drawn Correctly."

Step 6.   Distribute "Student Feedback Form—Situation 1" (shown on page 202).[1] Instruct the students to mark them according to how they felt

---

[1] Prepare a sufficient number of these forms ahead of time so that each student has a copy.

STUDENT FEEDBACK FORM—SITUATION 1

One way communication

In regard to my feelings concerning reproducing the rectangles correctly, I feel:

1	2	3	4	5
Very uncomfortable and frustrated		Somewhat comfortable and somewhat sure though perhaps a bit frustrated		Comfortable and sure

I think that I correctly reproduced_____rectangles.

STUDENT FEEDBACK FORM—SITUATION 2

Two way communication

In regard to my feelings concerning reproducing the rectangles correctly, I feel:

1	2	3	4	5
Very uncomfortable and frustrated		Somewhat comfortable and somewhat sure though perhaps a bit frustrated		Comfortable and sure

I think that I correctly reproduced_____rectangles.

during Situation 1. While they are completing these forms, you are to complete the "Teacher Feedback Form—Situation 1" (shown on page 213), indicating how you felt during the instructional exercise. Hold all feedback forms for future reference.

TEACHER FEEDBACK FORM—SITUATION 1

One way communication

In regard to my feeling concerning teaching the rectangles, I feel:

1	2	3	4	5
Very uncomfortable and frustrated		Somewhat comfortable and somewhat sure though perhaps a bit frustrated		Comfortable and sure

I think the student correctly reproduced_____ retangles.

TEACHER FEEDBACK FORM—SITUATION 2

Two way communication

In regard to my feelings concerning teaching the rectangles, I feel:

1	2	3	4	5
Very uncomfortable and frustrated		Somewhat comfortable and somewhat sure though perhaps a bit frustrated		Comfortable and sure

I think the students correctly reproduced_____ rectangles.

PROCEDURES FOR SITUATION 2 (TWO-WAY COMMUNICATION)

Note: Situation 2 immediately follows Situation 1.

Step 1. Advise the students as follows:

a. Again, the students are instructed to draw five rectangles, arranged properly on a piece of paper (these five are arranged differently than the first five). You, the teacher, will provide verbal instructions and information *on the spot* this time.

b. The students are permitted to ask any questions and/or make any comments that they feel will be helpful in reaching the goal of drawing the five rectangles correctly.

c. Any form of *verbal* communication, either between teacher and student or between students, is permitted. Students may ask you questions regarding the instructions. In addition, they may ask questions of or make comments to each other in order to facilitate the process. Any form of verbal behavior (talking) is permitted. *However, neither you nor the students are permitted to use any form of nonverbal cues, hand gestures, "sky writing," etc. as a means of communicating the proper arrangement of the rectangles on the paper.*

d. They may take as much time as they wish to complete the task. Again, the primary objective is to draw as many rectangles, properly arranged on the paper, as possible.

Step 2.   Provide each student with a piece of paper with "Situation 2" written at the top (to be prepared ahead of time). Instruct the students to write their names on the paper.

Step 3.   Note the starting time.

Step 4.   Instruct the students to draw the five rectangles as arranged on Rectangle Arrangement 2 For Situation 2 (shown on page 212). Follow through according to the instructions outlined above in Step 1. Allow the students as much time as they need to complete the exercise.

Step 5.   Note the finishing time. Calculate total amount of time required for Situation 2 and keep for future reference.

Step 6.   Upon completion of the instructional exercise, collect the students' rectangle drawings and hold for future reference. These drawings represent the part of Situation 2 called "Actual Number of Rectangles Drawn Correctly."

Step 7.   Distribute "Student Feedback Forms—Situation 2" (shown on page 212) [2] and instruct the students to mark them according to how they felt during Situation 2. While they are completing these forms, you should complete the "Teacher Feedback Form—Situation 2" (shown on page 213) indicating how you felt during Situation 2. Hold all of these completed feedback forms for future reference.

---

[2] Prepare a sufficient number of these forms so that each student has a copy.

RECTANGLE ARRANGEMENT 2—FOR SITUATION 2
(TO BE USED WHEN GIVING INSTRUCTIONS IN
FACE-TO-FACE SETTINGS; TWO-WAY)

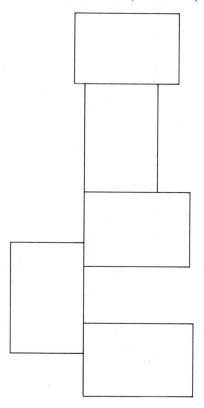

TREATMENT AND ANALYSIS OF DATA

1. The following raw data should be obtained for both Situation 1 and Situation 2:
   a. The number of rectangles drawn correctly as *predicted* by the *students*.
   b. The number of rectangles drawn correctly as *predicted* by the *teacher*.
   c. *Actual* number of rectangles drawn correctly (to be secured by grading students' drawings).
   d. The degree of comfort as recorded by *students*.
   e. The degree of comfort as recorded by the *teacher*.
   f. *Total time* required for the instructional exercise.
2. Draw a "recording table" (diagram on page 216) either on the blackboard or an overhead overlay so that treated data can be entered and studied thoroughly by the group.

RECORDING TABLE
(To Be Placed on Either Blackboard or Overhead Overlay)

	Situation 1	Situation 2
1. Average number of rectangles drawn correctly as predicted by students.		
2. Average number of rectangles drawn correctly as predicted by teacher.		
3. Average number of rectangles drawn correctly.		
4. Degree of comfort experienced by students.		
5. Degree of comfort experienced by teacher.		
6. Total time required.		

3. Using Rectangle Arrangement 1 (page 175) and Rectangle Arrangement 2 (page 177) determine the number of rectangles arranged correctly on each of the students' papers for both Situation 1 and Situation 2. (You will be able to facilitate this operation considerably if the students each grade a paper.) Calculate the mean (average) number of rectangles drawn (arranged) correctly for both situations and enter these numbers in their proper locations in the Reporting Table.

Note: When checking accuracy of rectangle drawings, actual size of the rectangles is not important. Rather, check: 1) to be sure that the student drew rectangles—not triangles, circles, squares, etc. and, 2) to be sure that the five rectangles are arranged in proper order.

4. From the "Student Feedback Forms," calculate the mean (average) number of rectangles drawn correctly as predicted by the students *for both Situation 1 and Situation 2*. (Again, this step can be facilitated considerably if you assign this task to two or three students.) Enter these figures in the Reporting Table in the spaces labeled "Average Number of Rectangles Drawn Correctly as Predicted By Students" for both situations.

5. From the data that you entered in "Teacher Feedback Form" for Situation 1 and Situation 2, enter in the Reporting Table the "Average Number of Rectangles Drawn Correctly as Predicted by Teacher" for both situations.

6. From the "Student Feedback Forms" calculate mean (average) degree (ranging from one to five) of comfort experienced by the students during both Situation 1 and Situation 2. Enter these figures in the Reporting Table in the spaces labeled "Degree of Comfort Experienced By Students" for both situations.

7. From the data that you entered in the "Teacher Feedback Form" for Situation 1 and Situation 2, enter in the Recording Table the "Degree of Comfort Experienced by Teacher" for both situations.

8. Enter in the Recording Table the "Total Amount of Time Required" for both Situation 1 and Situation 2.

9. Instruct the students to study carefully the data for both situations. After reasonable time for study, conduct an open discussion of the following questions.

Questions for Discussion

1. In which of the two situations did the students apparently feel more comfortable?

2. Why did they feel more comfortable in this situation?

3. In which of the two situations did the teacher apparently feel more comfortable?

4. Why did the teacher feel more comfortable in this situation?

5. Which of the two situations required the most total time?

6. Which of the two situations was apparently more efficient in terms of total time spent?

7. Is it reasonable to spend more time in order to produce more learning (i.e., "more rectangles drawn correctly")?

8. As a result of this exercise, what have you learned concerning the effectiveness of both the "one-way" and the "two-way" patterns of communication as they relate to the classroom and student learning?

Instructions for The Two-Minute Micro-simulation (Without Video or Audio Recording)

The general purpose of this exercise is to give the student an opportunity to plan a lesson according to a predetermined listing of RCS or ETC data, teach it under micro-simulated conditions, and compare the data describing his actual teaching performance with those in the original listing. This exercise is conducted with groups of either five or six students to allow each student an opportunity to plan and teach his lesson within the limits of a one to one-and-a-half hour period of time.

Prior to the exercise, the instructor should prepare a series of listings of either **RCS** or **ETC** data (depending upon which system is to be used). Examples of sample listings are shown on pages 183 and 218. These listings should be placed on the paper so that they can be cut into strips for easy distribution to the students. The instructor may use the sample listings shown in Table A.1 or he may choose to prepare different sequences to suit a particular situation.

Table A.1

SAMPLE LISTINGS OF RCS DATA FOR
TWO-MINUTE MICRO-SIMULATION

Pattern One	*Pattern Two*	*Pattern Three*	*Pattern Four*	*Pattern Five*	*Pattern Six*
7	6	1	9	4	1
7	6	1	9	16	7
10	4	4	4	2	7
10	15	1	15	1	10
7	2	3	6	4	10
7	4	16	4	16	1
10	15	3	15	3	7
10	2	16	6	16	7
7	4	1	4	2	10
7	15	6	15	1	10
10	2	6	6	4	1
10	1	4	6	16	7
4	4	16	9	3	7
15	15	3	9	16	10
2	2	16	4	2	10
4	1	3	16	1	1
15	4	16	16	6	6
2	16	1	4	6	6
4	3	1	16	1	4
15	16	7	16	4	15
2	2	7	6	15	2
1	4	10	6	2	1
6	16	10	9	4	4
6	3	1	4	15	15
4	16	1	16	2	2
16	2	4	16	4	1
2	6	16	6	15	7
7	6	1	9	2	7
		1		1	1

Organize the class into groups of five or six students and advise them according to the following instructions:

1. In a moment, they will receive a strip of paper upon which is printed a sequential listing of either RCS or ETC data.

2. Each student is to plan a short lesson, not to exceed five minutes, that, when taught, will generate data that will resemble as closely as possible the data listing on his strip of paper. Point out that, in the case of RCS, data generated during teaching does not have to follow exactly the precise number of a given category in sequence as shown on his strip, but that the sequential change from one category to another should be the same for the two sets of data. Arrange for all students to plan their lessons during the same planning period in order to conserve time.

3. After each student has planned his lesson, have the group members arrange themselves for the teaching exercises *per se*. One of the students should begin the lesson, while a colleague serves as the observer and records the data. The remaining group members should assume student roles.

   The skill with which a group member plays his student role is vital to the success of this exercise. Group members should try to play their roles as realistically as possible. They should not ask questions, volunteer contributions, or initiate any kind of verbal behavior in this exercise, since the listings that appear on the teacher's strip of paper do not provide for this sort of behavior. To generate these kinds of behaviors would result in a definite discrepancy between the planned and the actual data. *The purpose of this exercise is for teacher controlled behavior rather than for student controlled behavior.*

4. After each teacher has completed his lesson, the group members should compare the actual data collected with the data listing on the teacher's strip of paper. Things such as the following should be considered:
   a. How did the two sets of data compare?
   b. Were the observer's observations valid and realistic? Did he record certain observations inaccurately? (The observer and the teacher will need to resolve any discrepancies.)
   c. Did the group members playing student roles play them realistically?
   d. Of perhaps second importance in this exercise, did the group members learn anything? Was the goal achieved?
   e. What could the teacher do in future situations of this sort to improve?

5. Continue until each member has had an opportunity to present his lesson. At each change of teacher, rotate observers so that each group member will have an opportunity to observe.

6. Bring the smaller groups together for a large group discussion. The following points might be considered:
   a. Did the exercise help you to learn what is meant by "control of behavior"?
   b. Did you strive more to control your own behavior or to achieve the learning goal itself?
   c. Under average classroom conditions, which is more important, to control your own teaching behavior or to achieve the goal(s)?

d. Would you like to teach a twenty to thirty minute lesson under these same kinds of conditions? Why? Why not?

Note: An interesting variation of the procedures described above is to modify the predetermined data listings on the strips of paper by directing the students to list their own data on a piece of paper and to plan a lesson according to these data. This is a technique that might be used if a second two-minute micro-simulation is used.

Directions for Preparing the Fifteen-Minute Micro-simulation Critique

Below is a description of the format for preparing and organizing the critique. The descriptions and directions listed here are for your help and clarification. Please observe the following guidelines when preparing your critique:

A. Copy verbatim the statements that are printed below in *capital letters* at the top of each section. This statement will serve as a heading for that particular section. Parenthetical statements are intended for directions and should *not* be copied in your critique.

B. Organize the sections of your critique in the *same sequence* as they appear below.

SECTION   1.   *Discussion of the Behavioral Objective(s).* (Defend your behavioral objective(s) as being appropriate in terms of your hypothetical class.)

SECTION   2.   *A Copy of the Testing Instrument/Technique.* (An extra copy similar to those given the students is acceptable.)

SECTION   3.   *Report of Class Performance on the Testing Instrument.* (Include lowest and highest individual score, mean score for the class and a report of how many students responded correctly to each item included in the test. Use special form provided in class. Refer to form on page 221, Table A.2.)

SECTION   4.   *Discussion of Relationship between Class Performance on Testing Instrument and Behaviorally Stated Objective(s).* (Was the objective met? If not, analyze it and describe why it *is not* satisfactory. If it is satisfactory, explain.)

SECTION   5.   *Description of Hypothetical Class that You Taught.* (Diagnostic data. Use special form used in class. Refer to form on page 221, Table A.3.)

SECTION   6.   *RCS Matrix.* (Report your model and actual RCS data on one blank matrix as demonstrated in class. Include category percentages for both sets of data. Refer to page 194, Figure 6.8, for directions.)

Table A.2

REPORT OF CLASS PERFORMANCE ON THE
TESTING INSTRUMENT

A. Range:
   Highest score
   Number scoring highest score   _____
   Lowest score   _____
   Number scoring lowest score   _____
B. Mean score   _____
C. Median score   _____
D. Mode score   _____
E. Item analysis. Specify each item number of your test and the number of students who responded *correctly* and *incorrectly*. Refer to Part 2, Section 2.

Table A.3

DESCRIPTION OF ACTUAL (HYPOTHETICAL) CLASS TAUGHT
DURING THE PRESENTATION

A. Subject area   _____
B. Grade level   _____
C. Age of students   _____
D. Sex distribution   _____
E. Ability of students (high, low, average)   _____
F. Achievement level (over, under, etc.)   _____
G. Socio-economic background of students   _____
H. Ethnic background of students   _____
I. Race distribution of students   _____
J. Home cultural background of students   _____

SECTION 7. *ETC Data.* (Report your model and actual ETC data on one form as demonstrated in class. Refer to page 290 for directions.)

SECTION 8. *Description and Justification of Instructional Strategies and Techniques.* (Describe and defend your instructional strategies and techniques as being appropriate for facilitating learning in terms of described hypothetical class. Describe and discuss the implications of your RCS and ETC data *making reference to specific matrix areas, cells, and items.*)

SECTION 9. *Report of Teacher-Student Perceptions of Learning, Interest, and Involvement.* (Draw a single continuum ranging from one to five for each of the three measurement scales. Signify teacher's perceptions and students' perceptions in different colors for each of the three continua. Describe and discuss any discrepancies between the two ratings. Use special form distributed in class.)

SECTION 10. *Recorded Discussion/Critique.* (Write a discussion of the information that you secured from the video recording of the discussion and critique of your lesson.)

SECTION 11. *Instructor's Evaluation.* (Write a brief discussion of the instructor's evaluation.)

SECTION 12. *Specific Suggestions for Future Improvements.* (Be specific here. This is one of the most important sections.)

SECTION 13. *Additional Comments.* (Optional)

Below is a brief discussion of each of the thirteen sections to be included in the critique:

SECTION 1. *Discussion of the Behavioral Objective(s).* Copy the behavioral objective(s) verbatim. Discuss in detail why you selected them as being appropriate to the hypothetical class description. Is it (are they) suitable for this age group and student potential? Does the objective(s) describe learning that is meaningful and useful to the students as you have described them?

SECTION 2. *Copy of the Testing Instrument.* All that is required here is an actual copy or duplication of the test used in the presentation. If a technique other than a paper-pencil test is used, it should be described in detail in this section.

SECTION 3. *Report of Class Performance on the Testing Instrument.* Use the special form (Table A.1) shown on page 221 for this section. This section guides the student as he analyzes the construct of the test and how well the class members performed.

SECTION 4. *Discussion of Fit between Class Performance on Testing Instrument and Behaviorally Stated Objective(s).* Was the test valid? Was it too difficult? Was it inappropriate to either the behavioral objectives and/or the hypothetical class description? Questions of this type should be considered and treated in this section.

SECTION 5. *Description of Hypothetical Class that You Taught.* This section points out the nature and background of the hypothetical students that you taught. This information is helpful when comparing class performance to behavioral objectives. For learning to be assured, the learning objectives must be appropriate to the learners.

SECTION 6. *RCS Matrix.* With both the model and actual RCS data available for study in the same matrix, a comparison can be made between the two quite easily. Did you perform as you had predicted you would? Where are there discrepancies between model and actual data? What prompted these descriptions? Were they justified and defensible? Would you change anything in terms of your verbal behavior (as measured by the RCS) if you were to reteach the lesson? Answers to questions of this type provide the substance for this section.

SECTION 7. *ETC Data.* Considerations to be made in this section are similar to those described in Section 6 above. However, instead of considering your verbal behavior performance, you should consider how you controlled and manipulated the learning stimuli (content) in your performance. Would you change your behavior if you were to teach this lesson again?

SECTION 8. *Description and Justification of Instructional Strategies and Techniques.* This is perhaps the most important part of the critique. Here, consider all of the data and make value judgments concerning the effectiveness of overall performance. How well did you do? Were the strategies and techniques that you selected appropriate to the facilitation of the learning that was set forth in the learning objectives? Were you skillful in demonstrating these strategies and techniques? Do the RCS and ETC data shown in Sections 6 and 7 authentically reflect the strategies and techniques that you planned to use? Would you use the same strategies and techniques if you were to teach this kind of lesson again?

SECTION 9. *Report of Teacher-Student Perceptions of Interest, Learning, and Involvement.* With both the teacher's and the students' perceptions reported on a single continuum for each of the three measures, a clear view is available. Did the students perceive your performance in terms of these three measures to be more effective than you perceived theirs? What discrepancies do you note? How do you account for these? What would you do in order to overcome these if you were to teach such a lesson again.

SECTION 10. *Recorded Discussion/Critique.* What criticisms did your peers and the instructor have to offer concerning your teaching performance? Do you accept these to be valid? Are the suggestions offered relevant, and will they be helpful if you wish to modify your behavior for improvement in the future? Does your evaluation of the overall performance compare closely with those of your peers and the instructor?

SECTION 11. *Instructor's Evaluation.* The points that are considered by the instructor in this section are purposely slanted toward the more traditional techniques of judging teacher effectiveness. They are more subjective in terms of the factors considered. Voice, apparent ease, empathy displayed, and the like are a matter of personal opinion and do not lend themselves to the more objective forms of measurement. However, these data should provide interesting insights when considered by themselves, as well as when they are compared to the other forms of available data yielded in this exercise.

SECTION 12. *Specific Suggestions for Future Improvement.* This section culminates the exercise. If the teacher has analyzed and studied the data thoroughly and objectively, he should be able to identify areas of his performance that he feels can be improved. This requires introspection and an open mind.

The teacher should consider such questions as the following when preparing this section: What did I do well in the performance? What did I do poorly? What did the students indicate that I did well? What did they indicate I did poorly? How can I improve all of these in the future?

SECTION 13. *Additional Comments.* This section is optional.

Bibliography

Books and Monographs

Amidon, E. J., and N. Flanders, *The Role of the Teacher in the Classroom.* Minneapolis, Minnesota: Paul Amidon and Associates, 1963.

Amidon, E. J., and J. Hough, *Interaction Analysis: Theory, Research, and Application.* Reading, Massachusetts: Addison-Wesley Publishing Co., Inc. 1967.

Amidon, E. J. and E. Hunter, *Improving Teaching.* New York: Holt, Rinehart & Winston, Inc., 1966.

Anderson, H. H. and Helen M. Brewer, "Studies of Teachers' Classroom Personalities. I. Dominative and Socially Integrative Behavior of Kindergarten Teachers," Applied Psychology Monograph, No. 6, 1945.

Anderson, H. H. and J. E. Brewer, "Studies of Teachers' Classroom Personalities. II. Effects of Teachers' Dominative and Integrative Contacts on Children's Classroom Behavior." Applied Psychology Monographs, No. 8, 1946.

Anderson, H. H. and J. E. Brewer and Mary F. Reed, "Studies of Teachers' Classroom Personalities. III. Follow-up Studies of the Effects of Dominative and Integrative Contacts on Children's Behavior," Applied Psychology Monograph, No. 11, 1946.

Anderson, Richard C. and David P. Ausubel, *Readings in the Psychology of Cognition.* New York: Holt, Rinehart & Winston, Inc., 1965.

Ausubel, David P., *Educational Psychology—A Cognitive View.* New York: Holt, Rinehart & Winston, 1968.

Bales, R., *Interaction Process Analysis.* Cambridge, Massachusetts: Addison-Wesley Publishing Co., Inc., 1950.

225

Bellack, Arno A., et al., *The Language of the Classroom.* New York: Teachers College Press, Columbia University, 1966.

Bellack, Arno A. and J. R. Davitz, in collaboration with H. M. Kliebard and R. T. Hyman, *The Language of the Classroom: Meaning Communicated in High School Teaching,* U.S. Office of Education, Cooperative Research Project No. 1497, New York, 1963.

Bellack, Arno A., et al., *Theory and Research in Teaching.* New York: Teachers College Press, 1963.

Bentley, E. and E. Miller, *Teacher Evaluation: A Personal Responsibility.* Published monograph of the Supplementary Educational Center, Atlanta, Georgia, 1969.

Berlyne, D. E., *Structure and Direction in Thinking.* New York: John Wiley & Sons, Inc., 1965.

Bloom, Benjamin, et al., *Taxonomy of Educational Objectives: Cognitive Domain.* New York: David McKay Co., Inc., 1956.

Brown, Bob B., *The Experimental Mind in Education.* New York: Harper and Row, Publishers, 1968.

Bruner, Jerome S., et al., *A Study of Thinking.* New York: John Wiley & Sons, 1956.

Bruner, Jerome S., ed., *Cognition, The Colorado Symposium.* Cambridge, Massachusetts: Harvard University Press, 1957.

Bruner, Jerome S., *Learning About Learning.* Department of Health, Education and Welfare, Washington, D.C., 1966.

Bruner, Jerome S., et al., *Studies in Cognitive Growth.* New York: John Wiley & Sons, Inc., 1967.

Bruner, Jerome S., *The Process of Education.* Cambridge, Massachusetts: Harvard University Press, 1962.

DeCecco, John P., *The Psychology of Learning and Instruction; Educational Psychology.* Englewood Cliffs, N.J.: Prentice-Hall, Inc., 1968.

Flanders, N. A., *Analyzing Teaching Behavior.* Reading, Massachusetts: Addison-Wesley Publishing Co., Inc., 1970.

———, *Teacher Influence, Pupil Attitudes and Achievement.* Cooperative Research Monographs, No. 12, Washington, D.C., 1965.

Gagné, Robert M., *Learning and Individual Differences.* Columbus, Ohio: Charles E. Merrill Books, Inc., 1967.

———, *The Conditions of Learning.* New York: Holt, Rinehart & Winston, Inc., 1965.

Gordon, Ira J., *Studying the Child in School.* New York: John Wiley & Sons, Inc., 1966.

Guilford, J. P., *The Nature of Human Intelligence.* New York: McGraw-Hill Book Company, 1967.

Hughes, Marie, and associates, *The Assessment of the Quality of Teaching: A Research Report.* U.S. Office of Education Cooperative Research Project, No. 353. Salt Lake City, Utah: The University of Utah, 1959.

Kirk, Jeffrey, "The Effect of Teaching the Minnesota System of Interaction Analysis on the Behavior of Student Teachers." Unpublished Ed.D Thesis. Philadelphia, Pa.: Temple University, 1964.

Lohman, E., "A Study of the Effect of Pre-Service Training in Interaction Analysis on the Verbal Behavior of Student-Teacher," Unpublished doctoral dissertation. Columbus, Ohio: Ohio State University, 1966.

Miles, M. B., ed., *Innovation in Education.* New York: Teachers College Press, 1964.

Morphet, Edgar L. and Charles O. Ryan, *Implications for Education of Prospective Changes in Society.* New York: Citation Press, 1967.

Ober, R. L., "Predicting Student Teacher Verbal Behavior." Unpublished doctoral dissertation. Columbus, Ohio: Ohio State University, 1966.

Pankratz, R., "Verbal Interaction Patterns in Classrooms of Selected Science Teachers: Physics." Unpublished doctoral dissertation. Columbus, Ohio: Ohio State University, 1966.

Parsons, Theodore W., *Guided Self-Analysis System for Professional Development,* Education Series. Berkeley, California: privately printed, 1968.

Popham, W. James and Eva L. Baker, *Planning an Instructional Sequence.* Englewood Cliffs, New Jersey: Prentice-Hall, Inc., 1970.

Rappaport, David, *Organization and Pathology of Thought.* New York: Columbia University Press, 1951.

Ryans, D., *Characteristics of Teachers.* Washington, D.C.: The American Council on Education, 1960.

Sanders, Norris M., *Questions in the Classroom—What Kinds?.* New York: Harper & Row, Publishers, 1966.

Siegel, Irving E., *Logical Thinking in Children.* New York: Holt, Rinehart & Winston, Inc., 1968.

Staats, Arthur W., *Learning, Language and Cognition.* New York: Holt, Rinehart & Winston, Inc., 1968.

Taba, Hilda and Deborah Elkins, *Teaching Strategies for the Culturally Disadvantaged.* Chicago, Illinois: Rand McNally & Co., 1966.

Wood, Samuel E., "Analysis of Three Systems for Observing Classroom Behavior." Unpublished Doctoral Dissertation. Gainesville, Florida: University of Florida, College of Education.

Wrightstone, J. W., *Appraisal of Newer Practices in Selected Public Schools.* New York: 1935. (See also N. L. Gage (ed.), *Handbook of Research on Teaching.* American Educational Research Association, Rand McNally & Co., 1963.)

Articles

Amidon, E. J. and Elizabeth Hunter, "Implications of Interaction Analysis: Research for the Education of Secondary School Teachers," *High School Journal,* LI, No. 1 (October, 1967).

Amidon, E. J. and M. M. Giammateo, "The Verbal Behavior of Super Teachers," *Elementary School Journal,* LXV, No. 5 (1965), 283–85.

Anderson, H. H., "The Measurement of Domination and of Socially Integrative Behavior in Teachers' Contacts with Children." *Child Development,* X (1939), 73–89.

Bane, Robert, *Sequence Pattern Interpretation of Teaching Behavior,* Unpublished paper, 1969.

Birch, Daniel R., *Guided Self-Analysis and Teacher Evaluation,* Unpublished research paper read at ASCD Conference, Grand Rapids, Michigan, November, 1969.[1]

Brown, Bob Burton, "Experimentalism in Teaching Practice," *Journal of Research and Development in Education,* IV, No. 1 (Fall, 1970), 14–22.

Brown, B. B., R. Ober and R. S. Soar, *Florida Taxonomy of Cognitive Behavior,* an unpublished paper, University of Florida, 1968.

Bruner, Jerome S., "The Course of Cognitive Growth," *American Psychologist,* No. 19 (January, 1964), 1–15.

Campbell, J. R. and C. W. Barnes, "Interaction Analysis—A Breakthrough?" *Phi Delta Kappan,* II, No. 10 (June, 1969), 587–90.

Cogan, M. L., "Theory and Design of a Study of Teacher-Pupil Interaction," *Harvard Educational Review,* XXVI, No. 4 (1956), 315–42.

Flanders, Ned A., AERA Position Paper, Minneapolis, Minnesota, 1970.

Flanders, Ned A., "Personal-Social Anxiety as a Factor in Experimental Learning Situations," *Journal of Education Research,* XLV (October, 1951), 100–10.

Furst, Norma, "The Effects of Training in Interaction Analysis on the Behavior of Student Teachers in Secondary Schools." Paper read at the 1965 annual meeting of the American Educational Research Association, Chicago, Illinois.

Gallagher, J. J. and M. J. Aschner, "A Preliminary Report on Analysis of Classroom Interaction," *Merill-Palmer Quarterly of Behavior and Development,* IX, No. 3 (1963), 183–94.

Galloway, Charles, "Nonverbal Communication," *Theory Into Practice,* VII, No. 5 (1968), 172–75. (See also Sue S. Lail, "The Model in Use," in the same issue.)

---

[1] Guided Self-Analysis Conference, Grand Rapids, Michigan, November 11, 12, 13, 1969.

Hough, J. and R. Ober, "The Effect of Training in Interaction Analysis on the Verbal Teaching Behavior of Pre-Service Teachers." Paper read at American Educational Research Association annual meeting, Chicago, Illinois, February, 1966.

Katz, E., M. L. Levin and H. Hamilton, "Traditions of Research on the Diffusion of Innovations," *American Social Revolution,* XXVIII, No. 2 (1963), 237–52.

Kounin, J., W. Friesen and A. Norton, "Managing Emotionally Disturbed Children in Regular Classrooms," (dittoed report), Detroit, Michigan: Wayne State University Press, 1965. (See also Ira Gordon, *Studying the Child in School.* New York: John Wiley & Sons, Inc., 1966.)

Lippitt, R. and R. K. White, "The Social Climate of Children's Groups," in R. G. Barker, J. S. Lounin and H. F. Wright (eds.), *Child Behavior and Development,* New York, 1943, 458–508.

Medley, D. M. and H. E. Mitzel, "A Technique for Measuring Classroom Behavior," *J. Educational Psychology,* XLIX, No. 2 (1948), 86–92.

———, "Measuring Classroom Behavior by Systematic Observation." See also Gage, N. L., *Handbook of Research on Teaching.* Chicago, Illinois: American Educational Research Association, Rand McNally, Inc., 1963.

Minnis, D. L. and K. Shrable, "The Model in Use," *Theory Into Practice,* VII, No. 5 (December, 1968), 168–71.

Murray, C. Kenneth, "Systematic Observation," *Journal of Research and Development in Education,* IV, No. 1 (Fall, 1970).

Ober, Richard L., "Predicting the Verbal Behavior of Students from Data Collected During Student Teaching." Paper read at the annual meeting of the American Educational Research Association, New York, 1967.

———, "The Nature of Interaction Analysis," *The High School Journal,* No. 51 (October, 1967), 7–16.

———, "The Reciprocal Category System," *Journal of Research and Development in Education,* IV, No. 1 (Fall, 1970), pp. 34–51.

———, "Theory into Practice Through Systematic Observation," *Florida Educational Research & Development Council, Research Bulletin,* IV, No. 1 (Spring, 1968).

Perkins, H., "A Procedure for Assessing the Classroom Behavior of Students and Teachers," *American Educational Research Journal,* No. 1 (1964), 249–60.

Perkins, H. V., "Climate Influences Group Learning," *Journal of Educational Research,* No. 45 (October, 1951), 115–19.

Scott, W. A., "Reliability of Content Analysis: The Case of Nominal Coding," *The Public Opinion Quarterly,* XIX, No. 3 (1955), 321–25.

Smith, B. O. and M. Meus, et al., *A Study of the Logic of Teaching,* U.S. Office of Education, Cooperative Research Project No. 258 (7257), Urbana (1962).

Soar, Robert S., "Pupil Needs and Teacher-Pupil Relationships: Experience Needed for Comprehending Reading," in E. J. Amidon and J. B. Hough, *Interaction Analysis: Theory, Research and Application.* Reading, Massachusetts: Addison-Wesley Publishing Co., 1967, 243–50.

————, "Research Findings from Systematic Observation," *Journal of Research and Development in Education,* IV, No. 1 (Fall, 1970), 116–22.

Webb, Jeannine N., "Taxonomy of Cognitive Behavior: A System for the Analysis of Intellectual Processes," *Journal of Research and Development in Education,* IV, No. 1 (Fall, 1970), 23–33.

Webb, Jeannine N., Ernest L. Bentley and R. Robert Rentz, "Observation as a Methodology." Paper presented at 1970 annual meeting of American Educational RESEARCH Association, Minneapolis, Minnesota.

Withall, J., "Development of a Technique for the Measurement of Socio-Emotional Climate in Classrooms," *Journal of Experimental Education,* XVII, No. 3 (1949), 347–61.

————, "Development of the Climate Index," *Journal of Educational Research,* No. 45 (1951), 93–99.

Wood, Samuel E., "A Multidimensional Model for the Observation, Analysis, and Assessment of Classroom Behavior," *Journal of Research and Development in Education,* IV, No. 1 (Fall, 1970), 84–88.

Wrightstone, J. W., "Measuring Teacher Conduct of Class Discussion," *Elementary School Journal,* No. 34 (1934), 454–60.

Glossary

category system—an observational system consisting of a given number of behavior descriptions that are mutually exclusive, arranged such that the observer records the number of the behavior description that best describes a given, fixed interval of classroom interaction.

equivalent talk categories—an observational system designed to assess the cognitive activities of a given instructional-learning situation.

function—a teacher or learner behavior described by an item or category of an observational system.

instruction—the facilitation of learning.

microsimulation—a laboratory-controlled teaching situation which is shorter in terms of time, narrower in scope, and involves peers as student role players as compared to an actual classroom setting.

microteaching—a laboratory-controlled teaching situation which involves typical students but is shorter in terms of time and narrower in scope than an actual classroom setting.

multidimensionality—the incorporation of two or more observers, each using a different observational system simultaneously to observe the same instructional-learning situation.

observational system—any technique designed for the purposes of identifying, examining, classifying, and/or quantifying specific interacting variables of a given instructional-learning situation.

reciprocal category system—an observational system designed to assess the socioemotional climate of a given instructional-learning situation.

reciprocity factor—a principle purporting that for each teacher classroom behavior that can either be observed in the classroom setting or theorized, there exists a corresponding student classroom behavior.

reliability (as it pertains to systematic observation)—training two or more observers each using the same observational system to record identical data describing the same instructional-learning situation.

sign system—an observational system consisting of a given number of behaviors that are not mutually exclusive, arranged such that the observer checks (marks) once, in some manner, each behavior that is observed to occur during a fixed period of time.

strategy—one or more related functions which provide an instructional means for facilitating and/or accomplishing a given learning objective.

supervision—the facilitation of teaching by means of assisting the teacher to observe, analyze, and modify his own teaching behavior in order to improve his teaching effectiveness.

teaching—the related activities of establishing learning objectives, facilitating the learning, and measuring the learning produced in a given situation.

validity (as it pertains to systematic observation)—the operational ability of an observational system to measure the conditions of a given instructional situation in terms of the items or categories of the system itself.

Index

Accepts, 44–45
Act of learning, 145–46
Adoption curve, s-shaped, 32
Amidon, E. J., 15, 23, 30, 33
Amplifies, 45
Amplifies, ground rule, 45
Analyzing feedback data, 188–89, 193
Anderson, H. H., 22, 31
Aptitude-treatment interaction, 18, 35
Assessment of student feeling, 151
Assumptions, teaching-learning process, 3
Atlanta, Metropolitan Region, use of systematic observation, 32
Ausubel, David P., 144
Awareness and control, 1–14

Bacon, Sir Francis, 15
Bales, R., 22
Barnes, C. W., 34
Behavioristic: neo-behavioristic, 144
Behavior sequence, 72
Bellack, A. A., 22, 26, 31
Bentley, E. L., 32, 112
Birch, D. R., 18
Block, cell, 72
Bloom, B., 19, 92, 99
Bonnie and Clyde, 1
Branching, 125, 136
Branching chart, multipurpose, 126
Branching drills, 130
Brown, B. Burton, 18, 23
Bruner, J. S., 144, 145

Campbell, J. R., 34
Categories, ETC, 88–91
Categories, RCS, 38–40, 43–51
Category identification drill, 53
Category ratios, 134
Category recognition drill, 51, 52
Category system, 19, 231
Cell, 72
Cell loading, 72
Chaining, 146
Clarification strategy, 12
Clarifies, 45
Classroom learning, 139
Cogan, M. L., 31
Cognitive learning theory, 144
Collection procedures (ETC), 111–19
Comparative category ratio drill, 69
Comparative category ratios (RCS), 67
Computation drill (ETC), 129, 130
Computations (ETC), 123, 124
Computed ETC information, 134
Concept learning, 147
Concept of systematic observation, 15–36
Control variations, micro-simulation, 195
Cools the climate (RCS), 50
Corrects, 49, 50
Criteria for selecting an observation system, 36
Criterion scores (ETC), 111
Critique, instructional, 195
Cronbach, L. J., 35

Data bracketing, 59
Data collection
  functional guidelines, 114–15
  ground rules, 41
  practice script, ETC, 115
  RCS, 40–58
Data collection drills, 54–59
Data collection forms, 41, 52, 62, 80–81
Data collection procedures, ETC, 110–11
Data collection sheet (RCS), 58
Data interpretation drill, 74, 75
Data interpretation (ETC), 131–37
Data interpretation (RCS), 66–78
Data pairing, 59
Data pairs (ETC), 123
Data preparation drills (RCS), 64
Data preparation, RCS, 58–66
Desire to learn, 145
Dewey, John, 21, 144
Difference, RCS and ETC, 137
Differentiation drills, 53–54, 108–110
Directs, 49
Directs, ground rule, 49
Dogmatism scale, 9
Drills, ETC, 108–110, 115, 127–28, 129–30
Drills, RCS, 51–59, 64–65, 69, 74, 75, 78
Drill strategy, 11

Effect, indirectness, 34
Effect, systematic observation training, 34
Elicits, 46
Equivalent Talk Categories (ETC), 7, 16, 87–138, 231
  advantages, 137
  categories, 88–91
  category foci, 91
  functional guideline, 100, 102, 104, 106, 114, 115
  sample interaction, 95–97
  theory, 87
Evaluating results, 3
Exemplary systems, 21

Fifteen-minute micro-simulation, 190
Five-minute micro-simulation, 184
Flanders, N. A., 15, 19, 27, 31, 34, 38
Flanders' interaction analysis, 18, 23, 27
Flexibility in RCS matrix, 71
Florida Taxonomy of Cognitive Behavior, 18, 19, 20, 23
Foreign language, interaction analysis adoption, 35

Functional guidelines (ETC), 100, 102, 104, 106, 114, 115
Functions, 141–43, 155, 231
Functions for strategy building, 148–49
Furst, N., 10

Gage, N. L., 23
Gagné, R. M., 144, 146
Gallagher-Aschner, 26, 48, 92
Galloway, C., 15, 23
"Good observers," 33, 79
Gordon, I. J., 23, 29
Ground rules, RCS, 41, 45, 46–50
Guided self-analysis, 26, 35

Hough, J., 8, 9, 23, 33
Hughes, M., 22, 23, 137
Hughes' functions, 25

In-basket, 171
Indirect-direct ratios, 34
Indirectness, 34
Informalizes the climate, 44
Initiates, 47
In-practice uses, 171–200
In-service models, 32–33
Instruction, 231
Instructional situation, 139
Instructional strategies, 185, 186
Instructional strategy, 11
Interaction analysis, Flanders, 18, 23, 27
Interaction analysis categories, 28
Interaction analysis research group, New York University, 34
Inter-observer reliability, 79–85
Interpersonal Relations System (IRS), 18
Intra-observer reliability, 79–85

James, William, 144

Keys, ETC drills, 203–210
Keys, modification and in-practice uses, 210–30
Keys, RCS drills, 201–203, 204
Kirk, J., 10
Kounin, J., 23

Learning stimuli, 140
Learning theory, 143, 155
Lippit, R., 31

Live classroom observation, 177
Loading of cells, 72, 73
Lohman, E., 9, 34

Maintain-expand strategy, 12
Matrix (RCS), 65, 67, 70
Matrix plotting, 59–61, 63
Medley, D. M., 15, 22, 23
Micro-simulation, 173–74, 184–90, 231
Micro-teaching, 171, 231
Miller, E., 32, 88
Mitzel, H. E., 15, 22, 23
Modification, 143, 167, 171–200
Monitoring of teaching behavior, 18
Moskowitz, G., 35
Multidimensionality, 137, 172, 231
Multiple discrimination, 147

Ober, R. L., 18, 23, 29, 30, 31, 35, 36, 37
Objectives, 3, 139, 143, 155
Observational approaches, illustrative, 22–23
Observation and feedback, 155
Observation record sheet (ETC), 113, 127
Observation systems, 19–21, 232
Observe-record procedures (ETC), 111
Observer and valid observation, 79–86
Observer reliability, 80
Observing and recording, ETC, 93
Observing the teaching-learning situation, 5–7
One-way, two-way communication, 174
Operations of teaching, 140–41

Parsons, T., 18, 26, 35
Patterns, 76–78
Pavlov, 144
Penn, Arthur, 1
Percentages, 65, 66
Philosophy, 143
Planning, 3, 141–42
Planning, lesson, 185, 190
Plotting, RCS matrix, 60–61
Plotting, summary chart of ETC, 123
Positive reinforcement, 151
Practice opportunities, 125–30
Practice script, 115–19
Preparation procedures (ETC), 119–30
Presenting, 98
Principle learning, 147
Problem solving, 147–48
Process of strategy building, 143

Profile comparisons, 135
Purpose of book, 13–14

Qualities of observation systems, 34
Questioning and responding, 98–103
Questioning, extended response, 100
Questioning, functional guideline, 100
Questioning, restricted response, 100
Questions, prospective teachers, 7–11

Raw data tabulation form, 121, 128, 132
Reacting, 92, 103–106
Reacting, functional guideline, 104–106
Reacting, to extend, 105
Reacting, to maintain, 104–105
Reacting, to terminate, 106
Readiness, 145
Reciprocal Category System (RCS), 7, 16, 18, 29, 37–86, 232
  categories, 37, 43
  category identification drills, 48, 49
  category table, 39–40
  data collection, 40
  drills, 51–54, 55–59, 64–65, 69, 74, 75, 78
  ground rules, 41, 45, 46–50
  illustrative script, 42, 43
  operations, 38
  summary, 85–86
  theory of, 38
Reciprocity factor, 232
Recording (ETC), 114–15
Reliability, 232
Rentz, R. R., 112
Research efforts, 33–34
Respond, ground rule, 46, 47
Responding, 92, 101
Responding, extended, 101
Responding, functional guideline, 102
Responding, restricted, 101
Responds, 46
Results of systematic observation use, 31
Richmond Unified School District, use of systematic observation, 32
Ryans, D., 22

Sanders, N. M., 19, 92, 99
Schedules, guided self-analysis, 26, 27
Scientific method, 15
Selecting an observation system, 34–36
Self-evaluation, use of systematic observation, 32
Sequence of behavior, 72
Signal learning, 146

Sign system, 19, 232
Silence or confusion, 51
Simulation, 171
Skill, in planning strategies, 2
Skinner, B. F., 144
Smith, B. O., 22, 139
Smith's Categories, 25
Soar, R., 18, 34
Socio-emotional climate, 140
Staff development, use of systematic observation, 32
Steady state cells, 73
Stimulus-response learning, 146
Strategies
    cooling, 151
    designed to affect climate, 150
    designed to affect cognition, 152
    expanded questioning-responding, 152
    guided discovery strategy, 153–54
    illustrative, 149–55
    positive reinforcement, 151
    reacting to extend, 153
    reacting to maintain, 153
    reacting to terminate, 153
    restricted-questioning-responding, 152
    stimulus-response strategy, 150
    structuring, 152
    warming, 150
Strategy, 11–13, 93, 137, 141–42, 232
Strategy-building, process, 139–70, 143–49
Strategy development, simulated, 155–69
Strategy, moviemaking, 1
Strategy, television, 1
Structuring, 93, 94, 106, 107
Structuring, learning activities, 107
Structuring, silence or pause, 106
Student feedback form, 187
Submatrices, 68, 70
Summary chart of interchange, 122, 123, 133, 139
Summary, RCS, 85–86
Supervision, 232
Systematic observation, 6, 16–19
Systematic observation, feedback, 32
Systematic observation, research, 31, 33
Systematic observation, self-evaluation, 196–200
Systematic observation, strategy development, 196–200

Systematic observation in teaching operations, 30
Systems, exemplary, 21, 22, 23

Taba, H., 23
Tabulation drill, 127–29
Tabulations, 120
Taxonomy of cognitive behavior, **99**
Teaching, 232
Teaching behavior concepts, 31
Teacher feedback form, 187
Teacher situation reaction test, 9
Teachers Practices Observation Record, 18, 21, 24
Teaching-learning process, 2–5
Teaching operations, 140–41
Teaching the lesson, 186, 191–92
Teach-reteach, 189
Theory, ETC, 87
Theory, RCS, 38
Thorndike, R., 144
Two-minute micro-simulation, 182
Two-thirds rule, 19

Use of observation systems, 8, 29–34

Validity, 232
Validity of observers, 79–84
Variables of teaching-learning process, 5
Verbal association, 146–47
Vertical observation record form, 114, 115
Visual inspection of data, 131

Warming, 44
Watson, J., 144
Webb, J. R., 112
White, R. K., 31
Withall, J., 15, 22, 23, 31
Withall's categories, 21
Withall's system, 20
Wrightstone, J. W., 21, 22
Wrightstone's categories, 18
Written critique, 195